Tools for Complex Projects

*To Parmenides, Shakespeare, Douglas Adams and all those philosophers
and authors who recognised the interconnectedness of all things and
delighted in the random interference of human beings in any master plan.*

Tools for Complex Projects

KAYE REMINGTON and JULIEN POLLACK

GOWER

Published by
Gower Publishing Limited
Gower House
Croft Road
Aldershot
Hampshire
GU11 3HR
England

Gower Publishing Company
Suite 420
101 Cherry Street
Burlington
VT 05401-4405
USA

Kaye Remington and Julien Pollack have asserted their moral right under the Copyright, Designs and Patents Act, 1988, to be identified as the authors of this work.

British Library Cataloguing in Publication Data
Remington, Kaye
   Tools for complex projects
   1. Project management
   I. Title II. Pollack, Julien
   658.4'04
   ISBN-13: 9780566087417

Library of Congress Cataloging-in-Publication Data
Remington, Kaye.
   Tools for complex projects / Kaye Remington and Julien Pollack.
      p. cm.
   Includes bibliographical references and index.
   ISBN 978-0-566-08741-7
   1. Project management. I. Pollack, Julien. II. Title.

   HD69.P75R45 2007
   658.4'04--dc22

                                                                 2007010162

Reprinted 2008

Printed and bound in Great Britain by MPG Books Ltd, Bodmin, Cornwall.

Contents

List of Figures   *xi*
List of Tables   *xiii*
Acknowledgements   *xv*
Preface   *xvii*

Chapter 1   **What is a Complex Project?**   **1**
A new approach to project management   1
Aim of this book   3
A complex project is a complex adaptive system   3
Characteristics of a complex project   4
Recognizing the type of project complexity   6
Patterns of thinking about project management   8
More useful concepts from complexity theory   9
Summary   11
In the chapters to follow   12
References and further reading   12

PART I   **TYPES OF PROJECT COMPLEXITY: CHARACTER AND MANAGEMENT**   **15**

Chapter 2   **Where Complexity Comes From in a Management Context**   **17**
Complexity and perception   17
Logical problems arising from the process of categorisation   17
Focus in complex projects   18
Reflective practice   20
Quantity, ambiguity and interconnectedness   20
'Satisficing' zones   22
Problem and solution spaces   23
Summary   24
References and further reading   24

Chapter 3   **Structurally Complex Projects**   **27**
Explained in terms of Complex Theory   27
Project management challenges   32
Traps and consequences   36
References and further reading   37

Chapter 4   **Technically Complex Projects**   **39**
Explained in terms of Complexity Theory   40

Project management challenges   42
Traps and consequences   47
References and further reading   48

Chapter 5   Directionally Complex Projects   51
Explained in terms of Complexity Theory   52
Project management challenges   55
Traps and consequences   58
References and further reading   59

Chapter 6   Temporally Complex Projects   61
Explained in terms of Complexity Theory   62
Project management challenges   65
Traps and consequences   70
References and further reading   71

PART II   TOOLS AND TECHNIQUES   73

Chapter 7   Guide to the Tools   75
Relationship between theory, methodology and tools   75
How to select the tools   78
How the tools are set out   79
References and further reading   82

Chapter 8   Mapping the Complexity   85
Problem   85
Purpose   85
Types of complexity   86
Theoretical background   86
Discussion   87
The tool   87
Step by step   89
Caution   90
Example in practice   90
References and further reading   92

Chapter 9   System Anatomy   93
Problem   93
Purpose   94
Types of complexity   94
Theoretical background   95
Discussion   95
The tool   96
Step by step   100
Examples in practice   101
References and further reading   102

Chapter 10	**Target Outturn Cost**	**103**
	Problem	103
	Purpose	104
	Types of complexity	104
	Theoretical background	105
	Discussion	106
	The approach	106
	Step by step	110
	Caution	110
	Examples in practice	111
	References and further reading	112
Chapter 11	**Programme Tool**	**113**
	Problem	113
	Purpose	113
	Types of complexity	114
	Theoretical background	114
	Discussion	115
	The tool	116
	Step by step	118
	Caution	119
	Examples in practice	119
	References and further reading	120
Chapter 12	**Role Definition**	**123**
	Problem	123
	Purpose	123
	Types of complexity	124
	Theoretical background	124
	Discussion	125
	The tool	126
	Step by step	131
	Caution	132
	References and further reading	132
Chapter 13	**Jazz (Time-Linked Semi-Structures)**	**133**
	Problem	133
	Purpose	133
	Types of complexity	133
	Theoretical background	134
	Discussion	135
	The tool	136
	Step by step	138
	Caution	138
	Examples in practice	139
	References and further reading	139

Chapter 14   Multimethodology in Series   **141**
    Problem   141
    Purpose   141
    Types of complexity   141
    Theoretical background   142
    Discussion   143
    The tool   143
    Step by step   145
    Caution   145
    Examples in practice   145
    References and further reading   146

Chapter 15   Multimethodology in Parallel   **147**
    Problem   147
    Purpose   147
    Types of complexity   147
    Theoretical background   148
    Discussion   149
    The tool   149
    Step by step   151
    Caution   151
    Examples in practice   152
    References and further reading   152

Chapter 16   Virtual Gates   **155**
    Problem   155
    Purpose   155
    Types of complexity   155
    Theoretical background   156
    Discussion   156
    The tool   158
    Step by step   160
    Caution   160
    Examples in practice   161
    References and further reading   163

Chapter 17   Risk Interdependencies   **165**
    Problem   165
    Purpose   165
    Types of complexity   166
    Theoretical background   166
    Discussion   168
    The tool   168
    Step by step   170
    Caution   171
    References and further reading   171

Chapter 18   **Temporal Cost/Time Comparison (TCTC)**   **173**
               Problem   173
               Purpose   173
               Types of complexity   174
               Theoretical background   174
               Discussion   174
               The tool   175
               Step by step   177
               Caution   177
               References and further reading   178

Chapter 19   **Kokotovich Triad**   **179**
               Problem   179
               Purpose   180
               Types of complexity   180
               Theoretical background   180
               Discussion   181
               The tool   182
               Step by step   185
               Caution   185
               Examples in practice   187
               References and further reading   187

Chapter 20   **Stanislavski's Method**   **189**
               Problem   189
               Purpose   189
               Types of complexity   189
               Theoretical background   190
               Discussion   191
               The tool   192
               Step by step   192
               Caution   193
               Examples in practice   193
               References and further reading   193

Chapter 21   **Discursive Universe**   **195**
               Problem   195
               Purpose   195
               Types of complexity   195
               Theoretical background   196
               Discussion   196
               The tool   197
               Step by step   200
               Caution   200
               Example in practice   200
               References and further reading   201

Chapter 22   Conclusion   **203**

Index   *205*
About the Authors   *213*

List of Figures

2.1	Changing perspectives	19
2.2	Four possibilities	21
2.3	Sixty-four possibilities	21
2.4	65 536 possibilities, illustrating the rapid expansion of possible states	22
2.5	Interconnected problem and solution spaces	23
3.1	Uncertainty in structurally complex projects	28
4.1	Uncertainty in technically complex projects	40
5.1	Uncertainty in directionally complex projects	52
6.1	Uncertainty in temporally complex projects	63
7.1	Hierarchical relationship between the theoretical and practical	76
7.2	Derivation and design of methods	78
8.1	Goals-and-methods matrix: coping with projects with ill-defined goals and/or methods of achieving them	86
8.2	Base for mapping the project complexity	87
8.3	Mapping complexities for an IT development project	89
8.4	Complexity map at the definition phase for the hospital service project	90
8.5	Evolution of the map at the beginning of the planning phase	91
8.6	Evolution of the map at the beginning of the implementation phase	92
9.1	Example of the anatomy diagram developed for a telecommunications development project	97
9.2	Diagram showing the increments defined in terms of interdependencies in the anatomy	98
9.3	Integration plan	99
9.4	Context model with the System Anatomy shown circled in the centre	100
10.1	Reduction in cost uncertainties	107
10.2	Development and implementation of TOC under a CWA	109
11.1	Systemic model for thinking about complex infrastructure projects	116
11.2	Example showing how the programme changes in response to changing constraints and feedback	118
11.3	Example of programme model developed to meet particular organisational needs	119
13.1	Example of a project semi-structure model	137
14.1	Multimethodology in Series process	144
15.1	Multimethodology in Parallel process	150
16.1	Virtual Gate process model	159
16.2	Causal map for a construction project that went wrong	162
17.1	Circle of potential risks	170
17.2	Risk Interdependencies identified by one group	170
18.1	Temporal Cost/Time Comparison steps	176

19.1   Non-hierarchical mind map   182
19.2   Non-hierarchical mind map showing grouping and highlighting   183
19.3   Sample of intuitive leapfrogging   183
19.4   Example of a link matrix   186

List of Tables

7.1	Summary of tools chapters	80
12.1	Executive sponsor – ideal role definition	127
12.2	Executive sponsor – cultural/organisational fit	128
12.3	Manager role – capability definition	129
12.4	Project manager – cultural organisational fit	130
17.1	Interdependency matrix	169

Acknowledgements

The authors would like to thank the following people who, over recent years, generously shared their knowledge and experience and who contributed in many other ways to the intellectual content of the book. They are listed in alphabetical order.

Professor David Cleland
Kerry Costello
Katherin Coster
Professor Lynn Crawford
Raf Dua
Dr. Vasilije Kokotovich
Adjunct Professor Brian Kooyman
Dr. Elyssebeth Leigh
Dr. Joakim Lliesköld
Dr. Eunice Maytorena
Joan Opbroek
Professor Anders Söderholm
Dr. Lars Taxén
Professor Janice Thomas
Professor Terry Williams
Professor Rodney Turner
Dr. John Twyford

The following people have contributed to our health and well-being during the journey and we would like to thank them so much for their encouragement and endless emotional support.

John McInnes
Bruce Pollack
Rachel Ryan

Finally many thanks to Jonathan Norman, Fiona Martin and the rest of the team at Gower Publishing for their willingness to work with us to create the final product. It has been a relatively easy and very pleasant journey.

Preface

It has often been said that project management has little if any theoretical basis. The main way in which project management is discussed in practice, and often in the literature, is on the basis of 'best practice' – what practitioners feel is the best way to manage projects, or at least most projects most of the time. But our track record of planning and executing projects doesn't seem to get any better, and the public perception of major projects is that they are usually late and usually overspent.

We can manage straightforward projects. We can also manage certain types of large complicated projects, such as building large chemical plants. But it has been increasingly clear over recent years that projects are becoming more complex and it is the complex projects that we aren't very good at managing – in fact, we aren't very good at understanding how they behave at all.

The management literature has in recent years made considerable theoretical advances in our understanding of complexity, but this hasn't until now been applied to complex projects – or at least, not in any way that might help us actually manage those projects separately. Hence this book.

The book defines complexity in four ways: *structurally* complex projects, *technically* complex projects, *directionally* complex projects and *temporally* complex projects. It carefully takes us through each one and discusses some of the theory that might help understand these types of project.

The latter two-thirds of the book then looks firstly at approaches that might help us to think about complex projects better, and secondly at tools and techniques that can actually be applied to contribute to the better management of those techniques. These are not simply theoretical ideas – they are practical suggestions derived from the authors' own practice, their observations of experienced project managers and what works for them, as well as the suggestions of other authors and their experience in teaching post-graduate project management courses. A matrix shows when each approach could be adopted for which sort of complexity the project is exhibiting. As you go through, graphics show not only the applicability of the methods, but also the difficulty of using them, and how long they typically might take – essential pieces of information if the practitioner is thinking of using them – as well as some useful templates to use.

The overall flavour of the book allows us to look at projects with a variety of philosophical viewpoints. Conventional project management looks at projects with a rational, conventional philosophy; using a variety of philosophical 'lenses' allows us to recognise the complex intrarelationships within projects and approach them in a humbler spirit, but now with this book we are much better equipped to comprehend and manage those complexities.

Terry Williams PhD, PMP
Professor of Management Science
University of Southampton, UK

1 *What is a Complex Project?*

Nearly all large and many small projects exhibit characteristics of complexity. Nevertheless projects of all sizes continue to be managed using linear thinking strategies based on project management traditions that go back to the building of the great pyramids in Egypt during the third millennium BCE, when societies and workgroups were arranged hierarchically. Much of the thinking dominating project management as it is currently practiced and taught is still founded upon control theories which were developed in the early modern period to deal with nineteenth- and twentieth-century industrialization and imperial expansion. There is nothing intrinsically wrong with this. However, issues do arise when these ideas are applied unilaterally to all kinds of projects in all contexts.

In complex environments problems for management stem from the assumption that the outcomes, envisaged at the inception of the project, can be sufficiently determined early in the project and then delivered as planned. This approach to project management only works for a limited number of projects. Those projects tend to be rather small in scale and short in duration. However, once a project reaches a critical size, timeframe, level of ambiguity and interconnectedness, control-based approaches simply do not work for the entire project.

Several authors have recognized that projects are systems and should be addressed systemically. However the systemic view of the world presented is usually predicated upon what Peter Checkland (1981; 1999) refers to as 'hard systems thinking'. This kind of thinking is highly appropriate for mechanical systems but not so useful when people are the key elements in the design, operation and delivery of the system. The problem is that people are unpredictable in their behaviour. We are self-determining, self-willed, self-motivated and selfish. We can disrupt the most carefully planned project simply by refusing to play, doing something entirely unpredictable or acting in what we consider to be in the best interests of the organization, the project or ourselves. The high numbers of major project failures being observed suggests that project methodologies founded on control systems thinking alone are not appropriate for many of today's projects (Remington and Crawford, 2004; Williams, 1999; Baccarini, 1996). Projects are being subjected to numerous constraints, and project managers are expected to deliver outcomes in increasingly ambiguous and politically charged environments. In order to deliver satisfactory outcomes project managers need to adopt both a systemic and a pluralistic approach to practice.

A new approach to project management

'Systemic pluralism' is an approach that practitioners need to pursue if they are to survive and deliver successful project outcomes in complex contexts. Systemic pluralism requires two things from practitioners: that project managers recognize the systemic nature of projects; and that they adopt a pluralist approach to the tools and theories they apply. Systemic pluralism was developed as part of the systems field, under the banner of Critical Systems Thinking, a branch of systems thinking which emphasizes theoretical and methodological pluralism. Authors such as Midgley (1996; 2000), Mingers (1997; 2003) and Flood and Jackson (1991) all provide discussion on the development of Critical Systems Thinking and pluralist ideas in the systems, operational research and management science fields.

Management of most, if not all, projects can be aided by thinking of projects as systems. However, this does not mean the same thing to all people. Many different authors have placed different emphases on the systems concept, variously focusing on the attributes of open, closed, hard, soft, feedback and control systems. Although these different approaches all talk about systems, the different emphases they bring to the debate result in highly divergent forms of practice.

In this book we draw upon Complexity Theory, a cross-disciplinary branch of science which enquires into the nature of complex adaptive systems. Complexity Theory developed out of the observation of emergent, non-linear behaviour and particular sensitivity to initial conditions apparent in many natural systems. Its concepts have been developed through simulation and observation of complex behaviour in fields as diverse as biology, geology and meteorology. Lewin (1992) provides a good summary of the development of Complexity Theory. Ralph Stacey (1996) and others such as Griffin et al. (1999) and Lissack and Roos (1999) have applied ideas based on complex adaptive systems to general management. Complexity Theory also has considerable scope to provide insight into the systemic nature of projects.

Most projects can be more readily described as complex adaptive systems than as simple systems. In order to cope effectively with complex projects managers must adopt a pluralistic approach to practice. They must be able draw from a wide range of tools and ways of thinking to develop their own methods, their own patterns of practice, freely, according to the exigencies of the particular project. No one approach to project management is appropriate for all situations. There is no one size that fits all. Instead, project managers need to be equipped with a variety of different tools and ways of thinking about projects, a palette from which managers can pick and choose as the needs of the situation dictate. This is particularly true in environments characterised by confusion and transient conditions. Project managers should be able to select and vary the design of their methodologies or their approaches to managing different projects.

Complex projects vary dramatically, exhibiting different characteristics and aspects of systemicity. A single complex project may even demonstrate multiple kinds of systemicity, with various parts of the project showing markedly dissimilar characteristics and behaviour. Differences in systemicity will almost certainly vary considerably within any programme or group of interrelated projects.

Some projects can be described effectively as simple systems. For these projects the outcomes of the project might be so well defined that fully pre-determined control is possible. When this is the case traditional project management tools and processes are very efficient. However, in more complex contexts there will be aspects of the project for which control, in the sense of total predetermination of outcomes, is unlikely or even impossible to achieve. These parts of a project, or sub-projects, may benefit much more from approaches based on complex systems thinking. Faced with the pluralistic nature of the projects themselves, project managers have no choice but to adopt a pluralistic approach to practice. That means drawing flexibly and dynamically from a range of methods in order to deliver satisfactory outcomes to the stakeholders.

Aim of this book

This book is designed to assist practitioners to recognize the different sources of project complexity that might be confronted in a project context, as a guide to selecting the most appropriate management strategies. Based on the sources of complexity, we have defined various types of project complexity. We introduce whole-of-project approaches and individual tools that might assist practitioners to address different types of project complexity. The tools discussed in this book are not intended to be comprehensive. That would be impossible. In all cases it is the purpose behind the tool or approach, and the problem it is attempting to address, that are significant. Other tools can be selected if they fulfil the same purpose.

This book is a guide, not a step-by-step prescriptive methodology. Rather, it is a bag of tools and approaches from which managers can select in order to carry out the management activities needed for the project. The assumption is that the manager will make informed decisions about the most appropriate tools for the situation.

The focus is on tools and approaches which are not normally part of the project manager's palette of techniques. More traditional project management tools may be referred to in this book but will not be covered in any detail. However, there is no intention to dismiss the use of traditional tools. Traditional project management techniques and processes are entirely appropriate and effective in situations where project objectives are clear, fully understood, agreed and relatively stable over time. Traditional project management methods and tools are comprehensively addressed elsewhere (see excellent coverage in Harrison, 2004; Pinto and Trailer, 1999; Turner, 1999; and many others).

A complex project is a complex adaptive system

Complexity Theory in the form that has been applied to organizations (Anderson, 1999) may also be applied to projects (Williams, 2002; Baccarini, 1996). All projects exhibit the attributes of interconnectedness, hierarchy, communication, control and emergence, attributes which are generally useful in describing all kinds of systems. Most large and many small projects also exhibit the characteristics of complex adaptive systems. They exhibit characteristics such as phase transition, adaptiveness and sensitivity to initial conditions. These latter characteristics can be understood through reference to Complexity Theory.

It is commonly accepted that systems thinking is a way of looking at the world. Systems concepts, and the idea of systems, are frameworks which we use to interpret the world. We use these concepts in response to our recognition of stable relationships between different entities. Systems concepts aid our understanding of the relationships between parts and wholes. Thinking in terms of systems is something we do naturally. We intuitively make sense of the world by recognizing patterns of interaction and feedback. This book provides a selection of practical tools and techniques to allow managers to apply systems thinking and the concepts developed within Complexity Theory deliberately and with conscious effect.

An example of a system at a primitive level involves our ancestors who might have recognized that certain plants can be gathered at certain times of the year, that the bison pass through the lower ranges around 20 days after the solstice, and that if we follow the migrating bison we will arrive at the junction of the rivers in time to eat the spawning fish. This is a stable, repeatable pattern or system. The system is about us finding food in predictable way so that we can survive. We may not have understood why the system is stable or how the system fits into the greater ecosystem, but this does not prevent us from recognizing the relationships and taking advantage of them.

How we recognize systems and what is seen as a system is based on our points of view. Systems are based on stable relationships which must be recognized as existing and evolving over time. If there is no repeatable pattern, then we are looking at a single occurrence, not a system. When Douglas Adams' character, the detective Dirk Gently, noticed 'the interconnectedness of all things' he was recognizing the systemic nature of his universe:

> 'Whether we see a system in a situation is dependent upon what we are looking for at the time. For instance, most people are unlikely to perceive a simple pile of apples as a system. However, for very specific reasons, it may be useful to view this pile of apples as a system. If you were engaged by an apple producer to investigate the spread of a colony of bacteria in apple storage bins, thinking in terms of systems might be very useful. If you were an artist, and your intent and focus is the maintenance of a perfectly symmetrical pile of apples, then your focus changes again. Now, there is a perceived relationship between the apples and removing one apple fundamentally alters the properties of the pile of apples as a whole.'

Complex adaptive systems exhibit characteristics of all systems but it is the special additional characteristics that make them particularly difficult to understand and manage. Most authors agree that complex adaptive systems have the characteristics described as follows.

Characteristics of complex adaptive systems

HIERARCHY

Systems have sub-systems and are sub-systems for larger systems. This is often described as nested behaviour, like the Russian babushka dolls which fit one inside the other in seemingly endlessly diminishing replications.

In the same way, a chemist working on a drug development project is part of a project team. The interactions between the project team members can be considered to be a system. The team is one of many within a department, which can also be considered to be a system. The department is one of many within the organization, which is also a system. There are many organizations competing in this field, which together constitute another system.

Work breakdown structures are common ways of depicting a nested system of hierarchies, formally breaking down the activities in a project into manageable chunks. The project can be perceived at a number of levels, depending upon the focus of interest of the viewer.

COMMUNICATION

Information regarding the state of the system is passed between elements of a system. Information regarding the state of the system and the state of the environment is also passed across the system boundary. For example without anyone instructing them to do so, employees in an organization use the grapevine to rapidly communicate any changes to the organization that might affect them. Note however that rapidity and accuracy do not necessarily go together as anyone who has played the game Chinese whispers will agree. Projects have both formal and informal communications. The informal communications may both support and undermine the formal communications patterns.

CONTROL

Systems typically maintain the stability of the relationship between their parts, and so maintain their existence as a system. Control is what holds the system together. It maintains a stable state of operation. For example, a thermostat in the human body operates to maintain a comfortable body temperature by inducing sweating or shivering. In a workgroup, a congenial emotional climate and adherence to group norms are two of the conditions that hold the team together. If one team member does something to disturb this relationship other team members take action to re-establish the desired state of congeniality. Actions to control the behaviour and therefore maintain the system might be in the form of a joke, such as, 'I think we need to include the cost of an alarm clock for Fred in the next budget', which communicates acceptable group norms to a person who is habitually late for meetings. If the behaviour is allowed to escalate more serious control may be needed, such as exclusion of the member from the team.

EMERGENCE

At different levels of the system different properties emerge which may not be apparent from levels below. These properties are based on the stable interaction between different elements at a level of the system. Emergence is a property of the stable relationship between parts, not of any part in itself. In this respect the whole can be more than the sum of the parts. For example, when separated, the parts of a bicycle do not constitute a system of much interest. However, when combined, the capability of being able to be ridden emerges. This property only exists at the level of the whole bicycle but does not exist for any of the parts individually. It is a property which springs into being at a particular level of interaction with the system (see Dooley and Van de Ven, 1999).

PHASE TRANSITION

A complex adaptive system can suddenly take on a new form in response to changing conditions. It is the same system, just exhibiting different properties. This is usually an internal response to an external change. Descartes, in his *Meditations*, describes the transition of a piece of wax melting. When it melted he posed the question: How do we know is it the same piece of wax? It no longer looks the same. It doesn't feel the same. Nonetheless science now tells us that it is the same system of atoms and molecules, just in a different phase state. This in turn creates different emergent properties, such as runniness instead of solidity.

Another example can be illustrated with respect to specialized work teams. When a navy vessel changes from general operating conditions to battle stations the interactions between the people and within individuals themselves go through a phase change. People start behaving differently to each other. However, the system is still stable. It is just responding to a different environmental constraint.

NON-LINEARITY

Non-linearity is caused by 'positive feedback' and induces change (see Daft and Lewin, 1990). This is in contrast with control, a process of 'negative feedback' for maintaining stability, like a thermostat.

For example, the 1960's pop group, The Beatles, were only moderately successful until Ringo Starr replaced the original drummer. Although it could be argued that Ringo was no more proficient than the original drummer, he interacted with the group in such a way that they 'spun off each other' to create one of the most successful pop music groups in recent history. Something about the group interaction after Ringo joined allowed the creativity of each to be a positive influence on the others causing a spiral of creative output which had not been present before. This can also happen in project teams, particularly design teams.

ADAPTIVENESS

In response to changes in the environment a complex system adapts to accommodate and take advantage of the changes, to maintain or improve itself. The system adapts so that it can survive and maintain internal coherence in relation to the environment. Simple control involves maintaining the system against a fixed reference point. When a complex system adapts, the actual points against which the system regulates itself can be considered to move (see Lissack and Gunz, 1999). System adaptation can be in response to variation in the supply of resources which the system relies upon, new environmental constraints or the appearance of new possibilities.

For example, in the face of changing regulatory requirements for standards of production of vitamins it may not be possible for all companies to comply with production standards. Those companies that can adapt will survive and possibly expand. Others will be forced either to cease production or diversify.

SENSITIVE DEPENDENCE ON INITIAL CONDITIONS

This is the famous 'butterfly effect'. In 1972 the meteorologist Dr. Edward Lorenz pointed out that even tiny differences in initial conditions in a complex system (such as a butterfly flapping its wings in Brazil) can produce unanticipated and often catastrophic effects (such as a tornado thousands of miles away in Texas). As an example, the same team delivering the same project in a different environment with different initial conditions may achieve radically different levels of performance. This characteristic of a complex project, together with non-linearity and the positive feedback loops that may result, can cause risks, triggered by seemingly unimportant anomalies in initial conditions, to escalate out of control (see Arthur, 1989).

Recognizing the type of project complexity

Different kinds of complexity require different management methods. It is useful to be able to recognize different types of complexity as an aid to selecting the most appropriate tools and approaches to manage the project. Strategies for managing different kinds of complexity exhibited by different projects or project parts might need to vary enormously.

Based on the source of complexity and informed by the work of others (such as Turner and Cochrane, 1993; Williams, 2002) we suggest four types of project complexity as useful categories for analysis:

- structural complexity
- technical complexity
- directional complexity
- temporal complexity.

The source of project complexity will influence the project life cycle, including the critical review points and lengths of project phases within the life cycle, the governance structure for the project, selection of key resources, scheduling and budgetary methods and ways of identifying and managing risks. Different sources of project complexity will also have a major impact on choice of procurement method and approaches to contract management. Any large project, and many smaller ones, will exhibit one or more types of complexity.

STRUCTURAL COMPLEXITY

This kind of complexity may be found in most large and certainly all very large projects. Because the project management discipline has developed its knowledge based on management of such projects, they are often referred to as complicated rather than complex. We would argue that this classification is influenced by familiarity with the project type and that the dividing line between what can be considered as simply complicated and what can be thought of as complex is very unclear. The complexity in these projects stems from the difficulty in managing and keeping track of the huge number of different interconnected tasks and activities. This kind of complexity is commonly associated with large construction, engineering and defence projects. To manage these projects, outcomes are decomposed into many small deliverables which can be managed as discreet units. The underlying assumption is that the individual units, when delivered, will come together to make the required whole. The major challenges come from project organization, scheduling, interdependencies and contract management.

Structural complexity and its implications for managing projects in which it occurs will be discussed in more detail in Chapter 3.

TECHNICAL COMPLEXITY

This type of complexity is found in projects which have technical or design problems associated with products that have never been produced before, or with techniques that are unknown or untried and for which there are no precedents. Here the complexity stems from interconnection between multiple interdependent solution options. It is commonly encountered in architectural, industrial design, engineering, explorative IT projects and R & D projects, such as those found in the chemical and pharmaceutical industries. The project management challenges are usually associated with managing the critical design phases, managing contracts to deliver solutions to ill-defined design and technical problems and managing the expectations of key stakeholders.

Technical complexity and its implications for managing projects in which it occurs will be discussed in more detail in Chapter 4.

DIRECTIONAL COMPLEXITY

Directional complexity is found in projects which are characterised by unshared goals and goal paths, unclear meanings and hidden agendas. This kind of complexity stems from ambiguity related to multiple potential interpretations of goals and objectives. The management challenges tend to be associated with the allocation of adequate time during project definition (initiation of the project) to allow for sharing of meanings and revelation of hidden agendas. Managing relationships and organisational politics often become the keys to success. Political awareness and cultural sensitivity are two fundamental capabilities needed to manage these projects successfully.

Directional complexity and its implications for managing projects in which it occurs will be discussed in more detail in Chapter 5.

TEMPORAL COMPLEXITY

These projects are characterised by shifting environmental and strategic directions which are generally outside the direct control of the project team. This kind of complexity stems from uncertainty regarding future constraints, the expectation of change and possibly even concern regarding the future existence of the system. Temporal complexity can be found in projects which are subjected to unanticipated environmental impacts significant enough to seriously destabilise the project, such as rapid and unexpected legislative changes, civil unrest and catastrophes, or the development of new technologies. Often associated with this kind of complexity are paranoia and anticipation on the part of the personnel within the organisation. Changes of government can create this climate within the public sector, while a similar effect can be found in the private sector during periods of mergers and acquisitions and projects which have very long durations. This kind of complexity relates to change in external influences over time that may happen at any time during the project life cycle. Temporal complexity can be found in apparently straightforward projects, particularly those of long duration where delays due to external factors, such as monopolies on supply of vital goods or services, can occur at any time during the project life cycle.

Temporal complexity and its implications for managing projects in which it occurs will be discussed in more detail in Chapter 6.

Each one of these types of project complexity exhibits characteristics found in a complex adaptive system. Any project or programme of projects can exhibit one or more of these types of complexity.

Patterns of thinking about project management

Thinking and research in project management have emphasized structurally complicated projects. Therefore many project management techniques can be adapted to the needs of structural complexity. However, these approaches, and the broad patterns of thought which have spawned them, do not always translate effectively to the needs of technical, directional or temporal complexity. In order to address these radically different requirements, it has been necessary to do more than just extend the current thinking in project management by tweaking existing tools. What we have done is appeal to a wide range of thinking, starting with Complexity Theory and systems thinking, but also extending to include design theory, cognitive and behavioural psychology and various aspects of organisation theory.

COMPLEXITY IN COMBINATION

The bigger the project or programme the more likely it is to exhibit all four types of complexity, albeit in varying degrees.

For example, an international telecommunications company initiated an organisational change project involving the introduction of new, company-wide human resource management processes. The initiative had been stimulated by a perceived need to restructure and consolidate some departments. The organisation was also dealing with a volatile legislative environment which had different impacts in different countries. This kind of initiative exhibited elements of structural, technical, directional and temporal complexity. The structural complexity came from the sheer size of the programme and the number of component parts and dependencies. The technical complexity was related to the design and implementation of a new IT system and its integration with the huge variety of existing processes. The directional complexity was derived from the lack of shared understanding amongst key departments within the global organisation of the project objectives and lack of agreement on how to proceed. Temporal complexity came from difficulties in anticipating and responding to the frequent changes in legislation due to a volatile, international, political environment. Different management approaches were needed to deal with each of the types of complexity.

However not all parts of a project or programme will necessarily exhibit complexity.

Some parts of the telecommunications initiative described above were able to be rolled out as relatively standard discreet projects. These individual project elements within the programme were fully understood by key stakeholders, they were able to be thoroughly defined with very clear objectives and they involved standard technologies. Therefore they could be successfully managed by project managers using standard project management tools and processes.

This is an example of how systemic pluralism works in practice. The whole programme is viewed as a system with various sub-systems. Those sub-systems or parts that do not exhibit characteristics of a complex adaptive system may be more suited to hard systems approaches to management and may be successfully managed using standard project management procedures. However other sub-systems might require different approaches (see Turner and Cochrane, 1993; Shenhar, 2001; Payne and Turner, 1999; Engwall et al., 2005).

More useful concepts from complexity theory

ORDER TO CHAOS – A CONTINUUM

At this point it is useful to mention the continuum that exists between order and chaos. Fully ordered systems are not complex. They obey very tight, stable sets of rules and lack the ability to adapt to environmental change. Similarly, a chaotic system is not complex either. Neither is it random. Completely chaotic systems may appear to be random but the actions of individual parts within the system are predictable at a local level. Chaotic systems lack the stable relationships and patterns of interaction between parts which allow for emergent properties. Chaotic systems also do not react as a whole in response to environmental change. They lack internal coherence (see Stacey, 1991; Griffin et al., 1999 and Lissack and Roos, 1999).

All complex systems exist somewhere between order and chaos. More ordered complex systems tend to be highly efficient in relation to a limited range of functions. As a consequence of this level of specialisation their propensity for adaptation is lower. The area of focus in an ordered complex system is very tight and it may only be open to very specific information from the environment. Systems tending more towards chaos are open to a wider range of information from the environment and are able to explore multiple options and aspects of the environment at any one time. This is because while the system maintains cohesion, different sub-systems may be engaged in very different functions. As a consequence there is less efficiency through economy of scale, repetition and specialisation of tasks. Complex systems closer to chaos also face a greater danger of losing coherence and breaking up, and ceasing to be systems.

A metaphor for the difference between order and chaos can be seen in the changes in city planning policy which occurred during the sixteenth and seventeenth centuries in Europe. Prior to this time mediaeval cities had grown up in organic, apparently haphazard configurations of buildings and thoroughfares. Inspired by publications such as Antonio Filareti's *Trattato di architettura* ('Treatise on Architecture') of 1465, the Renaissance brought a desire to plan cities based on ideal models. The careful geometry of the Renaissance city plan permitted no building to take place outside the idealized geometry of the city boundary wall and city functions were carefully segregated within. Mediaeval towns by contrast grew as the population increased, and evolved organically over time in response to topography and available resources and social needs. However, judging by the political turmoil that characterised the Renaissance, social order did not necessarily follow the imposition of architectural order. When built, these geometrically perfect cities, planned with wide streets radiating from a symbolic centre, were easier to defend in times of attack. Nevertheless the populations soon outgrew them and the cities expanded, often in a chaotic manner beyond the walls.

We should expect that any large project or programme will attract very different approaches to management depending upon the various levels of order and chaos within the project and within the larger systems of which it is also a part – the organisation and the environment (Turner and Cochrane, 1993; Shenhar, 2001; Payne and Turner, 1999; Engwall et al., 2005). The key is to identify those parts of the project which exhibit characteristics of complex adaptive systems so that they can be handled differently from simpler parts of the project. Simpler parts or projects which have clear, shared objectives, use standard technologies and are able to be delivered over relatively short time spans will be more effectively handled using standard project management control processes.

FITNESS LANDSCAPES

Complexity theorists talk about the concept of fitness landscapes. Imagine a rugged landscape with rolling hills. Within that landscape your fitness is measured by your height relative to others' positions in the landscape. This can be thought of as having a better view. If you find yourself on a slope the tendency is to move up the hill if you want to improve your view and therefore your fitness. Once you reach a relatively high level of fitness, a local peak, you tend to stay there because leaving that peak, even to get to another higher nearby peak means becoming less fit during your progress to the higher peak. You have to travel through valleys to get to the second, more advantageous position, a process which might take considerable time. There may be little incentive to leave your local peak or position of advantage, especially if you cannot see any higher peaks nearby (see Griffin et al., 1999 and Lissack and Roos, 1999).

Being on the current peak may not necessarily be the optimum level of operation or the fittest position in the landscape. It may simply be a level sufficient to sustain activity. We often see this kind of adaptiveness in projects, particularly those involving technical innovation or design components. There is a point at which the design phase must come to a close so that something can be delivered. Enough of the needs of the key stakeholders are met and the urgency to deliver the product outweighs the need to make further refinement to 'perfect' the design. The local peak may be good enough to meet client needs. There may be no point striving for a better solution, moving to another peak, and there may possibly even be some level of risk as the situation may have changed by the time you get there.

A fitness landscape is not static. The landscape surrounding a complex adaptive system, such as a large organisation, might best be thought of as a moving sea, or shifting sand dunes in a desert. It changes over time. It also changes in response to your movement within it.

You are in and also part of the landscape, changing it for yourself and for others who may share the landscape with you. Movement in the fitness landscape can cause risks, particularly if what was once a local peak changes over time to become a valley. This can become even more problematic if your position within the landscape does not change. Therefore there can be great advantage in being aware of the need to take as many positions and viewpoints as possible and having the skills to do so.

EDGE OF CHAOS

The edge of chaos is a theoretical point between order and chaos (see Crutchfield and Young, 1990; Beinhoffer, 1997). When a system is at the edge of chaos it is in a poised state, able to readily react to environmental change. It is a state close to chaos, but just before the system starts to break down into truly chaotic behaviour. At the edge of chaos the system gets the benefits of a high level of creativity and diffuse sensitivity to the environment, whilst maintaining sufficient coherence and internal consistency to survive. For an organisation delivering part or all of its business by projects, the edge of chaos occurs at a point that permits maximum use of information both internally and from the environment (see Stacey, 1996; Griffin et al., 1999).

Where the edge of chaos is for a system will vary. It partly depends upon how rugged the fitness landscape is at that particular time. For instance you can be quite ordered while moving towards greater fitness in a relatively flat environment. You can see a long distance when on a hill surrounded by plains. In such a situation you may be able to move reasonably safely across a flat landscape to the next high vantage point. You can focus on control and efficiency as the situation is well structured and clear. On the other hand, in a rugged environment where observation is obscured by other hills or valleys, less order and consequent wider boundaries will be useful in noticing and moving towards points of greater fitness. In this kind of landscape you would be wise to send out investigating expeditions to get a sense not only of the actual lie of the land but also what surprises it may hold behind the hills and ridges where you cannot see.

Where the edge of chaos occurs for any project at any one time depends on the context and will move in relation to changes in context. For instance, for a very well-defined project the edge of chaos will be very close to order. Because the project is in a stable and well-defined context it is possible and useful to apply traditional techniques, such as decomposition of work and specialisation, defined by clear objectives. There is less need to be exploratory. In a project characterised by turbulence and lack of clarity the edge of chaos may be more towards chaos. This is because the project team needs to have greater awareness of the environment and may need to trial multiple options. Specialisation might not be a possibility until the context is more stable.

Summary

This chapter discussed the following concepts:

Systemic pluralism   Managing within complex environments requires the ability to observe systems from many different perspectives and to apply a range of tools and methodologies to suit the needs of the situation at that time.

Types of complexity   Based on the source of complexity, four different types of complexity have been identified, each exhibiting distinctly different characteristics, and presenting different management challenges.

Complexity types in combination   All large projects and many smaller ones can exhibit more than one type of complexity. It must also be recognised that complex projects may also have aspects that are straightforward. These are most efficiently managed using standard project management processes.

Order to chaos – a continuum   There exists in any system a continuum between order and chaos. Complex systems will exhibit a varying degree of order and chaos. Neither a fully ordered nor a fully chaotic system is complex.

Fitness landscapes   This is a concept used by complexity theorists to describe different positions of advantage in a system. The concept uses the idea of peaks and valleys which are not static but move over time. Being higher on the landscape implies greater fitness, but it is not always worthwhile trying to reach a higher peak. You may have to walk through many valleys of lower fitness to get there.

Edge of chaos   This is another concept developed by complexity theorists. It is a point between order and chaos where the system gets the benefit of some level of chaos and the resulting creativity whilst the system still has enough order to survive, maintain coherence and specialisation in some functions.

In the chapters to follow

The book is divided into two parts. Part I will explore the special conditions characterising each of the four types of project complexity summarised above and issues related to managing complex projects in organisational settings. Part II will describe a series of tools and techniques influenced by and developed from complexity theory, design theory, soft systems thinking, behavioural psychology and adult education theory which can be used to help unravel and manage the various types of complexity.

References and further reading

Anderson, P. (1999), 'Complexity Theory and Organization Science', *Organization Science* 10:3, 216-323.

Arthur, B. W. (1989), 'Positive Feedback in the Economy', *Scientific American* 262, 2.

Baccarini, D. (1996), 'The Concept of Project Complexity – A Review', *International Journal of Project Management* 14:4, 201-4.

Beinhoffer, E. (1997), 'Strategy at the Edge of Chaos', *McKinsey Quarterly*, No.1.

Checkland, P. (1981), *Systems Thinking, Systems Practice*, (Chichester, UK: John Wiley & Sons).

Checkland, P. (1999), 'Soft Systems Methodology: a 30-Year Retrospective', in Checkland, P. and Scholes, J., (eds.) *Soft Systems Methodology in Action*, A1 - A65 (Chichester, UK: John Wiley & Sons).

Checkland, P. and Howell, S. (1998), *Information, Systems and Information Systems – Making Sense of the Field*, (West Sussex, UK: John Wiley & Sons).

Crutchfield, J. and Young, K. (1990), 'Computation at the Onset of Chaos', in *Entropy, Complexity, and the Physics of Information*, W. Zurek, (ed.), SFI Studies in the Sciences of Complexity, VIII, (Reading, MA: Addison-Wesley) 223-69.

Daft, R. L. and Lewin, A. R. (1990), 'Can Organization Studies Begin to Break Out of the Normal Science Straight Jacket: An Editorial Essay', *Organization, Science* 1, 1-9.

Dooley, K. J. and Van de Ven, A. (1999), 'Explaining Complex Organizational Dynamics', *Organization Science* 10:3, 358-72.

Eisner, H. (2005), *Managing Complex Systems: Thinking Outside the Box*. (Hoboken, NJ: John Wiley & Sons).

Engwall, M., Kling, R. and Werr, A. (2005), 'Models in Action: How Management Models are Interpreted in New Product Development', *R & D Management* 35:4, 427-39.

Flood, R. and Jackson, M. (1991), *Creative Problem Solving: Total Systems Intervention.* (NY: John Wiley & Sons).

Griffin, D., Shaw, P. and Stacey, R. (1999), 'Knowing and Acting in Conditions of Uncertainty: A Complexity Perspective', *Systemic Practice and Action Research* 12 (3), 295-309.

Harrison, F.L. (2004), *Advanced Project Management: A Structured Approach.* (Aldershot, UK: Burlington, VT: Gower).

Jackson, M.C. (2000), *Systems Approaches to Management.* (NY: Plenum Publishers).

Kerzner, H. (2005), *Project Management: A Systems Approach to Planning, Scheduling and Controlling.* (NY: John Wiley and Sons).

Lewin, R. (1992), *Complexity: Life at the Edge of Chaos.* (NY: Macmillan Publishing).

Lissack, M. and Gunz. H. (1999), *Managing Complexity in Organizations: A View in Many Directions.* (Westport, USA: Quorum Books).

Lissack, M. and Roos, J. (1999), *The Next Common Sense.* (London, UK: Nicholas Brealey Publishing).

Maguire, S. and McKelvey, B. (1999), 'Complexity and Management: Moving From Fad to Firm Foundations', *Emergence* 1:2.

McKelvey, B. (1999), 'Complexity Theory in Organization Science: Seizing the Promise or Becoming a Fad?', *Emergence* 1:1, 5-32.

Midgley, G. (1996), 'What Is This Thing Called CST?', in Flood, R. and Romm, N. (eds.), *Critical Systems Thinking: Current Research and Practice.* (NY: Plenum Publishers) 11-24.

Midgley, G. (2000), *Systemic Intervention: Philosophy, Methodology, and Practice.* (NY: Plenum Publishers).

Midgley, G. (2003), *Systems Thinking.* (London, UK: Sage).

Mingers, J. (1997), 'Multi-paradigm Multimethodology', in *Multimethodology: The Theory and Practice of Combining Management Science Methodologies.* Mingers, J. and Gill, A. (eds.), (Chichester, UK: John Wiley & Sons) 1-20.

Mingers, J. (2003), 'A Classification of the Philosophical Assumptions of Management Science Methods', *Journal of the Operational Research Society* 54, 559-70.

Payne, J. H. and Turner, J. R. (1999), 'Company-wide Project Management: The Planning and Control of Programmes Of Projects of Different Type', *International Journal of Project Management*, 17:1, 55-9.

Petzinger, T. (1999), 'Complexity – More than a Fad?' in Lissack, M. & Gunz, H (eds). *Managing Complexity in Organizations: A View in Many Directions.* (Westport, USA: Quorum Books) 29-34.

Pidd, M. (2004), *Systems Modelling: Theory and Practice.* (Chichester, UK: John Wiley & Sons).

Pinto, J. K. and Trailer, J. W. (Eds) (1999), *Essentials of Project Control.* (Newton Square, PA: Project Management Institute).

Remington, K. and Crawford, L. (2004), 'Illusions of Control: Philosophical Foundations for Project Management', *IRNOP VI Conference*, Turku, Finland, August 25–27 2004 (Abo Akademi University Press).

Richardson, K. A. and Lissack, M. (2001), 'On the Status of Boundaries, both Natural and Organizational: A Complex Systems Perspective', *Emergence*, 3:4, 32-49.

Shenhar, A. J. (2001), 'One Size Does Not Fit All Projects: Exploring Classical Contingency Domains', *Management Studies* 47:3, 394–414.

Stacey, R. (1991), *The Chaos Frontier: Creative Strategic Control for Business.* (Oxford, UK: Butterworth-Heineman).

Stacey, R. (1996), *Complexity and Creativity in Organizations.* (San Francisco, CA: Berrett-Koehler Publishers, Inc.).

Turner, J. R. (1999), *The Handbook of Project-Based Management.* 2nd Edition. (London, UK: McGraw-Hill).

Turner, J. R. and Cochrane, R. A. (1993), 'Goals-and-Methods Matrix: Coping with Projects with Ill Defined Goals and/or Methods of Achieving Them', *International Journal of Project Management* 11, 93.

Warfield, J.N. (1999), 'Twenty Laws of Complexity: Science Applicable in Organizations', *Systems Research and Behavioral Science* 16, 3-40.

White, L. (2001), 'Effective Governance Through Complexity Thinking and Management Science', *Systems Research and Behavioral Science* 18, 241-57.

Williams, T. M. (1999), 'The Need for New Paradigms for Complex Projects', *International Journal of Project Management* 17, 269-73.

Williams, T. M. (2002), *Modelling Complex Projects.* (Chichester, UK: John Wiley & Sons).

Types of Project Complexity: Character and Management

2 Where Complexity Comes From in a Management Context

Complexity and perception

Complexity in a management context is a matter of perception and ambiguity. Whether or not you see a situation as complex has to do with how you perceive it. Some may not see a situation as complex because their range of perception is too narrow. Perhaps they are focusing too intently on a single area of expertise, and ignoring anything that does not directly relate to it. Some others may not see a situation as complex because they have extensive experience in the area, and know what to look for, ignoring extraneous information as background noise. They may look at a situation that others see as complex, pick out the significant markers in the environment, and then steer easily through what others may consider a storm. Most of us see the complexity and wonder what to do with the mess we are surrounded by. We might be assailed on all sides, with the situation developing on all fronts at once. We might spend half our time following false leads, trying to work out which bits of information are important, and which can be ignored. For further discussion see Lissack and Gunz (1999).

In China, particularly during the Ming Dynasty, very special gardens were created which were really metaphors for the complex world outside the garden. When you are inside the garden it is very, very difficult *not* to get lost. Finding your way out becomes a real challenge as you explore the beautiful vistas which unfold. At every turn more choices unfold and more delights appear to distract the traveller. It is not until you see an aerial perspective drawing of the garden that the design, in all its intricacy, is able to be fully comprehended.

What we inevitably do in a complex situation is focus on some areas, to the exclusion of others. This is necessary and natural, as our attention can only be in so many places at once. We focus on some areas, and let others take their course. We consciously or unconsciously categorise things and events in order to make some sense of the mess. As we can't possibly deal with everything at the same time, it is important that our attention is focused on the most significant areas, the pivot points around which the direction of the project can be steered at the moment. We need to recognise also that these pivot points might change as we move down the track.

Logical problems arising from the process of categorisation

To help us think about complexity in a project context we have classified complex projects into four types; structural, technical, directional and temporal, based on the sources of complexity. Projects have been classified using a range of other categories, such as scale or cost of project, degree of risk to the owner, the sector in which the project is managed, the technological characteristics of the project, where the methods and goals are clear, etc. (see Crawford et al., 2006, for a more thorough discussion).

For our purposes the source of complexity has proved to be useful as a basis for categorisation because it helps us think about causes and therefore possible remedies. Also, with the exception of structural complexity, which is associated mostly with projects that are large in scale, projects of all sizes can be affected by complexity arising from technical design issues, lack of agreed direction and temporal constraints. Equally these sources of complexity can be found across industry sectors. Even a very low cost project can have high risk implications for the project owner, as anyone who has managed a politically sensitive project will verify. However, we acknowledge that these categories aren't necessarily distinct. Combinations are likely and the real world consistently defies any attempts to be bounded by categories. The danger in categorising anything is that there will be situations, events or things that do not fit into any of the pre-determined categories. References on the subject include Bowker and Star (1999) and Foucault (1970).

Therefore categories are useful but the very act of categorisation results in omissions and the focus then becomes the categories rather than the potential spaces between the categories or the super-categories created by the amalgamation of categories and the spaces between them. These are issues of systemicity of which we try to remain mindful.

Focus in complex projects

We return to the problem of focus in complex projects. Given that we cannot focus on everything at once, how do we know which are the most significant areas on which to focus? This is where categorisation is helpful, bearing in mind its intrinsic limitations. The four types of project complexity are categories which we have developed to help structure thinking about project complexity.

NAVIGATING COMPLEXITY

When you see the right markers in a situation, it can become relatively easy to steer through the complexity. What looked like a complex situation can then resolve into something simpler and more manageable. With the right markers your perception can be given anchors amongst the maelstrom. Your attention can be focused on what is of significance. We can't tell you exactly what to look for to resolve a complex situation into one that can be managed, as this will vary from project to project, and from person to person. However, you can use the tools in this book and other fully developed tools and approaches, some of which we have referred to, to help identify the most significant markers in your context.

There is no magic formula for complexity. No one framework fits all situations; but our research has indicated that expert practitioners tend to develop an almost intuitive understanding of how a complex situation can be appropriately simplified. Until then, you have to look at each situation you are presented with, assess it by its own merits, then consciously and explicitly apply tools to develop your understanding of what's going on.

DIFFERENT PERSPECTIVES

With all types of project complexity an important management skill is being able to deliberately change between different levels of analysis. It is necessary to be able to adopt an overview of a situation as well as a detailed view. This can be thought of as the difference between being an eagle or a mouse. However, being able to change perspective well involves not only the ability to look at the fine detail and to look at the big picture, but also being able to choose different points in between and to choose how each point in between is looked at.

In theory, while looking at a system in overview it should be possible to see in all directions; to see everything at once. However, it is important to recognise that any system can be viewed from multiple perspectives, and that all perspectives both highlight some aspects of a situation and blind you to others. It is possible, not only to move up and down to different levels of abstraction, but also to change the way in which you are looking at the situation, to move up and down on different planes. When managers swoop down from their clouds to intervene on a particular occasion it doesn't mean the next time they will be swooping in the same way or in the same plane in which they did last time.

A simple example, involving standard project management tools, might involve looking at a project from an organisational perspective using an organisational breakdown structure, then changing to another perspective, focusing on products or outcomes of the project using a product breakdown structure. Both of these everyday project management tools provide different perspectives on the project as a whole. They direct attention towards particular aspects of the project. Either tool allows the manager to move up and down a hierarchy. When managers change between the tools they are changing their perspective, and can now move up or down a hierarchy on a different plane (see Figure 2.1).

In many cases more than one tool may be appropriate for a situation. Alternating between the tools will help alternate between different perspectives, help find new perspectives from which to view the situation, and provide insight into new ways to take action in a situation. The ability to change perspectives at will is a vital skill when managing complex projects and programs. The simplest way to do this is through consciously selecting different tools or methodologies.

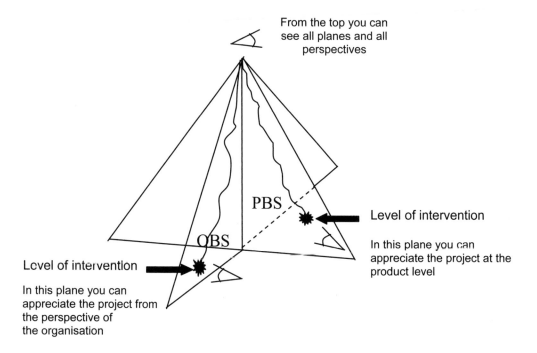

Figure 2.1   Changing perspectives

Reflective practice

There is then one final step in developing an understanding of how complex projects work. This step is often ignored or pushed to the side, and in a busy working environment it is understandable why. However, its value cannot be overstated. In order to improve, we must reflect on the project. This can be reflection on the ways in which our project aligned with the four types of complexity, how it didn't and how this changed over time. We can reflect on the effectiveness of the tools chosen, and how they could be applied differently to greater effect. We can also reflect on the relationship between the tools, the general approach that was employed for the project, and how these addressed the specific needs of a project of that kind of complexity. Reflective practice is one of the most effective ways to achieve deep learning.

The literature on reflective practice is well developed. Interested readers are referred to Jarvis (1999) who provides practical insight into how reflection and practice can be combined. The Action Research community also provides a great deal of information on ways to effectively cycle between periods of reflection and action. Stringer (1999) provides a good overview of the field. Checkland and Holwell (1998) detail ways that Action Research can be structured before and during a project, to facilitate learning afterwards. Interesting, and more specific, commentaries are also provided by Baskerville and Wood-Harper (1998), Champion and Stowell (2003) and Swepson (2003).

Quantity, ambiguity and interconnectedness

A good place to start developing a greater understanding of complexity is by looking at where complexity comes from.

Complexity, very generally, is a result of interrelationships and feedback between increasing numbers of areas of uncertainty or ambiguity. When there are few areas of uncertainty in a project and little interconnection between then, then complexity is generally seen as low. When all other aspects of a project are well defined, dealing with a single area of uncertainty is not too difficult. For instance, it is not a particularly complex situation if all aspects of a project are going to schedule, but uncertainty remains regarding the completion date for a single work package being handled by a contractor.

However, the complexity of the situation is generally seen to rise when the number of areas of uncertainty increases, especially if these areas are interdependent. For instance, if multiple interdependent aspects of a project are being handled by contractors who cannot give you firm completion dates, managing the project becomes significantly more complex. It is this ambiguity between different interconnected aspects of a project which creates the perception of complexity.

Below a certain threshold, the complexity in a situation is easily understood by the human mind. Past this threshold, the variety of potential links between areas of ambiguity and the consequences of these different links become too much to hold at once. As we keep adding more and more ambiguous elements to a project, the project passes from being merely difficult to being complex. At some point, the project goes through phase transition, and starts to exhibit emergent properties which could not be predicted from looking at the individual parts. The project will start to show non-linear behaviour. This change in quality is a function of the number of different elements in the project and their interconnectedness.

A similar effect can be seen when you compare the brains of different creatures. The neurons which make up the brains of humans and of other creatures are fundamentally the same. The complexity and the emergent behaviours associated with it arise from the number of neurons in the human brain. Smaller brains contain fewer neurons. The range of possible ways in which these neurons can interact and form complex networks is prohibitively limited by the number of neurons. However, once the number of neurons and interconnections between them grows past a certain threshold level, emergent behaviours become apparent, which were not previously possible. This is not a linear progression, but one where huge leaps are taken once a threshold is passed. There may be multiple thresholds that a system could potentially pass. As each threshold number of interacting elements is passed there is an increased possibility for interaction, and thus new behaviours in the system can emerge.

In a management context, the phase transition from complicated to complex has to do with our ability to understand and predict the behaviour of the system. Below a certain threshold number of project elements, we can see the whole system at once, or at least enough of it to know what the whole is doing. Above this threshold, we can't any more. It becomes too difficult to hold all the different pieces in your head at once. As a consequence, it becomes impossible to monitor all the interrelationships between these different project elements, or to work out which are the important elements and interrelationships, and which can be ignored. It also becomes more difficult to move between levels of analysis, to move from looking at the parts to looking at the whole. As a result, the ability to predict and understand emergent properties is significantly diminished.

Imagine a project described by Figure 2.2. The dark circles represent aspects of the project which are well defined, which are stable, or about which there is considerable confidence. The grey circle represents an aspect of the project which is ambiguous or uncertain. The area of uncertainty

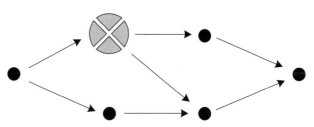

Figure 2.2   Four possibilities

may have to do with the potential completion times for a deliverable, or perhaps possible design solutions. For the sake of discussion, let's assume that there are four likely states into which this aspect of the project could resolve. Although this uncertainty may cause some difficulty in the project, it is unlikely to produce an overly complex situation, especially if the other aspects of the project with which it is interconnected are relatively stable, defined or predictable.

In Figure 2.3, we have the same structure. This time we have three ambiguous aspects of the project, each of which could take one of four possible values. These three areas are interconnected, and potentially interdependent. In this case, planning becomes more difficult, as it may be necessary to resolve the uncertainty in one area of the project before planning for subsequent areas can continue in earnest. However, in this example,

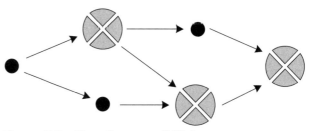

Figure 2.3   Sixty-four possibilities

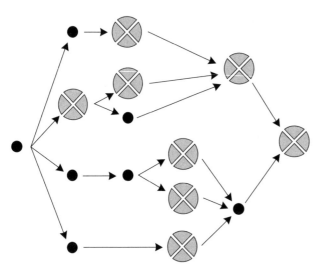

Figure 2.4   **65 536 possibilities, illustrating the rapid expansion of possible states**

there are only 64 different possible ways in which the project can play out, and planning and managing the project should not prove too problematic.

Figure 2.4 provides a model for a larger project involving fifteen different aspects. In this case, eight of these project areas are described as uncertain, each of which can take one of four possible states. With eight areas of uncertainty, we have a staggering 65 536 different possible ways in which the project can play out. Managing under this level of uncertainty certainly now becomes a significantly more complex task.

Project situations can be much more complex than implied by the diagram above. Before we discuss this further it is useful to briefly examine how thinking about complex problem solving has progressed in other disciplines, such as cognitive psychology and design.

'Satisficing' zones

In a project context limitations of time and other resources lead the project team to the decision that satisfies – the so-called 'satisficing' solution. The term 'to satisfice' was coined by Herbert Simon to describe the situation where people seek solutions or accept choices or judgements that are 'good enough' for their purposes (Simon, 1957, cited in Kunda, 1999). In the tradition of rationalistic decision making, it was conventionally assumed that individuals seek the optimal result. Instead, as Simon argues, it is often rational to seek to satisfice, in that the process of looking for better solutions expends resources. A better solution would thus have to justify the extra costs carried in finding it. Middleton (1998) includes a satisficing zone as the part of the problem-space, an area within which agreement is reached that a satisfactory resolution has been achieved.

In a complex project the satisficing zone may be unable to be specified with any precision. Extending Middleton's (1998) argument to the project environment, the project may move towards closure when the project team or key stakeholders agree either that set goals have been achieved or that old goals have not been achieved but the project satisfices under a more current set of criteria. The project team may also abandon problem solving at any stage on realising that pursuing it any further becomes redundant under a new state that has emerged or when they are not able to make adequate sense to solve it effectively.

The satisficing zone in design problems is ambiguous because precise goal criteria are typically unknown (Simon, 1981). For example, the goal criteria for a project to design a car to suit a newly identified market are ambiguous because the criteria that determine the success of the new design may only become apparent after the product has reached the market.

Identifying the satisficing zone for a complex project, whether technically or directional complex, can be further complicated by linked or contradictory goal criteria.

Problem and solution spaces

In the rapid expansion of possibilities in a complex project we can see that the areas of a project which are ambiguous do not tend to fall into neat possible outcomes. Typically, an ambiguous aspect of a project will eventually take one of a range of possible outcomes. This final value can be thought of as a point within a multidimensional space, instead of one of a selection of predefined options. For projects, these can be thought of in terms of problem and solution spaces.

Each area of ambiguity in a project can be thought of as a paired problem and solution space (see Figure 2.5), both of which may change as the project develops. A problem space is the range in which the final definition of a problem will exist. The problem space may change in response to changing client demands, or in the light of developments in interconnected areas of the project. The solution space is the range in which a solution to the problem will be found. The solution space may change in response to changes in the problem space or in response to an increased understanding of which solutions are possible, given available resources.

Each area of ambiguity in a project can then be thought of, not as a selection between distinct possibilities, but as a range in which the problem and solution can be found. These are malleable ranges which may change in size, shape and quality as a project progresses. Most work packages, tasks or deliverables can be defined in terms of problem and solution spaces and can be thought of as occupying a range of possibilities, rather than a single defined point. There is some ambiguity associated with every piece of project work.

Different kinds of ambiguity have different effects on a project. These different kinds of ambiguity result in four distinctly different kinds of complexity. This is discussed in greater detail in the next four chapters, each of which focuses on one kind of complexity.

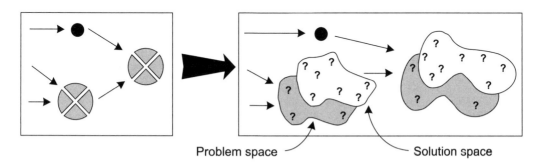

Problem space   Solution space

Figure 2.5   Interconnected problem and solution spaces

Summary

This chapter discussed the following concepts:

Complexity is a matter of perception   Not everyone will see complexity in a situation. Whether you do is a function of how you are looking at it. Both people who have too narrow a focus and those who are very experienced in a situation may not see a situation as complex, although for different reasons.

Categorisation   How we categorise and the categories we develop to understand, communicate and manipulate the world are dependent upon the methods that we are using to categorise. Categories enable communication, but also blind us to certain characteristics of an object.

Problem and solution spaces   The definitions of the problem and solution for a project can both be thought of as occupying a point within a range of possible outcomes. The problem and solution may both be developed throughout the life of the project.

Where perception of complexity comes from   Perception of complexity in a management context comes from the varying influence of the quantity of different elements in play, how ambiguous they are, and the level of interconnectedness between different elements. The four kinds of complexity outlined in this book exhibit these qualities in different ways.

Quantity   The greater the number of interconnected elements, the more complex the project is likely to appear, as it becomes increasingly difficult to keep track of the state of all elements, and as the number of possible outcomes rapidly increases.

Ambiguity   Greater ambiguity in the problem and solution spaces of the various project elements will result in the project appearing more complex, as ambiguity prevents detailed planning, instead requiring ongoing monitoring and definition.

Interconnectedness   The more interconnected different project elements are, the more complex the project will appear, requiring that the project be seen as an interdependent whole, instead of as separable parts.

References and further reading

Baskerville, R. and Wood-Harper, A. T. (1998), 'Diversity in Information Systems Action Research Methods', *European Journal of Information Systems* 7, 90-107.

Bowker, G. C. and Star, S. L. (1999), *Sorting Things Out: Classification and Its Consequences*. (Cambridge, MA and London, UK: MIT Press).

Champion, D. and Stowell, F. (2003), 'Validating Action Research Field Studies: PEArL', *Systemic Practice and Action Research* 16:1, 21-36.

Checkland, P. and Holwell, S. (1998), *Information, Systems and Information Systems – Making Sense of the Field*. (West Sussex, UK: John Wiley & Sons).

Crawford, L., Hobbs, B. and Turner, J.R. (2006), 'Aligning Capability with Strategy: Categorising Projects to do the Right Projects and to do Them Right', *Project Management Journal* 37:2, 38-51.

Dey, I. (1999), *Grounding Grounded Theory*. (London, UK and California, USA: Academic Press) 48-57.

Foucault, M. (1970), *The Order of Things. An Archaeology of the Human Sciences* (first published in 1966 in French under the title, *Les Mots et les Choses*, Paris: Éditions Gallimard) (London, UK: Tavistock Publications).

Glaser, B. and Strauss, A. (1967), *The Discovery of Grounded Theory: Strategies for Qualitative Research.* (Chicago, USA: Aldine).

Jarvis, P. (1999), 'Global Trends in Lifelong Learning and the Response of the Universities', *Comparative Education* 35:2, 249-257.

Kunda, Z. (1999), *Social Cognition: Making Sense of People.* (Cambridge, MA: MIT Press).

Lissack, M. and Gunz. H. (1999), *Managing Complexity in Organisations: A View in Many Directions.* (Westport, USA: Quorum Books).

Middleton, E. (1998), *The Role of Visual Mental Imagery in Solving Complex Problems in Design,* PhD. Thesis. (Queensland, Australia: Griffith University).

Simon, H. A. (1957), *Administrative Behavior: A Study of Decision-making Processes in Administrative Organization.* (New York: Macmillan).

Simon, H. A. (1973), 'The Structure of Ill-Structured Problems', *Artificial Intelligence* 4, 181-201.

Simon, H. A. (1981), *The Sciences of the Artificial,* 2nd Edition (Cambridge, MA: MIT Press)

Stringer, E.T. (1999), *Action Research,* 2nd Edition. (Thousand Islands, CA, London: Sage Publications).

Swepson, P. (2003), 'Some Common Ground that can provide a Basis for Collaboration between Action Researchers and Scientists: A Philosophical Case that Works in Practice', *Systemic Practice and Action Research* 16:2, 99-111.

3 *Structurally Complex Projects*

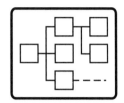

The questions associated with this kind of complexity are:

'How does it all fit together so that we can manage it?' or
'How can we keep track of all the interdependencies?'

Words or phrases you might hear or think when confronted with this type of complexity are:

- You can't see the forest for the trees.
- How do we coordinate this nightmare?
- This is impossible to schedule.
- There are too many potential risks to be able to track or manage.
- How do I keep all this in my head?
- There is too much going on at once.

Structural complexity is found most frequently in large-scale engineering, construction, IT and defence projects which are able to be broken down into many small tasks and separate contracts. They are usually managed through clearly defined hierarchies; they have complex communication structures and many interrelated and dependent parts. The myriad of risks that have to be identified and managed make it very difficult to keep a grasp on risks that trigger other risks in a kind of chain reaction. The sheer size of the project and the numbers of interdependent tasks mean that non-linear behaviour will emerge, making control of the project very difficult.

In Chapter 1 we mentioned that this kind of complexity is often referred to as being complicated rather than complex. The complexity stems from the difficulty in managing and keeping track of a huge number of different tasks and activities which are interrelated and coupled. The major challenges relate to project organisation, scheduling, interdependencies, contract management, keeping track of the risks and spotting interconnected and dependent risks.

Explained in terms of Complexity Theory

From close up, many of the elements (for example sub-projects) of a structurally complex project look significantly like the elements of other non-complex projects, especially those undertaken in a similar industry. When each element of the project is taken separately, it may appear that nothing significant is going on. When five or six such elements are operating in the same environment, there still may not be any real complexity. However, as we keep adding more elements something significant happens. As we pass a critical number of elements the project crosses a threshold and goes through a phase transition. It becomes a structurally complex project. It starts to exhibit emergent characteristics, it becomes significantly more dependent on initial conditions, and shows very particular patterns of communication and control.

In Chapter 1 we introduced the idea that perception of complexity in a management context is a function of the number of elements, their interconnectedness and the ambiguity involved. One factor which distinguishes a structurally complex project from other kinds of complex projects is the kind of ambiguity involved.

Figure 3.1 represents a project at a particular point in time. Six interconnected areas of ambiguity are depicted, each showing a different solution space for a different aspect of the project. These could represent the solutions being developed by six interdependent aspects of the project, such as six sub-project teams. Constraints are also shown on the figure, implying that some solution spaces are unavailable. This may be because of client requirements, environmental constraints, or time, cost and resource constraints.

WHAT COMPLEXITY LOOKS LIKE IN THESE PROJECTS

The complexity in a structurally complex project is qualitatively different from other kinds of complex projects. In structurally complex projects the complexity comes from the uncertainty regarding time, cost and resource requirements. Even if the scope, time and cost of each element can be estimated with a high degree of accuracy, the sheer number of interdependent

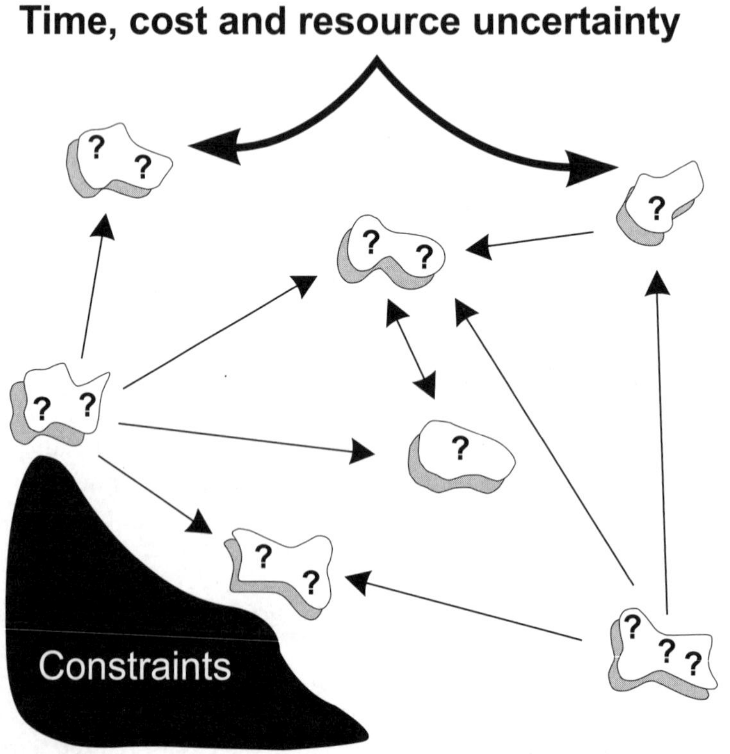

Figure 3.1   Uncertainty in structurally complex projects

elements means that a single change in terms of scope, time, cost or quality has the potential to set off a chain reaction involving the other interrelated elements. Although there may not be a high level of uncertainty in any one element, the massive degree of interconnectedness between a large number of sub-projects provides the main source of complexity.

Time, cost and resource estimating and planning are amongst the central foci of project management. Many techniques developed in these areas are highly sophisticated, and capable of very accurate estimates. As such, it is often possible to have solution spaces for these projects which are quite tightly defined, that is, it is known that the solution to a problem will fall within a relatively narrow range. Similarly, the problem space for these projects may also be tightly defined, often before the project even begins.

As both problem and solution spaces can be well defined, it is possible to have many interconnected areas of the project in play at one time. As a result, these projects can become quite large, before the ambiguity between interconnected areas compounds and the project becomes complex, creating emergent effects which cannot be predicted merely from a selection of sub-projects.

Structures developed to manage time, cost and resource uncertainty typically take very specific forms. Hierarchy is usually quite clearly defined in a structurally complex project. Systems and sub-systems are usually expressed through the formal management structure and there are often distinctive dividing lines between separate subsystems.

COMMUNICATION

Structurally complex projects also demonstrate particular patterns of communication. It should be noted that in the project management literature communication typically refers to how communication is planned so that information is transferred efficiently in order to achieve objectives and monitor performance. In Complexity Theory, communication refers to how information is passed between the sub-systems of a system, and between the system as a whole and its environment.

Structurally complex projects are usually characterized by rule-bound communication channels that are formal and very efficient at passing information defined by stable system rules. The system becomes very proficient at passing designated information in designated ways. The information channels almost become hard wired to only pass specific information, and in so doing the system becomes particularly efficient at responding to some external stimuli. For instance project information security requirements determine who gets the information. However, when the predetermined rules result in key people being unable to access vital information the system may be unable to respond efficiently enough to accommodate change in a timely manner.

As the communication system is strongly rule-bound it will be highly selective about which information is passed on. Other information will be completely ignored by the formal communication network. It should also be noted that the ability to efficiently pass some information in this kind of network is unrelated to any ability to efficiently source the information required for a specific task. Information which is required to complete one-off tasks is usually sourced through the informal network, an overlay of interaction between individuals within the organisation.

Communications pathways in structurally complex projects are usually defined by small groups of people who base their decisions on their prior knowledge of similar projects using an input–output model. If the decisions about communication protocols and pathways are found to be inefficient, people will set up informal communication pathways in order to get the job done. The larger the project, the greater is the likelihood that alternative informal pathways will operate within the system. If formal pathways do not meet communications needs and are only geared to providing information other than that needed by the project team at that time, adequate information will be sourced elsewhere. If information gathered informally is at variance with information provided though formal networks, then the project team may lose trust in the accuracy of the information which can in turn affect efficiency.

CONTROL

Control in Complexity Theory refers to the ability of a system to maintain its stability of form. This is considerably different from the project management literature, where control refers to achieving performance according to plan.

In structurally complex projects, such as large projects in the engineering, construction and defence industries, patterns of behaviour develop and protocols are introduced which will usually result in the system maintaining form very stubbornly. Personal roles and responsibilities are usually firmly defined, and patterns of interaction resist change throughout the life of the project. Internal controls are generally explicit and carefully managed, which contributes to a rigid form of stability.

Structurally complex projects do not tend to be particularly adaptive. Parts of the project will respond to environmental changes. However, due to the general size of structurally complex projects, they do not tend to adapt quickly as a whole. Think of trying to pick up a sleeping cat. Lifting your hand under part of it will only raise that part. Other parts will stay limply on the floor. In an allegorically similar way, structurally complex projects exhibit inertia in adaptation.

This can have both positive and negative effects. For instance, imagine that one subsystem in a large structurally complex project (such as a team working on one sub-project) uncovers evidence that there has been a significant environmental change, and that the whole project must change course. A structurally complex project will be slow as a whole to adapt to any significant environmental changes and, just like changing the course of a large container ship at sea, it will be difficult to make the necessary structural changes to change direction. However, on the positive side, imagine that the subsystem has overreacted or is wrong about the significance of the evidence they have found. In such a case, a structurally complex project may also easily absorb momentary shocks without flinching, with the majority of the system carrying on work, while the sub-system brings itself back into line.

Lack of adaptation can also be related to communication within the system. Communication is essentially hardwired and the system is very efficient for passing some, but only some, specific kinds of information. As a consequence, these hardwired communication channels can quickly alert the whole system to some situations, while information regarding other situations has to pass haphazardly through more informal networks. The system as a whole is only capable of quickly reacting to very specific kinds of signals.

SENSITIVITY TO INITIAL CONDITIONS

The initial conditions for a project can influence the way in which the project is defined and the direction in which the project is headed. Once the initial conditions have been addressed, structurally complex projects become very robust and the project will stubbornly march up the local peak, irrespective of change to the landscape. Think again about the large container ship in the process of changing direction. Once the command to commence the turn is implemented the ship gathers momentum. Stopping the ship from completing its turn becomes more and more difficult as the operation progresses. Structurally complex projects tend to be sensitively dependent on initial conditions in that once started, inertia will keep the project heading in the same direction, even if that direction is leading it into a local valley on the fitness landscape.

ORDER TO CHAOS

The closer the system is to order the easier it is to manage this kind of project, provided there are few externally imposed changes. The edge of chaos is relatively close to order for a structurally complex project. As chaotic behaviour within the system increases, non-linear and emergent effects will rapidly start to appear, due to the number of individual elements involved. Indeed, if a structurally complex project becomes too internally chaotic, it is likely to collapse. Although structurally complex projects may be robust in relation to shocks from the environment, it is typically difficult for them to reform in different configurations. This means that if environmental change is too significant, or the project becomes too internally chaotic, the system is more likely to break up than significantly restructure. This phenomenon also occurs in large bureaucracies which are rigidly controlled (see Stacey, 1991).

Ship-building provides a good example of a type of project which is prone to structural complexity. Although industry practice aims at solving most of the technical issues prior to building, constructing or doing a major refit of a ship is a big, complicated, expensive project. Ships are often built as one-offs or short runs with an emphasis on time to market and availability of dry-dock facilities. Ship repair and conversion is a large part of the industry. Most shipyards are functionally organised for maximum efficiency. In the constant search for additional efficiencies shipyards are also cutting down on staff. Environmental legislation is proliferating making the constraints on practices, particularly regarding waste management, more and more stringent. Concurrent working occurs across the entire supply chain on all phases of the projects, therefore the schedule networks are multi-layered, with many activities occurring in parallel. The costs and degree of specialisation required mean that each project is rarely the work of one shipyard.

Sources of complexity come from the number of people, groups and separate organisations involved. In order to manage all these elements there is usually a complicated hierarchy of supervision and governance as ship-building incurs very comprehensive auditing protocols. Complexity arises, therefore, from the huge number of interdependent activities which have the potential to affect each other in terms of delays, cost and quality issues and the equally complicated communication networks.

Inspection and testing must be carried out stringently on all critical components. If one component is found to be faulty it can affect hundreds of other dependent elements. For this reason quality checks must be exhaustive and the information generated is enormous.

Information and decision-making pathways are susceptible to delays and errors due to the amount of information being communicated and the fact that it needs to be communicated across several shipyards, with their own entrenched work practices. Special ship-building simulation programs have been developed to model and visualise the construction activities as well as the management decision processes in order to manage the interdependencies (McLean and Shao, 2001).

Given the number of people, organisations and components that have to be procured, sequenced, assembled and verified it is reasonable to expect that this kind of project must operate under a strict formal organisation. The communication networks must be carefully planned and the system must tend towards control if it is to be maintained. However, with the current trend to reduce personnel to a minimum the lack of redundancy in the system means that a key technician who is absent for a few days may cause major delays throughout the system, which may escalate, developing emergent properties very rapidly. In addition, informal communications systems which have supported formal networks are now undermined revealing inadequacies in the formal communication systems.

Project management challenges

In structurally complex projects project management challenges revolve around project organisation, including communications, scheduling, interdependencies and contract management. The challenge in relation to project organisation is how to obtain the shock-proofing associated with a clearly defined and robust structure while allowing for adaptation to changing environmental conditions once the project is underway.

An added constraint is that many structurally complex projects are high budget projects and subject to a great deal of public scrutiny. Therefore key stakeholders demand very high levels of certainty about budgets, timeframes and how risks will be managed. In reality that certainty can rarely be guaranteed but project directors and managers are expected to provide it, often very early in the project life cycle. This need to provide an appearance of control tends to influence choices of procurement systems, which are often selected from the more conservative options which produce the illusion of guaranteed certainty. As many authors, including Flyvbjerg et al. (2003) and Williams (2002), have pointed out, the failure rate, particularly in terms of cost overruns, for these very large, structurally complex projects is very high indeed.

CRITICAL PROJECT PHASES

In structurally complex projects critical project phases are usually distributed over all phases. However the early phases, such as definition and feasibility, are being identified as key. One major contributor to project failure in structurally complex projects is poor analysis of options and cost estimation, during the feasibility analysis phase, particularly if the scope is not fully understood, developed and detailed. Insufficient analysis can be due to political and social pressure to get the project underway. This has the effect of stripping away the time and resources needed to properly assess options and perform full and detailed cost analyses (see Flyvbjerg, et al., 2003).

Another contributor to project failure has been identified as poor risk analysis. This applies to planning and implementation phases. Once the project is in the implementation phase decisions must be made and implemented very quickly, as risks are triggered. It is difficult for the project manager to maintain an holistic perspective when there is a tendency to address risks individually as they appear. Terry Williams (2004) has also identified problems associated with risk mitigation actions which have themselves triggered further peripheral risks. If foundation budget estimates and risk analyses are not thorough the project manager has little robust information upon which to make rapid decisions. Once a number of risks accumulate, emergent characteristics which are non-linear and very difficult to predict can eventuate.

Adding to this, the rate of decision making required to address the emergent risks is often too great for any normal human being to cope with efficiently and accurately. Unfortunately the pressure to get these projects underway means that detailed planning is often rushed with resulting negative effects on implementation. Handover can also be problematic in that the focus on getting the project completed can result in loss of focus on the larger contextual issues associated with operation of the project.

EXECUTIVE SUPPORT

The most important aspects of executive support needed in structurally complex projects involve recognition of the need for detailed options analysis, cost estimation and risk analysis during the feasibility phase of the project. This might mean that executive sponsors have to fend off those stakeholders who want to rush the project, ensuring that space and time is available for the project team to complete the detailed planning needed for wise financial decisions. It usually requires a very high level of influence and may also take enormous courage to provide this kind of support.

Executive support is also vital during implementation and handover phases. During these phases, the project manager will be concerned with monitoring project risks on a daily basis. The project manager must be able to depend on rapid and effective escalation procedures and decision making in order to be able to control cost and time variances and manage risks as they are triggered.

Also during these phases, when the project team members are focused on the day-to-day detail, it is easy for them to lose sight of the big picture. The executive sponsor plays an important role during these phases in keeping the project team aware of contextual issues in the larger environment which might influence the project so that they can plan ahead and be ready to respond.

PROJECT MANAGER CAPABILITIES

These include many of the traditional project management capabilities such as the ability to programme, schedule, organise and integrate a multitude of tasks and activities; ability to see the overall picture as well as the detail; and strong contract management abilities. However, in structurally complex projects project managers also need the ability to think creatively and to be able to quickly respond with a range of possible options as risks are triggered. To do this the project manager needs to maintain a multi-perspective focus on the project. This ability to change focus has been referred to by a number of authors, who describe it as like being in a helicopter and landing briefly from time to time to deal with issues in detail as they arise, or alternating between the eagle and the mouse (Turner, 1999). Some of the tools in this book are designed to help project managers and their teams to break out of detailed thinking and look at situations through other frames.

Project managers engaged in structurally complex projects need to be able to assess a given situation, act quickly and decisively and often with substantial courage. There is some anecdotal evidence that in these kinds of projects the ability to make quick decisions is preferable to delays or no decision at all, even if a small percentage of decisions are wrong. This is because the delays caused by slow decision making can trigger even more risks. Project managers need to be fully capable of using all the standard project management planning and control tools, including advanced scheduling techniques and cost-control techniques, such as Earned Value. In addition they should have a sound knowledge of the organisational financial processes (Lundsten and Zimmerman, 2006).

In an investigation of large software projects Verner et. al (2007) have found that, from the point of view of the developer, success is more likely if the project manager is involved in all aspects of the project planning from the beginning. This research is fully supported by others (see for example Cleland and Ireland, 2006; Pinto, 1998).

TEAM SUPPORT

Generally project team members will be drawn from highly specialised disciplines, such as project scheduling, contract management, estimating, cost engineering, quality control and risk management, together with those charged with maintaining vigilant document control and reporting procedures. Such tasks require high levels of accuracy and attention to detail.

Although there are critics of personality testing (see particularly Mischel, 1996) it is probably reasonable to say that most people have preference for either detailed work or work which involves the big picture. It is common to find within project teams, particularly in fields like engineering and IT, that there is a greater preference for detail rather than the big picture. Although this level of focus on detail is essential to achieve control, it can also mean that project team members might be less inclined to take a multi-perspective approach to their work. This can result in oversight of systemic issues which cross boundaries. The project manager must look for ways to track the multiple interfaces which do not interfere with or overly stress team members who have detailed tasks to complete. This might simply involve regular meetings to discuss interface issues. Alternatively project teams might include extra team members who have an integrating function and who are good at making connections between team members and others associated with the project, as a way of assisting the project manager in identifying cross-boundary issues. It is false economy to save small amounts by reducing the project team to a minimum. Some redundancy in the project team is necessary for safety and sustainability (see Perrow, 1984) and knowledge management (Grant, 1996) especially if the project has a long duration.

FINANCIAL ISSUES

Structurally complex projects, being very large projects, usually have very large budgets. These may or may not be tied to government or organisational funding cycles and other external constraints. The record of cost control on very large projects is not good (DeMarco, 2005). However there is a great deal of literature in the field of cost estimating or cost engineering (see for example, Humphreys, 2005; Loch, 2004; Goodpaster, 2004).

Contributing factors, such as lack of time and resources allocated to the feasibility phases of such projects, resulting in poor estimating, have been discussed earlier. In addition to more rigorous approaches to estimating and risk planning, attitudes of governing authorities and promoters need to change to become more realistic about potential risk patterns which can emerge and the need for much larger contingencies to manage stakeholder expectations if costs do escalate. Researchers have identified the need for more appropriate contingencies and the dangers associated with over-optimistic estimating (see Dillon et. al., 2005; Flyvbjerg et al., 2003).

During implementation, variance control must be vigilant so that stakeholders are kept informed of possible cost blow-outs. Techniques like Earned Value Management (EVM), a tool which links scope with time and cost, can be used to translate schedule slippages into budgetary terms. Tools like EVM can assist the project manager to predict the cost variance caused by schedule variances and therefore the long-term implications for the project as a whole (references include, AS 4817-2006; Budd and Budd, 2005; Fleming and Koelman, 2005; Webb, 2003).

SCHEDULING ISSUES

Planning, monitoring and controlling the schedules of structurally complex projects are major tasks which are highly specialised and must be fully resourced with appropriately skilled people. Scheduling is recognised as a specialised profession in construction and engineering but in other sectors it is often under-resourced, being left for the project manager to manage alone. It is not uncommon in some disciplines for schedules to be produced for project approval but after that put in a drawer and not updated regularly after approval. As a result, schedules are often not fully utilized as project control and prediction tools.

Using the schedule as an effective project control tool requires a detailed knowledge of how to prepare and work with precedence networks, including time-scaled networks and critical path networks. Structurally complex projects also require considerable expertise in the use of top-end scheduling software products in order to monitor the project process. Some industries, such as defence and large-scale engineering, also favour scheduling methods that involve calculations of durations involving probability estimates, such as PERT and other similar techniques. On large, structurally complex projects more than one full-time scheduler may be required. The schedule is closely linked to scope, cost, risk and quality and the latest schedule update is often the place for evidence of risks being triggered which might lead to compound risk events. For this reason schedules in structurally complex projects must be reviewed and updated frequently, often daily, to detect where slippages will have impacts on deliverables. In the construction and engineering industries this is common practice, but such an intense focus on scheduling has not been common practice in other disciplines. Recently there has been a successful entry by construction and engineering project management firms into the IT project arena, because of the traditional emphasis by the former on managing large, structurally complex schedules. There are many excellent text books explaining the range of scheduling techniques for large projects (see for example, Lester, 2006; Cleland and Ireland, 2006; Lewis, 2005; Lock, 2004).

Fast-tracking, like concurrent engineering, involves the start of implementation before the final design and detailed specifications have been completed. This approach is usually adopted because of pressure from key stakeholders to get started. The overall level of complexity is increased exponentially in fast-tracked projects because of the additional sources of complexity. Fast-tracked projects have high propensities for significant cost overruns because they are likely to experience all four types of complexity – technical and directional complexity in addition to structural and temporal complexity. Cost and schedule overruns in fast-tracked projects have been the subject of much research (see Eatham, 2002).

RISK ISSUES

In structurally complex projects risks can escalate rapidly. A detailed risk management plan should be prepared and published. Usually risk analysis produces lists of risks which become the basis for decisions whether to accept or mitigate the risk, with each risk considered on an individual basis (see Edwards and Bowen, 2005). As the number of risks identified in a risk analysis increases, the propensity to miss possible associations between risks also increases dramatically. The tendency when identifying and managing risks is to avoid seeing the forest for trees. Risks may be identified and treated, but not in such a way that possibilities for emergent risk patterns are identified in advance. There is also some anecdotal evidence that commonly used risk identification techniques, involving panels of experts, are not consistently reliable, as experts may be constrained by their past experience.

In structurally complex projects there is the ever-present danger that risks will compound in emergent ways. Through positive feedback loops or 'vicious circles' they can escalate to dangerous proportions. The potential for risks to compound and escalate in this way is very difficult to identify using linear analysis techniques based on lists and matrices. Ackerman et al. (1997) and Williams et al. (2003) have used causal mapping and systems dynamics to investigate the cause of delays on major projects. These techniques may also assist in prediction of likely vicious circles or other emergent risk characteristics (Williams, 2004).

During implementation of large projects it is common practice to use a technique, such as Monte Carlo simulation, which applies probability modelling to predict impacts of risks to the schedule. However, as Williams (2004) points out, the usefulness of the technique may be undermined by project managers who must act quickly to recover late-running projects. The actions of the project manager are ignored in most models.

PROCUREMENT IMPLICATIONS

Selection, tendering and contract management procedures are generally connected with risk. Risks associated with selection and tendering are often related to lack of rigour in estimation. As noted above, this can be a result of inadequate time frames in the early stages of the project. It is important to think creatively and explore options for procurement, especially where suppliers have virtual monopolies on key commodities or services.

Usually structurally complex projects are managed via traditional procurement systems in conjunction with strict and regular supervision. In some cases, particularly if the project can be fully defined, standard procurement systems may provide the most efficient ways to control the many contracts involved. However, if risk events multiply there may be a need for directly affected contracts, associated contracts and downstream contracts to be terminated in order to stop the project and make decisions about the project viability and direction. Since the 1960s most contracts contain a 'termination for convenience' clause which gives the power to the principal to terminate the contract when circumstances indicate that the project needs to be terminated or halted to allow re-appraisal. However, as discussed later, there are a number of reasons why the powers under such a clause are not often invoked.

Some structurally complex projects are now being successfully managed through collaborative working arrangements, such as partnerships or alliances, as opposed to standard contracts (Dua, 2006). However these approaches are not without difficulty, particularly in relation to the cultural changes needed, such as 'trust', which are difficult to implement in industries which have a history of high levels of litigation (Zhang and Flynn, 2003).

Traps and consequences

A number of traps need to be watched for in structurally complex projects. The consequences of falling into these traps can have devastating results.

There is often inadequate attention to detail in the early phases of the project, resulting in poor estimation of time and cost. This can be a result of pressure to proceed from influential outside parties.

During implementation there is a tendency to focus on detail while ignoring the big picture during implementation. Similarly, there is often a lack of systemic investigation of risks, and reliance on linear risk analysis techniques, which prevents revelation of emergent risk patterns. This can result in an inability to capture potential for positive risk feedback loops and consequent emergent characteristics.

There is also a tendency to ignore growing problems which cross over traditional boundaries and areas of expertise. Disputes also need to be settled quickly before the internal chaos can spread. Both of these factors can contribute to vicious circles. When positive feedback loops are triggered they often cause sudden state change – one minute everything appears to be going relatively smoothly and then there is suddenly a crisis coming from all directions.

References and further reading

Ackerman, F., Eden, C. and Williams, T. (1997), 'Modelling for Litigation: Mixing Qualitative and Quantitative Approaches', *Interfaces* 2, 48-65.

AS 4817-2006, *Project Performance Measurement using Earned Value*. (Sydney, Australia: Standards Australia).

Budd, C. I. and Budd, C. S. (2005), *A Practical Guide to Earned Value Project Management*. (Vienna, VA: Management Concepts).

Cleland, D. I. and Ireland, L. R. (2006), *Project Management: Strategic Design and Implementation*. (NY: McGraw-Hill).

DeMarco, A. A. (2005), 'Six Steps to Project Success', *Cost Engineering* 47:9, 12-4.

Dillon, R. L., Pate-Cornell, M. E. and Guikema, S. D. (2005), 'Optimal Use of Budget Reserves to Minimise Technical and Management Failure Risks During Complex Project Development', *IEEE Transactions on Engineering Management* 52:2, 382-95.

Dua, R. M. (2006), 'Making Performance Happen using Collaborative Working Arrangements in the Construction Industry', *IRNOP VII Proceedings*. (Xi'an, China: Northwestern Politechnical University Press).

Eatham, G. (2002), *The Fast Track Manual: A Guide to Schedule Reduction for Clients and Contractors on Engineering and Construction Projects by the Fast Track Projects Study Task Force*. (Loughborough, UK: European Construction Institute).

Edwards, J. and Bowen, (2005), *Risk Management in Project Organisations*. (Sydney, Australia: UNSW Press).

Fleming, Q. W. and Koelman, J. M. (2005), *Earned Value Project Management*. (Newtown Square, PA: Project Management Institute).

Flyvbjerg, B., Bruzelius, N. and Rothengatter, W. (2003), *Megaprojects and Risk: An Anatomy of Ambition*. (Cambridge, UK: Cambridge University Press).

Goodpaster, J. C. (2004), *Quantitative Methods in Project Management*. (Boca Raton, FL: J. Ross Publishers).

Gould, F. E. (1997), *Managing the Construction Process : Estimating, Scheduling, and Project Control*. (Upper Saddle, NJ: Prentice Hall).

Grant, R. M. (1996), 'Toward a Knowledge-Based Theory of the Firm', *Strategic Management Journal* 17 - Special Issue, 109-122.

Grey, S. (1995), *Practical Risk Assessment for Project Management*. (Chichester, UK; Brisbane, Australia: John Wiley & Sons).

Harrison, F. L. (2004), *Advanced Project Management: A Structured Approach*. (Aldershot, UK: Burlington, VT: Gower).

Humphreys, K. K. (2005), *Project and Cost Engineers' Handbook*. (Morgantown, W. VA: AACE International; NY, USA: M. Dekker).

Lester, A. (2006), *Project Management, Planning and Control: Managing Engineering, Construction and Manufacturing Projects to PMI, APM and BSI Standards*. (Oxford, UK: Butterworth-Heinemann).

Lewis, J. (2005), *Project Planning, Scheduling, and Control: A Hands-On Guide to Bringing Projects in on Time and on Budget*. (NY: McGraw-Hill).

Loch, C., De Meyer, A. and Pich, M.T. (2006), *Managing the Unknown: A New Approach to Managing High Uncertainty and Risk in Projects*. (Hoboken, NJ: John Wiley & Sons).

Lock, D. (2004), *Project Management in Construction*. (Aldershot, Hants, UK; Burlington, VT: Gower Publishing).

Lundsten, D. J. and Zimmerman, S. E. (2006), 'The Financial Aspects of Project Management', *Contract Management* 46:4, 14-21.

McLean, C. and Shao, G. (2001), 'Simulation of Shipbuilding Operations', Manufacturing and Visualisation Group (NIST) in Peters, B. A., Smith, J. S., Medeiros, D. J. and Rohrer, M. W. (eds.) *Proceedings of the 2001 Simulation Conference*, Gaithersburg, USA.

Mishcel, W. (1996), *Personality and Assessment*. (Mahwah, NJ: Lawrence Erlbaum Associates).

Nicholas, J. M. (2004), *Project Management for Business and Engineering: Principles and Practice*. (Amsterdam, The Netherlands; Boston. MA: Elsevier Butterworth-Heinemann).

Perrow, C. (1984), *Normal Accidents: Living with High Risk Technologies*. (NY: Basic Books).

Pinto, J. K. (Ed.) (1998), *The Project Management Institute: Project Management Handbook*. (San Francisco, CA: Jossey-Bass Publishers).

Project Management Institute (2005), *Practice Standard for Earned Value Management*. (Newtown Square, PA: Project Management Institute Inc.).

Stacey, R. (1991), *The Chaos Frontier: Creative Strategic Control for Business*. (Oxford, UK: Butterworth-Heineman).

Turner, J. R. (1999), *The Handbook of Project-Based Management*. 2nd Edition. (London, UK: McGraw-Hill).

Verner, J. M., Evanco, W. M. and Cerpa, N. (2007), 'State of the Practice: An Exploratory Analysis of Schedule Estimation and Software Project Success Prediction', *Information and Software Technology* 49:2, 181-93.

Webb, A. (2003), *Using Earned Value: A Project Manager's Guide*. (Aldershot, Hants, UK; Burlington, VT, USA: Gower Publishing).

Williams, T. (2002), *Modelling Complex Projects*. (Sussex, UK: John Wiley & Sons).

Williams, T. (2004), 'Why Monte Carlo Simulations of Project Networks can Mislead', *Project Management Journal* 25:3, 53-61.

Williams, T., Ackermann, F. and Eden, C. (2003), 'Structuring a Delay and Disruption Claim: An Application of Cause-mapping and System Dynamics', *European Journal of Operational Research* 148:1, 192-204.

Wysocki, R. K. (2003), *Effective Project Management: Traditional, Adaptive, Extreme*. (Indianapolis, USA: John Wiley & Sons).

Verner, J. M., Evanco, W. M. and Cerpa, N. (2007), 'State of the Practice: An Exploratory Analysis of Schedule Estimation and Software Project Success Prediction', *Information and Software Technology* 49:2, 181-93.

Zhang, H. and Flynn, C. (2003), 'Effectiveness of Alliances Between Operating Companies and Engineering Companies', *Project Management Journal* 34:3, 48-52.

4 *Technically Complex Projects*

The questions associated with this kind of complexity are:

'How do we do or make it?' or
'How do we solve the technical or design problems?'

Words or phrases you might hear or think when confronted with this type of complexity are:

- There is nothing like this out there.
- I have never seen anything like this.
- No one has ever done this before.
- How can we make or solve it?

Technical complexity is found in projects which have design characteristics or technical aspects that are unknown or untried. There are no precedents on which the team can rely although there might be aspects of other projects that can be used to inform decision making. There are many risks associated with such projects. There is the real possibility in some technically complex projects that a solution will not be found and the product or service cannot be delivered at all. However, generally speaking an acute awareness of constraints such as stakeholder expectations, time, cost and reputation of the designers and technical experts themselves, results in a solution of some kind. The aim in this kind of project is generally to solve the technical issues early in the project so that implementing or building the project becomes a straightforward exercise. This is not always possible and protracted technical problems can increase the level of complexity of the project as time progresses. One of the most difficult aspects associated with this kind of project complexity is the black-box syndrome and the resultant power that the designers and technical experts can wield because they alone have a day-to-day grasp on the extent of any design problems, and whether a solution is imminent or a long way off.

In project management the project must reach an end or it is deemed a failure. This is particularly problematic in complex technical design situations because the desired end state might be continuously redefined as solutions are explored, particularly if there are no universally acceptable criteria to determine where one should stop or no criteria to determine whether a solution is right or wrong. Simple notions such as right and wrong, or best option, tend to be meaningless labels which cannot be applied to complex problems. Alternatives are always possible.

Explained in terms of Complexity Theory

Technically complex projects are qualitatively different from projects exhibiting other kinds of complexity. In Chapter 1 we introduced the idea that the perception of complexity is a function of the number of different elements in play, their interconnectedness and the ambiguity involved.

Whereas structurally complex projects involve a multitude of interconnected elements or sub-projects, with the complexity arising as a result of the sheer number of interconnections, technical complexity can arise with significantly fewer elements. This difference is because the level of ambiguity in individual elements of technically complex projects is significantly higher. Furthermore, the kind of ambiguity involved is qualitatively different from structural complexity. In a technically complex project, areas of uncertainty and ambiguity relate to issues of how we will find solutions to problems and the implications that different potential solutions will have on interconnected areas of the project. Figure 4.1 illustrates the difference.

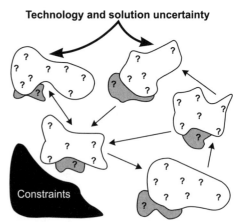

Figure 4.1   Uncertainty in technically complex projects

UNCERTAINTY IN TECHNICALLY COMPLEX PROJECTS

In a technically complex project the solution space (shown in white) is considerably larger than the problem space (shown in grey). Complexity in a technically complex project arises because of uncertainty regarding the outcomes for the many interdependent design solutions which may be reached. In this kind of project we typically know what we need to do, but not how we are going to do it.

There is often a significantly large range of possible outcomes for many of the individual elements of a technically complex project. As the uncertainty in any one element of a technically complex project is usually quite high, the level of complexity will rise quickly. The consequence of this is that a technically complex project may become unmanageably complex with significantly fewer elements than in a structurally complex project.

STRUCTURE

Structures developed to manage technical complexity are typically very flat hierarchies. Team members in these kinds of projects are often highly skilled professionals who value their autonomy. It is the expertise which typically defines the functional groups. Different functional groups are often left to manage their own parts with a great deal of autonomy. In these kinds of projects there is usually a titular head but this role may be exercised in an informal, almost egalitarian manner. Control is usually based on implicit understanding of specialist roles of individuals or groups. Each sub-system has a very well-defined internal identity based on expertise, and these groups typically maintain an internal order of their own. For instance, the division of roles and responsibilities is very clear on a film set, with actors, designers and musicians all having specific areas of expertise.

The internal structure of different groups within a technically complex project may vary, with each group finding their own way to work together. Uniformity should neither be expected nor enforced between the various groups. Rather, the internal structure of each group will emerge based on the nature of those involved and the work they are performing. It is more important that all groups be supported in doing their work.

COMMUNICATION

The pattern of communication in a technically complex project is typically rich and chaotic. Communication is characterized by lots of informal meetings and discussion. Indeed, the vast majority of information vital to the project will be distributed through informal networks. Formal communications networks will exist, but are less structured and rule bound than those found in structurally complex projects. As a result, a wider variety of information can be passed through the networks, and in many cases it may not be possible to see a clear division between formal and informal communication networks.

The frequency and intensity of information transfer tends to be cyclic, with information sharing becoming most rapid at nodal points, such as design review meetings or production meetings. Between these nodal points are periods of seemingly chaotic activity as groups go in different directions to work on separate work packages. This kind of repeating pattern of expansion and contraction governed by nodes is sometimes referred to by complexity theorists as 'periodic attractors'.

As technically complex projects may have multiple semi-autonomous groups, if communication between groups is not frequent or rich enough there is some danger of a group progressing in a way which does not synchronize with the development directions of other groups. In such a situation, one group may proceed with development within their area of expertise, on the mistaken assumption that other sections will harmonize with their work.

CONTROL

As mentioned in the previous chapter, control in Complexity Theory refers more to the ability of the system to maintain form in response to environmental change, as opposed to the traditional project management interpretation of control, which emphasises control to predetermined objectives, criteria and measures. Communication in a technically complex project provides an avenue for control and maintenance of system form by providing a way for different groups to maintain consistency of direction. Lack of consistency of direction amongst groups within the project is a significant threat to maintaining the internal integrity of the project system.

Although different groups in a technically complex project will be separately working in their areas of expertise, effective communication will transfer information about where tentative solutions have been found, where new areas of uncertainty have been uncovered, and which areas of uncertainty have been resolved. Regular communication regarding these issues is essential if the project as a whole is to react in response to development, as it provides the opportunity for each semi-autonomous group to separately take new information into account in their ongoing design efforts.

Control for consistency is most clear at these nodal points of communication, when information is more formally exchanged, and where decisions may be made regarding the consequences of any recent developments. These points give the opportunity to check that all groups are moving in the same direction; that if adaptation is necessary, then all groups adapt in reaction to the same stimuli. The design process depends upon creating new ideas. Opportunities which emerge during the design process need to be recognised and embraced, and these nodal points of communication provide a formal chance to do this. Furthermore, regular communication is vital in ensuring that no groups have been left behind. This last point can be an issue, as design teams can become very focused at times, dedicating themselves to their part of the problem, while blanking out external signals.

ORDER TO CHAOS

Technically complex projects tend to be quite chaotic, especially when compared to structurally complex projects. The edge of chaos tends to be quite close to chaos for this kind of project, with multiple different teams all working on separate, but interconnected, pieces of work. The project will be quite flexible, responsive to environmental changes, and able to assume new forms. The project will be simultaneously exploring multiple peaks on the fitness landscape.

Although a technically complex project tends to be chaotic, the project must maintain some internal consistency, if it is to produce a viable result. The project must not drift too far towards chaos, otherwise it risks breaking down and losing its cohesiveness as a whole. The main danger here is that different teams will wander off during their own design processes, and what was once a collection of separate groups working on different aspects of the same problem will become separate groups working on problems that can no longer be related.

If the project becomes too ordered, if there is too much control, then creativity is likely to be stifled. One way in which this can occur is if unequal power relations between different groups occur, and people start to apply influence in areas outside their direct areas of expertise. For example, during the production of a film, if the producers lose confidence in the director of a film, they may start to interfere. Similarly, artists with high artistic capital are famous for being able to manipulate directors. However, most directors will argue that a good production is essentially a cooperative association of creative minds.

Project management challenges

The major challenge for project management in technically complex projects is supporting the need for experimentation and discovery while maintaining a realistic hold on the schedule. Research now suggests that some structure is important but the structure should not be so rigid as to stifle innovation. This recent thinking is in direct contrast to earlier thinking (see March and Simon, 1958) which argued that reliance on formal role definitions discourages people from deviating from expected behaviour, making experimentation and creativity very unlikely. Kiesler and Sproull (1982) argue that explicit rules and procedures create a frame for the interpretation of new information and decrease the likelihood that relevant data will be ignored. On the other hand, Katz and Allen (1985) found that some types of constraints, such as formal incentive systems, caused engineers and scientists to become wary about experimenting because of the uncertainty of outcomes. Benner and Tushman (2003) also found that formalized and rigid management systems that push the organisation towards high productivity levels tend to discourage the pursuit of new ideas. We have explored these ideas further in a tool entitled 'Jazz'.

Adequate design and development time must be allocated in early or critical stages. Recognising the level of technical complexity as early as possible is very important so that realistic milestones can be set. This often means fending off interested parties, whilst providing the space for designers to work, and keeping the designers on track. This can be especially difficult when other stakeholders, such as the marketing department, have promised delivery; or there is a time-to-market issue.

CRITICAL PROJECT PHASES

The critical project phases for technical complexity tend to be the initiation and design/ development phases. These phases can be protracted, as discussed above. The initiation phase of the project usually involves other interested parties, such as research and development teams whose interests are discovering new market needs, or the marketing department who might pre-sell the idea or the actual end product to eager customers. The ever-present danger is that, despite the best efforts of the designers involved, it might not actually be possible to solve the technical or design issues and to produce the product or service within the time and budget promised to customers.

Some industries, such as the pharmaceutical industry, are well geared to deal with these uncertainties and there is an expectation that a very small percentage of ideas will actually reach the market as viable products. Associated losses are typically factored into the organisation's annual budget. In other industries, which are not similarly organised, such as engineering consultancies, there is an expectation that a satisficing solution will be found for each design problem presented. Part of the challenge in this kind of project is framing the problem in such a way that it can actually be solved.

The next critical project phases are detailed design and development, during which prototypes or models may be built and tested. By these phases resources have been committed to the project and there is an expectation of an outcome. Success during these phases is very much related to how the solution has been defined and communicated to key stakeholders. A great deal of concurrent activity occurs during these phases. These phases often overlap and are contiguous rather than sequential.

An example can be found in an annual design competition that culminates in a race for low-energy vehicles across the Australian desert. The competition attracts university teams and teams from industry. In order to better understand the organisational processes involved, design teams from one university were observed over two years (Remington, 2004, 2005). During the design and development process industrial design and engineering teams worked on different aspect of the vehicles. Project phases were not sequential but overlaid as the teams defined the problem space and explored and developed solutions, building prototypes to test ideas, discarding those that didn't work and going back to redefine the problem. All this took place as a series of complex iterations which looked very messy to the outsider. The organisational structure that worked most effectively was based purely on the strict definition of roles and responsibilities, clear and frequently emphasised milestones and regular meetings which formalized the informal communication. The project managers found that they were most effective if they acted to support the communications and protect the teams by providing space for them to work. When they tried to apply more rigid control procedures the design teams reacted very negatively and became more difficult to manage.

EXECUTIVE SUPPORT

Industries, such as the pharmaceutical industry, which are very good at managing projects that involve technical complexity also have learned to develop realistic expectations of outcomes. This involves implementing executable policies and procedures to optimize use of design phases within the project life cycle. It is normal practice to include appropriate project gateways at which the project can be formally evaluated. At these gateway reviews it may be necessary to terminate the project. Project termination policies are necessary to make sure that projects which are not able to be technically resolved within specified constraints are discontinued.

Fields such as theatre, film and the design professions have evolved into relatively flat structures to support the different technical or design specialisations. The flat structure, in which executive support is distributed and shared along lines which support the creative enterprise, appears to be more successful in these industries than more hierarchical structures which are functionally derived and have more and steeper layers of decision responsibility.

PROJECT MANAGER CAPABILITIES

Project managers need high level skills in communication and relationship management for technically complex projects. In particular they need the ability to protect, nurture and motivate design and research teams. They must be able to communicate critical design issues to stakeholders and manage their expectations throughout the design phases. They also need the ability to achieve closure to the design phase at the critical time. Obtaining agreement on the satisficing solution can be particularly difficult when designers know that the 'optimum' solution is 'just around the corner'. However, experience has shown that designers and researchers alike tend to be highly motivated people who are often very familiar with deadlines. Therefore the project manager must be able to communicate a level of trust and autonomy to the designers but, at the same time, maintain a grasp on what design teams are doing at any one time.

The project manager can also play a very useful role as integrator in technically complex projects. An ability to determine when exchanges of information between design teams might be opportune and to make sure exchanges happen in a timely fashion is crucial (see Büchel, 2005).

TEAM SUPPORT

As with the performance arts and the design industries, research and development teams tend to be highly skilled, very specialised and relatively autonomous. However most design teams resist any kind of micromanagement. In some industries, such as IT, the level of autonomy attributed to system architects can make it particularly difficult for the project manager to achieve the right balance between autonomy and delivery to a deadline. Roles within the teams are often quite fluid with individuals within the specialised teams assuming several roles at any one time (Sonnenwald and Lievrouw, 1997).

Although communication within the teams is usually high there is some evidence that communication between teams can be problematic. In an investigation of design teams in the New Zealand telecommunications industry, Whybrew, et al. (2002) found particular weaknesses in the level of communications between engineering and marketing functions, and recurrences of task clarification and conceptual design activity late in the overall product development process. This is supported by Büchel (2005) who concludes that teams working on new product development not only have to explicitly manage their relationships within the team, but also within the organisation and across the organisation. While both strong internal team networks and many external contacts certainly contribute to success, the need for strong knowledge networks between the team and their internal stakeholders is less obvious. Lack of consciousness of this need might mean that important perceptual differences are not revealed early enough in the project.

Due to time-to-market pressures it is not unusual for designers to work in virtual teams, internationally around the clock. These virtual teams have unique communication and integration challenges which have been the subject of much research (see for example, Duncan and Panteli, 2001)

FINANCIAL ISSUES

Depending upon the nature of the industry financial issues arising from the technical complexity can be an important source of complexity for the project. Again it is the uncertainty of outcome which makes financing these projects so difficult. As discussed above some industries, such as the pharmaceutical industry, with extensive experience in managing research and development projects, have developed effective measures to manage and control costs during periods of technical complexity. The number of project phases is determined according to the level of uncertainty. The number of 'control gates' relates to the number of points at which the project can be stopped, the number increasing with the perceived level of project complexity (see NASA, Procedural Requirements, undated, for example). In these contexts there is an expectation that a large proportion of the technically complex projects will fail. Therefore finance for such projects is bulked at the program level, rather than the individual project level.

The major financial consideration in technically complex projects is whether to go ahead with the project and when to stop it if it no longer becomes viable in terms of return on investment. Net present value (NPV) remains a frequently used tool for decision making in product research and development but it is often criticized for not properly accounting for uncertainty and flexibility, including the high possibility of abandonment (see Vlahos, 2001). Decision tree analysis, using probability-based expected monetary values, more effectively captures the many stages in research and development. An alternative to decision tree analysis is real options, a technique that applies financial options theory to non-financial assets and encourages financial managers to consider the value of such projects in terms of risks (see Reupper and Leiblein, 2001). Davis (2002) has developed a framework for evaluating product development which he calls net present value risk-adjusted (NPVR). This model adjusts the NPV calculations by including factors to account for the probability of risks, using a simple to use factor of 5 (high risk) to 1 (low risk), under the categories of marketing risk, technical risk and user risk (see Davis, 2002 for a full explanation of the technique). When adjusted for risk the results produce substantially different internal rates of return (IRR) than for simple unadjusted NPV calculations .

SCHEDULING ISSUES

Creating accurate schedules is also difficult when unknowns are involved. What counts as a satisficing solution will usually involve issues related to time and budget constraints. It is important that key stakeholders understand the design issues involved, so that it is possible to manage the expectation that an optimum solution can always be obtained.

As mentioned earlier these projects are often more effectively managed using milestones rather than detailed schedules such as precedence networks (Turner, 1999). The milestones can be based on estimated decision points, at which information exchange takes place, and major decision points, at which the project is reviewed and a decision made to carry on or abandon it. Estimating when decision points should be scheduled is based on the level of complexity of the problem, the level of risk to the organisation and the degree of expertise and experience of the design teams involved. It is very helpful to involve the design teams in setting intermediate milestones whilst keeping them aware of overall major milestones.

However, approaches to scheduling can and should vary according to the level of uncertainty. Van Oorshot et al. (2005) found that, generally speaking, design engineers in the product development industry were good at estimating durations for all but a few types of work package. Schedule overruns were mainly the result of a few work packages that were very difficult to estimate because of the high level of uncertainty. This suggests that time buffers should be attached to those activities.

In a low-uncertainty product development project, the project will consist of a stable network of work packages. Time and resource requirements can be established with a high level of accuracy for each work package (see for example Wheelwright and Clark, 1992). Conventional project scheduling techniques, such as CPM and PERT, are readily applicable here (see for example Meredith and Mantel, 1989; Ulusoy and Ozdamar, 1995). Where there is a high level of technical complexity it is not possible to accurately define time and resources. Therefore detailed planning is often more effective if it is incremental, with the level of detail inversely proportional to the level of uncertainty, starting with simple milestone planning (Turner, 1999) and progressing to precedence networks once the product is fully developed.

RISK ISSUES

As for financial control, risk is best managed overall through a 'control-gate' process. For high-uncertainty new product development projects, Khurana and Rosenthal (1997) recommend managing the risk with thorough contingency planning, generating multiple product concepts, developing alternative solutions in parallel, or even creating competing design teams for products or subsystems. During development, it should be expected that engineers will discover new problems or opportunities resulting from cross-functional problem solving. Newly discovered problems usually result in new work that cannot be foreseen at the start of the project. Such an approach would work effectively with a control-gate process.

In technically complex projects the ideal is to solve the majority of problems during the initiation and design phases before going into production. Often the pressure to start production outweighs the desire to resolve problems and complete detailed specifications. In these cases, it is very important that the risks involved be clearly communicated to all parties, prior to contracts being signed. High levels of risk, particularly in terms of cost overruns, occur when production begins before technical issues are resolved. Concurrent engineering, like fast-tracking, involves teams of engineers working simultaneously to design the various pieces of a product. The approach allows companies to get products to market much faster than they could before. However, like fast-tracking in the engineering and construction industry, concurrent engineering introduces considerable uncertainty into the development process and considerable levels of associated risk.

When contracts are let while the design phase is still in progress, emergent design issues may result in changes to work already started or completed. Often affected work packages will flow on to infect other sub-contracts or work packages, resulting in delays and escalating costs, particular if there is a pressing need to bring the project back on schedule.

PROCUREMENT ISSUES

Two major procurement issues are associated specifically with technically complex projects. The first is how best to manage procurement while solutions for technical problems are still being developed. Traditional contract management systems require the product to be fully defined and specified for a contract to be drawn up and enacted upon. Therefore, the first phases of technically complex projects may best be achieved using non-traditional forms of contract such as alliances or partnerships, founded on shared key success factors. While most studies point to the potential advantages of inter-organisational collaboration in order to achieve technical innovation there are issues about the governance of these collaborative working arrangements (Gerwin 2004). These can include risks of opportunistic behaviour and high coordination costs. Faems et al. (2006) recognise that formal governance mechanisms are needed to mitigate the risk of opportunistic behaviour as well as coordination costs. However they are also cautious that strict governance can hamper creativity. They propose instead that alliances should be structured, which involves embedded relationships in which heterogeneity is maintained and there is a balance between formal and relational governance.

The second procurement issue occurs in concurrent engineering or fast-tracked projects which may involve letting contracts for production prior to full resolution of all technical and design issues. The project manager must ensure that the contracts are written in such a way that the principal is protected from ambit claims from contractors who may see opportunities to make up losses through variations caused by the rework.

Traps and consequences

There are a number of traps which are worth considering.

Research has shown that dependence upon earlier experience may cause blind spots. This is often seen as the 'technical expert syndrome' in which there is reliance on existing technical expertise rather than on thinking laterally to solve the problem in a different way.

There may also be a tendency for technical experts to drive the project with the result that important people's views and ideas within other sectors of the organisation are not addressed. A balance needs to be found between giving technical experts the space to work, and ensuring that any technical solutions developed do actually fall within clients' satisficing zones.

The original objectives can also become lost during the development process. This can happen for two main reasons: focusing on finding an optimal solution; and defining the problem at the wrong level. If designers focus on finding the best solution, rather than one which satisfices, then technical innovation may become a goal in itself, replacing the original goal of contributing to strategic objectives. Furthermore, this path tends to be time dependent and costly, as some designers may find it difficult to let go of the possibility of finding the perfect solution. If you spend too much time trying to find the best design solution the environmental constraints may change, leaving you with a highly specialised, beautiful solution, which is no longer relevant.

Focus on technical solutions can mean that the problem is identified at the wrong level. For example, if we need to get material from A to B the problem might logically be given to structural engineers who see the problem as how to build a bridge, while other solutions might be obtained if different perspectives are adopted. Similarly, a consultant may talk to a limited number of people within an organisation and produce a solution that meets the needs of those specific end users very well, but does not meet the needs of other potential stakeholders very effectively. Likewise, 'better' to a programmer might mean efficiency of program code, whereas 'better' to the end user might mean clarity of layout on the screen.

It is important that some compromise is found between different stakeholder perspectives, and that the satisficing zone for the project is negotiated and current, rather than assumed.

References and further reading

Benner, M. J. and Tushman, M. L. (2003), 'Exploitation, Exploration, and Process Management: The Productivity Dilemma Revisited', *Academy of Management Review* 28, 238-56.

Büchel, B. (2005), 'New Product Development Team Success: The Team's Knowledge Network Makes a Real Difference!', *Perspectives for Managers* 129, 1-4.

Davis, C. (2002), 'Calculated Risk: A Framework for Evaluating Product Development', *MIT Sloan Management Review* 43:4, 70-7.

Duncan, E. and Panteli, N. (2001), 'Virtual Team Working: A Design Perspective'. *IEE CONF PUBL* 481, 115-9.

Faems, D., Janssens, M., Bouwen, R. and Van Looy, B. (2006), 'Governing explorative R&D alliances: Searching for effective strategies', *Management Review* 17, 9-29.

Gerwin, D. (2004), 'Coordinating New Product Development in Strategic Alliances', *Academy of Management Review* 2, 241-57.

Katz, R. and Allen, T. J. (1985), 'Organizational Issues in the Development of New Technologies', in P. R. Kleindorfer (ed.), *The Management of Productivity and Technology in Manufacturing*. (NY: Plenum Press) 275-300.

Kiesler, S. and Sproull, L. (1982), 'Managerial Responses to Changing Environments: Perspectives on Problem Sensing from Social Cognition', *Administrative Science Quarterly* 27, 548-70.

Khurana, A. and Rosenthal, S. R. (1997), 'Integrating the Fuzzy Front End of New Product Development', *Sloan Management Review* 38, 103-20.

Lester, D. H. (1998), 'Governing Explorative R&D Alliances: Searching for Effective Strategies. Critical Success Factors for New Product Development', *Research Technology Management* 41:1, 36-43.

March, J. G. and Simon, H. A. (1958), *Organizations*. (NY: John Wiley & Sons).

Meredith, J. R. and Mantel, S. D. Jr. (1989), *Project Management: A Managerial Approach*. (Singapore: John Wiley & Sons).

NASA, 'Flight Systems and Ground Support Projects, 6.1.1', *Procedural Requirements* (undated, accessed 20-12-06), http://nodis3.gsfc.nasa.gov/displayDir.cfm?Internal_ID=N_PR_7120_005C_&page_name=Chapter6

Remington, K. (2004), 'Managing creativity: Observations on the UTS Ecodesign Projects, 2004', Working paper series, *Colloquium* (University of Technology Sydney, Australia).

Remington, K. (2005), 'Managing creativity: Observations on the UTS Sunrace Project, 2005', Working paper series, *Colloquium* (University of Technology Sydney, Australia).

Reupper, J. J. and Leiblein, M. J. (2001), 'Real Options: Let the Buyer Beware', in Pickford, J. (ed.) *Mastering Risk*, Vol. 1 Concepts. (Upper Sandle River, NJ: Prentice-Hall), 79-85.

Sonnenwald, D. H. and Lievrouw, L. A. (1997), 'Collaboration during the Design Process: A Case Study of Communication, Information Behavior, and Project Performance. Information Seeking in Context.' Vakkari, Savolainen, R. and Dervin, B. (eds). *Proceedings of the International Conference on Research in Information Needs, Seeking and Use in Different Contexts, August 1996*, (Tampere, Finland; London, UK: Taylor Graham).

Turner, J. R. (1999), *The Handbook of Project-Based Management*, 2nd Edition. (London, UK: McGraw-Hill).

Ulusoy, G. and Ozdamar, L. (1995), 'A Heuristic Scheduling Algorithm for Improving the Duration and Net Present Value of a Project', *International Journal of Operations & Production Management* 15, 89-98.

Van Oorschot, K. E., Bertrand, J. W. M. and Rutte, C. G. (2005), 'Field studies into the dynamics of product development tasks', *International Journal of Operations & Production Management* 25:8, 720-739.

Vlahos, K. (2001), 'Tooling Up for Risky Decisions', in Pickford, J. (ed.) *Mastering Risk*, Vol. 1. Concepts. (Upper Sandle River, NJ: Prentice-Hall), 47-52.

Wheelwright, S. C. and Clark, K. B. (1992), *Revolutionizing Product Development: Quantum Leaps in Speed, Efficiency and Quality.* (NY: The Free Press).

Whybrew, K., Raine, J. K., Dallas, T. and Erasmuson, L. (2002), 'A Study of Design Management in the Telecommunications Industry', *Proceedings of the Institution of Mechanical Engineers B, Journal of Engineering Manufacture* 216(B1), 13-23.

5 *Directionally Complex Projects*

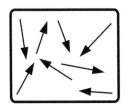

The questions associated with this kind of complexity are:

'How do we share understanding?' or
'How do we agree about what we have to do?'

Words or phrases you might hear or think when confronted with this type of complexity are:

- No one seems to be on the same page.
- No one is listening to anyone else.
- Why are we doing this?
- We are talking to each other but there is no actual communication.
- Both sides are nodding but we are not actually sharing meaning.
- Hidden agendas drive the project.
- This project is politically motivated.
- All we're doing is arguing. When are we going to actually start the project?

Directional complexity is found in projects where there is no consistently understood or agreed direction for the project, where goals are unclear or undefined, or where progress towards superficially agreed goals is being hampered by undisclosed political motivations and hidden agendas. Directionally complex projects typically involve disagreement between stakeholders, or issues which are difficult to appreciate. Directional complexity may emerge when a project manager is handed a project which is not well defined, or where a project has been started, but has broken down because previously unknown inconsistencies between how stakeholders view the project have been revealed. Directional complexity is often found in change projects, when it is clear that something must be done to improve a problematic situation, but it is unclear what this 'something' should be.

Directional complexity is not typically addressed by most approaches to project management, which assume that goals can be clarified in the early stages, that the project team is receiving consistent information from stakeholders and that the project plan can be followed once it has been developed and agreed. However, if the project goals are not shared, or if the project team is receiving conflicting information from stakeholders, it may not be possible to meet these assumptions. Instead, facilitating the development of some sort of agreed position or working direction might be half the battle to successfully completing the project. Unlike in a technically complex project, where design issues might determine which directions are taken for the project, in a directionally complex project decisions about the direction are more likely to be based on issues of cultural and interpersonal alignment. The most important and time consuming part of a directionally complex project is often reaching a mutually agreed definition that all stakeholders will work towards.

Explained in terms of Complexity Theory

Like other kinds of complex projects, directionally complex projects are perceived as complex because of three main factors: the number of different elements involved in the project; the interconnections between the different elements; and the ambiguous nature of the different elements.

In structurally complex projects, the number of interconnected elements is very high. However, like technically complex projects, in directionally complex projects a situation can become unmanageably complex with significantly fewer elements in play. This is because although in a structurally complex project there may be a multitude of interconnected elements, each element is relatively well defined. In directionally and technically complex projects there is significantly more ambiguity involved in each of the elements.

Once again the kind of ambiguity involved in a directionally complex project is qualitatively different from other kinds of complex projects. In a directionally complex project the main sources of ambiguity relate to issues of problem definition, developing understanding of stakeholder needs and expectations, and negotiating an agreed direction for the project. This is in contrast to time, cost and resource ambiguity in a structurally complex project, and to technology and solution ambiguity in a technically complex project. Directional complexity is represented in Figure 5.1.

In a directionally complex project the problem space (shown in grey) is much larger than the solution space (shown in white). Directional complexity arises through uncertainty regarding the specific goals, objectives or success criteria for the different interconnected elements of the project. It may be that some aspects of the project are well defined, but in this kind of project many other project elements will be lacking clear definition, or different stakeholders' definitions will be contested. When directional complexity is found in a project, without being in combination with the other kinds of complexity discussed in this book, we often feel that we could deliver the project if only we knew exactly what we're supposed to be doing.

These situations often mean that it is difficult to directly link effects to actions (Vickers, 1965). Also it may be difficult to identify a single factor as being responsible for change (Van der Meer, 1999), with 'problems of causality often confounding attempts to clearly measure outcomes' (Rose and Haynes, 1999, 6). The difficulty can be due to the number of variables which are operating at the same time (Vickers, 1967), although directional complexity is unlikely to involve as many variables and interdependencies as you would find in structural complexity. In a directionally complex project the strength of the interdependencies is likely

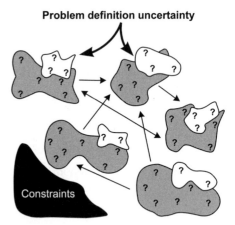

Problem definition uncertainty

Constraints

Figure 5.1   Uncertainty in directionally complex projects

to be high, causing tensions which are sometimes difficult to grasp. Decisions reached about the direction of one element of the project are likely to have significant influences on decisions about other areas of the project. It is likely that areas of ambiguity in the project will have to be considered as an interconnected whole, instead of separate elements.

Project teams may be aware of directional complexity early on in a project, although directional complexity can arise later in a project as a result of emergent phenomena, or simply because influential stakeholders have changed their minds regarding the appropriateness of the current direction. However, it often happens that key stakeholders are unaware of directional complexity until it is revealed that others have quite different goals or needs. It is not uncommon for projects to be well into the planning phase when it becomes clear that key stakeholders are not on the same page. Therefore the most desirable tactic when faced with directional complexity is to try to resolve the ambiguity as quickly as possible, so that the project can then be managed using standard project management techniques.

As directional complexity is most commonly encountered during the early phases of a project, the project may not yet have any clear structure. The system may not have entirely formed yet, having no clear and stable processes, direction, hierarchy or power relationships.

ORDER TO CHAOS

This kind of system is usually quite chaotic, and the edge of chaos for a directionally complex project will be closer to chaos than to order and it will certainly feel that way to those trying to manage it. Different parts of the project will be exploring different parts of the fitness landscape, either because they are lost and wandering in the fog, trying to find a local peak, or because different project members have settled on what they consider to be the most promising peak, irrespective of what may have been found by other project members.

As always, a balance must be maintained between order and chaos but the edge of chaos for a directionally complex project will be nearer to chaos, moving closer to order as better alignment is attained. In a directionally complex project it is important that order is not imposed on the situation by one party too early (Beinhoffer,1997; Brown and Eisenhardt, 1998). Other people's opinions should not be quashed for a superficial version of order. A high level of uncertainty should be expected, and needs to be managed rather than eradicated, until such a time that an agreed direction can be achieved which will be sustainable enough to allow the project to be planned in detail and implemented. Forcing an ordered state in the system involves prematurely choosing a local peak before all information regarding the state of the environment has been considered.

The system needs to find an order, not have one imposed on it. Order in a directionally complex project should arise as a result of all participants having sufficient understanding of what's going on and what has to be done. A sustainable order will not arise from one person or stakeholder group dictating the direction to be taken. A centralised authoritarian approach will only give the appearance of consistency. It will provide the comforting illusion that the situation has been simplified. However, the directional complexity will remain under the surface, ignored while feedback loops potentially create ever-increasing problems for the project.

Likewise, the system must not be allowed to move too far towards chaos. The project needs to be held together, while it finds the kind of order that is appropriate for it. This can be done through non-standard approaches to management that favour partnering and alliances, as opposed to forcing standard contractual relationships before directional stability has been achieved. The role of the executive sponsor is also vital in helping the project manager to maintain the necessary balance between order and chaos. This is discussed in greater detail below.

COMMUNICATION AND STRUCTURE

Communication during a directionally complex project can often become heated, especially if different stakeholder groups have conflicting views about the project direction and if strong-willed personalities are involved. In such cases, there is the potential for communication in the project to break down. If a directionally complex project is becoming too chaotic, it is likely that communication will be typified by ongoing arguments which don't seem to be leading anywhere.

It is important that some structure and order is brought to a directionally complex project. A good way to do this is by providing structure for the process of discussion and exploration of potential project directions. It is possible to structure the process of communication without imposing structure on the content or result of any discussions. In this way, you can provide sufficient structure for the project to build on, without overly constraining the result. It should not be a surprise that methodologies developed to clarify goals and negotiate meaning in project situations are referred to as 'problem structuring' methodologies in the operational research community (see Ferrari, et al, 2002; Ormerod, 1999, for examples from practice).

SENSITIVITY TO INITIAL CONDITIONS

A directionally complex project is particularly sensitive to some kinds of initial conditions. The structure which is brought to a directionally complex project will influence the way in which goals are defined, meanings are negotiated and accommodated positions are developed. As directionally complex projects often lack structure, they tend to be very sensitive to any structure brought to them. As the project develops, this structure will become embedded in the project process, as an acculturated way of doing things, and will become increasingly difficult to change as the project progresses.

Although periods of directional complexity can be chaotic and uncomfortable, it is important that the project team doesn't settle on a local peak too quickly. It is often important to focus on maintaining the structure of communication, while the remainder of the project is left as chaotic. Don't rush to resolve all aspects of the project. Instead, only resolve those parts of the project which are ready to be settled and agreed upon.

Taking this approach demands that the project manager be prepared to admit that the project team don't know some details at the moment. This is contrary to the standard approach to directional complexity, which emphasises trying to resolve the complexity and simplify the situation as quickly as possible, and can be a very challenging role for project managers used to environments which encourage the view that certainty and self-assurance are sources of power.

CONTROL

Issues of control in directionally complex projects relate to how the project will maintain form and develop a sustainable structure. In a structurally or technically complex project, control is related to issues of how consistent and unifying project form and direction are maintained. However, when directional complexity arises at the start of a project, the project typically does not yet have a sustainable structure to be maintained. In this case, issues of control relate to patterns of communication. If the project is to maintain some form long enough to develop something more sustainable, it is important that communication continues. If communication breaks down during periods of directional complexity, so will the project.

Project management challenges

Once potential directional complexity has been identified, the challenges for management include planning for adequate time to address the complexity while it persists. This is often during the initial phases of the project; however, it can also occur during later stages of the project. It is important to provide sufficient time and space to allow for the uncertainty and the necessary unravelling of the project goals.

The project management approach taken needs to be flexible enough to accommodate the level of uncertainty experienced during this time. As with technical complexity strict processes are often counter-productive (Benner and Tushman, 2003). The management approach should draw from a broad range of tools with an emphasis on soft rather than hard or closed systems thinking. Midgely (2000) offers an excellent coverage of systemic intervention practice. Problem structuring methodologies developed to clarify goals and negotiate meaning in project situations should be used. See Koberg and Bagnall (2003) for a readable overview of some of the soft systems methods.

Directional complexity more than any other requires an interpretive approach, rather than a rigid, rule-bound methodology. Approaches can be classified as interpretive if we assume that our knowledge of reality emerges during the process through increasing consciousness, shared meanings, documents and other artefacts (Klein and Myers, 1999). Approaches designed to address unclear goals tend to focus on exploration and discovering patterns (Fitzgerald and Howcroft, 1998).

Depending upon the nature of the uncertainty a variety of meaning-making tools can be used such as dialogue (see Kotter and Cohen, 2002; Levine, 1994; Schein, 1993) to build trust and openness among members of a group. Appreciative Inquiry (Cooperrider and Srivastra, 1987) aims through discovery and shared understanding to build a constructive bridge between and among members of the stakeholder group, with emphasis on the achievements, potentials, innovations, strengths and visions of valued and possible futures (Cooperrider and Whitney, 2001). Critical systems heuristics also offers ways to manage situations of non-alignment which are characterised by competing political agendas (Ulrich, 1983). See the Discursive Universe tool chapter for more discussion.

A tool like Value Management (Kelly et al., 2004; Woodhead and Downs, 2001) are useful to refine the agreed requirements and optimize design solutions. Generally this tool is used once alignment has been obtained and the problem defined but it has also been used successfully where groups have been in conflict. Developed essentially in the construction and engineering disciplines the process can be applied to any problem situation requiring optimization of design approaches and hence value for money. Value management, also known as value engineering, draws upon explorative, analytical, creative and evaluation techniques from a variety of disciplines to achieve the desired functions in a design or process while minimising costs. It is used to eliminate unnecessary costs without sacrificing safety, quality, environmental compliances or other functional requirements. In addition, innovation is used to improve cost effectiveness, enhance performance and foster partnering (Lane Davis, 2004).

Based on functional analysis and creative solution finding, the process can often bring people with very different agendas together in a problem-solving mode.

The project manager will need to use a range of methods depending upon the nature of the directional complexity. When faced with directional complexity, one standard project management tool that should be included is thorough stakeholder identification (see for example Curtin, 2007; Cleland, 2006; Huber and Palls, 2006; Scharioth and Huber, 2003). Identifying and keeping track of stakeholders and their needs is fundamental to the success of such a project. See also the chapters Multimethodology in Series and Multimethodology in Parallel.

CRITICAL PROJECT PHASES

The critical project phases tend to be the initial phases of the project during which the project goals are being defined and agreement from key stakeholders is being sought. Many directionally complex projects have failed because of a very common tendency to want to proceed to detailed planning too early. These early phases are critical to project success. The tendency to rely on control through good planning as the major management approach should be resisted. Research, including a study of 448 projects by Dvir and Lechler (2004), has shown that changes in directions and goal paths may have a negative effect on project outcomes, effects far outweighing any positive effects of good planning. Adequate exploration of goals at the beginning of a project can help to mitigate this.

EXECUTIVE SUPPORT

The role of the executive sponsor is vital. It is more likely that the executive sponsor, rather than the project manager, will have access to information at the strategic decision-making levels of the organisation or organisations involved. The executive sponsor should keep the project team aware of relevant political agendas and issues so that the project team can maintain and develop relationships during goal definition (Helm and Remington, 2005).

The project executive sponsor also has a key role in fending off those who press for early milestones for what might prove to be inappropriate deliverables. The role of the executive sponsor in a directionally complex project is much like that of an artistic director sponsoring the introduction of a new and highly experimental ballet. Artistic influences will come from many people, the choreographer, the composer, the designer and the dancers themselves until, at some point, the vision comes together and the ballet is conceptualised. Only at this point can the ballet go into production and rehearsals take place in preparation for the performance. The artistic director must provide ad hoc support and guidance and demonstrate trust in the choreographer and the company in order to produce a master-work.

PROJECT MANAGER CAPABILITIES

Standard project management practice tends to favour the early attainment of control. However, as the goals of a directionally complex project are usually fuzzy, project managers working on these projects need to feel comfortable with a high level of ambiguity together with a sense of lack of control. It is likely that many people associated with the project will not be comfortable with ambiguity. In order to promote a sense of comfort for the stakeholders and the project team a key responsibility for the project manager is to communicate to others that this kind of uncertainty is quite normal at this stage of this kind of project.

Part of this necessary high-level expertise in communication is the ability to translate ambiguity into an acceptable form for stakeholders, while not losing sight of the complexity itself. Recognising the need to look from different perspectives, to observe the project holistically and from a variety of angles will help the project manager develop the ability to recognise pathways through the chaos. The project manager also needs to be able to recognise the point when detailed planning should start and to resist the tendency to plan too early, before goals have been agreed by key stakeholders. Dvir and Lechler's study (2004) clearly indicates that over-detailed planning can be a waste of time when goals are not clarified and agreed.

TEAM SUPPORT

As directional complexity is likely to be highest in the early phases of a project, the project team might only consist of one or two people performing coordinating activities. People are likely to be chosen to join the project team for the specialist expertise which they bring to the project. Rather than a permanent co-located team a variety of people may consult to the project.

Specialist consultants may be required to communicate with key stakeholders, such as the media, facilitate meaning-making sessions, apply soft and critical systems thinking with groups of stakeholders, conduct value-management studies and use other kinds of problem-structuring activities.

FINANCIAL ISSUES

These projects present enormous challenges to senior executives and auditors. Developing budgets for directionally complex projects early in the project life cycle is particularly fraught. It is not until the goals have been clarified that the project can be planned in enough detail to allow a realistic budget to be determined. Often an initial budget is based on other considerations, usually a combination of available funds and a degree of guesswork. It is essential that key stakeholders are aware that a real budget cannot be determined until goal directions have been clarified and agreed. This makes forward planning at the corporate level and management of stakeholders very difficult.

The use of control gates can assist in some respects. In this kind of project the control gates function as points of review at which the project progress is assessed. For example, at the first control gate the budget might have an expected variance of approximately 200 per cent or greater. At the second control gate the expected budget variance might be approximately 120 per cent, at the third approximately 70 per cent. See the Virtual Gates tool for further explanation.

However there are several problems with a strict control-gate approach. For example, gates tend to be linked with the major reporting schedules for the organisation, such as finance board meetings. Often in directionally complex projects, as with some technically complex projects, it is difficult to obtain stakeholder agreement on a schedule which fits in with the major decision-making meetings. Therefore there must be an expectation that the timing of the control gates might also need to be flexible. For instance, several scheduled meetings might pass before the project can move from gate 1 to gate 2. In order to move to gate 2, agreement on goals should have reached a sufficient level of alignment to allow some planning to be undertaken. It is impossible to plan the unknown.

SCHEDULING ISSUES

Scheduling directionally complex projects presents similar kinds of challenges to those hindering determination of the project budget. Rodney Turner (1999) argues that milestone planning is the only form of scheduling suitable for projects which suffer from unclear goal direction. Milestones may act like periodic attractors in that they provide a focus and a sense of urgency for the stakeholders. However a stakeholder who is deliberately obstructing the project will be unlikely to be affected by a list of dates. In some cases, depending upon the context, milestone dates will also need to be very flexible.

In our experience with directionally complex organisational change projects, the time required during the early definition phases of the project can often be much greater than the time needed to plan and roll out the projects. Once defined, with fully agreed goals, these projects are often extremely straightforward to roll out, requiring proportionately little time during implementation and handover phases in comparison with the early definition phases of the project. Once clearly defined many directionally complex projects do not exhibit high levels of structural complexity.

RISK ISSUES

The major risks are associated with delivery of assumed goals before the project direction has been agreed by all key stakeholders. This wastes resources and can disenfranchise those key stakeholders who were not in agreement. In some cases it is better to envisage the project as a series of projects, the first project being to agree on a goal or direction. This reduces the level of expectation of key stakeholders and therefore makes management of their expectations less difficult. In directionally complex projects it is likely that each key stakeholder will hold a different initial view of the ultimate goal of the project. Therefore many stakeholders will be under the impression that delivery of their own version of the goal is relatively simple – they don't understand what the fuss is about! The first task is to demonstrate that different views exist and convince stakeholders that it is necessary to sort out the ambiguity before even contemplating the deliverables.

PROCUREMENT IMPLICATIONS

As with technically complex projects traditional contracts cannot be effectively implemented until the project goals are determined and the project can be planned in detail. Until the point when directions are agreed, non-traditional contracts such as alliances or partnerships are preferable, especially when key success factors are frequently revisited. Refer to the previous chapters for some discussion on collaborative partnerships and alliances.

Traps and consequences

There are a number of traps which are worth considering.

It is important not to give into the urge towards thinking that 'At least we're doing something' or 'It's better to be doing anything than to keep sitting around discussing it'. This attitude will lead to rework, unhappy stakeholders, commitment to inappropriate solutions, or further complication to an already problematic situation if your hasty option turns out to make the situation worse.

If the appearance of progress is needed to keep major stakeholders satisfied that something is happening it is better to define small sub-projects which definitely must be done and deliver those while allowing time for definition of the major parts of the project.

Planning and implementation should not go ahead before an accommodated position has been reached. Similarly, the project should not go ahead without a true agreed direction or without sufficiently shared meaning and understanding.

Periods of directional complexity can be very uncomfortable for project personnel and for stakeholders. However it is important that, in the rush to bring order to the project, the project team does not adopt particular directions too quickly. It is often more important to focus on maintaining the structure of communication, while the remainder of the project is left as chaotic. Don't rush to plan all aspects of the project. Instead, only resolve those parts of the project which are ready to be settled and agreed upon.

Directionally complex projects also tend to lack structure. Therefore, there is often a tendency to try to impose structure as a way of creating a sense of control. Directionally complex projects are particularly sensitive to attempts to impose structure. As the project develops, any imposed structure may become embedded in the project process, and may become increasingly difficult to change as the project progresses, even if it becomes obvious that the structure will not deliver satisfactory outcomes. Instead, it is important to let a structure emerge as mutual understanding of the project goals develops.

In directionally complex projects there is often the belief by some stakeholders that everyone shares the same goals and meanings. As a result, any lack of shared understanding or agreement may not be revealed until much later in the project life cycle when resources have been committed.

Sharing meanings is vital but it is a time-consuming early activity. It is very difficult to return to meaning making once superficial agreement has been reached.

Vocal stakeholders tend to dominate meaning making leaving quieter participants in potential disagreement without the opportunity to voice their opinions. If this is the case, project outputs may only meet the needs of a limited number of stakeholders, and this may only become apparent later or even after delivery. Often the result is that the products of the project are not taken up or used fully.

Dominance of the meaning-creation process may result in the learning needs of only some stakeholders being met. A lack of shared meaning may then result in some risks not being identified. If stakeholders don't understand what is going on and are not given the opportunity to fully understand the situation, then their contribution will be limited. Therefore, risks that they may have been able to identify, monitor or find solutions for have not even been recognised.

Similarly, dominance by some parties when trying to create shared meaning can result in marginalization and lack of commitment from key stakeholders. Lack of commitment from key stakeholders who are not engaged or who have different understandings of the objectives may result in confusion and conflict during the later stages of the project. This can cause delays and even abandonment of the project.

References and further reading

Beinhoffer, E. (1997), 'Strategy at the Edge of Chaos', *McKinsey Quarterly* 1.

Benner, M. J. and Tushman, M. L. (2003), 'Exploitation, Exploration, and Process Management: The Productivity Dilemma Revisited', *Academy of Management Review* 28, 238-256.

Brown, S. L. and Eisenhardt, K. M. (1997), 'The Art of Continuous Change: Linking Complexity Theory and Time-Paced Evolution', *Administrative Science Quarterly* 42:1, 1-34.

Brown, S. L. and Eisenhardt, K. M. (1998), *Competing on the Edge: Strategy as Structured Chaos*. (Boston, MA: Harvard Business School Press).

Cleland, D. I. (2006), *Project Management: Strategic Design and Implementation*. (NY: McGraw-Hill).

Cooperrider, D. and Whitney, D. (2001), *Appreciative Inquiry. An Emerging Direction for Organizational Development*. (Champaign, Il: Stipes Publishing).

Cooperrider, D. and Srivastra, S. (1987), 'Appreciative Inquiry in Organizational Life', in Passmore, W. and Wodman, R. (eds) *Research in Organization Change and Development: Volume 1t*. (Greenwich CT: JAI Press).

Curtin, T. (2007), *Managing Green Issues*. (NY: Palgrave Macmillan).

Dvir, D. and Lechler, T. (2004), 'Plans are Nothing, Changing Plans is Everything: The Impact of Changes on Project Success', *Research Policy* 33:1, 1-15.

Ferrari, F., Fares, C. and Martinelli, D. (2002), 'The Systemic Approach of SSM: The Case of a Brazilian Company', *Systemic Practice and Action Research* 15:1, 51-66.

Fitzgerald, B. and Howcroft, D. (1998), 'Towards Dissolution of the IS Research Debate: From Polarization to Polarity', *Journal of Information Technology* 13, 313-326.

Fordor, J., de Baets, B. and Perny, P. (2000), *Preferences and Decisions Under Incomplete Knowledge*. (NY: Physica-Verlag).

Hazen, M.A. (1993), 'Towards Polyphonic Organization', *Journal of Organizational Change Management* 6:5, 15–6.

Helm, J. and Remington, K. (2005), 'Effective Sponsorship, Project Managers' Perceptions of the Role of the Project Sponsor', *Project Management Journal* 36:3, 36-51.

Huber, M. and Palls, M. (eds.) (2006), *Customising Stakeholder Management Strategies: Concepts for Long-Term Business Success*. (Berlin, Germany; NY: Springer).

Kelly, J., Male, S. and Drummond, G. (2004), *Value Management of Construction Projects*. (Malden, MA: Blackwell Science).

Klein, H. K. and Myers, M. D. (1999), 'A Set of Principles for Conducting and Evaluating Interpretive Field Studies in Information Systems', *MIS Quarterly* 23:1, 67-94.

Koberg, D. and Bagnall, J. (2003), *The Universal Traveller: A Soft-Systems Guide to Creativity, Problem-Solving and the Process of Reaching Goals*. (Menlo Park, CA: Crisp Learning).

Kotter, J. and Cohen, D. S. (2002), *The Heart of Change: Real Life Stories of How People Change Their Organisations*. (LLC, USA: John Kotter and Deloitte Consulting).

Lane Davis, K.E. (2004), 'Finding Value in the Value Engineering Process', *Cost Engineering* 46:12, 24-7.

Levine, L. (1994), 'Listening with Spirit and the Art of Team Dialogue', *Journal of Organisational Change Management* 7:1, 61-73.

Ormerod, R. (1999), 'Putting Soft OR Methods to Work: The Case of the Business Improvement Project at PowerGen', *European Journal of Operational Research* 118:1, 1-29.

Midgley, G. (2000), *Systemic Intervention: Philosophy, Methodology, and Practice*. (NY: Kluwer Academic/ Plenum).

Pinto, J. (ed.) (1998), *The Project Management Handbook*. (San Francisco, CA: Jossey-Bass Publishers).

Rose, J. and Haynes, M. (1999), 'A Soft Systems Approach to the Evaluation of Complex Interventions in the Public Sector', *Journal of Applied Management Studies* 8, 199-216.

Scharioth, J. and Huber, M. (eds.) (2003), *Achieving Excellence in Stakeholder Management*. (NY: Springer).

Schein, E. H. (1993), 'On Dialogue, Culture, and Organizational Learning', *Organizational Dynamics* 93:2, 22.

Turner, J. R. (1999), *A Handbook of Project-Based Management*, 2nd edition. (London, UK: McGraw-Hill).

Ulrich, W. (1983), *Critical Heuristics of Social Planning*. (Bern, Germany: Haupt).

Van der Meer, F. (1999), 'Evaluation and the Social Construction of Impacts', *Evaluation* 5, 387-406.

Vickers, G. (1965), *The Art of Judgment*. (London, UK: Chapman and Hall).

Vickers, G. (1967), *Towards a Sociology of Management*. (London, UK: Chapman and Hall).

Woodhead R. and Downs C. (2001), *Value Management: Improving Capabilities*. (London, UK: Thomas Telford Publishing).

6 *Temporally Complex Projects*

Questions associated with this kind of complexity are:

'How can we be in a position to anticipate, survive or take advantage of the changes?' or
'How do we keep some control over the changes when they can occur at any time?'

Words or phrases you might hear or think when confronted with this type of complexity are:

- It is like standing on quicksand.
- Everything keeps shifting.
- We don't know what is going to change next.
- My work keeps being thrown out because it is no longer relevant.
- We have seen this kind of thing all before – let's just sit back and wait until it settles.

Temporal complexity is found in projects experiencing significant environmental change outside the direct influence or control of the project. In this kind of project it may be known that significant changes will occur, but it may be unclear exactly what these changes will be or when they will happen. In the private sector this kind of complexity is commonly found during periods of mergers and acquisitions, changes of leadership and major periods of organisational change. In the public sector temporal complexity is common during changes of government and legislative change, and has been referred to as 'public sector paranoia'. Seemingly straightforward projects with long durations can also be vulnerable simply because the longer the duration of the project the higher the likelihood that it will be exposed to externally imposed changes. In all these cases, the exact result of the change and when the effects will filter through are extremely difficult to predict.

Managing a project in a temporally complex context will challenge ideas about what is normally assumed to be stable in a traditional project management context. In periods of considerable change, it may still be necessary to manage and deliver the project, even though areas as fundamental as the ongoing involvement of the project team, or even the continued existence of the organisational department overseeing the project, are in question. In a temporally complex project it is less a case of whether goals will change and more a case of when will the goals change, in which direction they will change and whether we can possibly anticipate the nature of the change.

Increasingly common are projects marked both by large scale and very long duration (De Maio et al., 1994). These include development projects, such as new aircraft (Sabbagh, 1996), new vehicles (Quinn and Pacquette, 1998, Clark et al., 1987), aerospace initiatives and defence contracts (Argyres, 1999; Scudder et al., 1989; Hoffman, 1997), transport and infrastructure (Ivory and Alderman, 2005) and public sector reforms, particularly internationally funded aid projects (Uddin and Tsamenyi, 2005). Although the enormous sizes of these projects means that they are also characterised by a high level of structural complexity, the time-related aspects, such as changes in customer profile, changes in the market, imposition of regulatory constraints and accompanying expanding knowledge requirements, seem to provide the major sources of complexity (Ivory and Alderman, 2005; Alderman et al, 2003). This is probably because most aspects of structural complexity can be managed by the project team using existing knowledge. Other aspects, such as a customer or major contractor going bankrupt in the middle of the project or suddenly imposed regulations, which are politically driven, are not within the sphere of influence of the project team.

Timing and positioning through analysis and predictive mapping may be more significant to success in temporally complex projects than efficiency and control. The situation is acknowledged as turbulent and changing, but despite changing goals and environmental influences it is necessary for the project to deliver something that is relevant and appropriate at the time of delivery. This requires careful timing for delivery and an approach to positioning deliverables that accounts for multiple possible outcomes and an ongoing sensitivity to where the problem areas are likely to occur. It is important to make sure that what is delivered by the project is actually what is needed at the time of delivery. This will not necessarily be what was originally specified during project initiation.

Explained in terms of Complexity Theory

Temporally complex projects, much like the other types discussed so far in this book, are perceived of as complex because of the combined influence of the number of different elements involved, the interconnection between these different elements, and ambiguity. In each different kind of complexity introduced, the most significant sources of complexity have been different.

For structural complexity, the high number of different elements in play and the number of interconnections between elements creates the perception of complexity, and can mean that the project team can easily find themselves past the point where emergent effects can be holistically appreciated. In technically and directionally complex projects the number of elements involved may be lower than in structurally complex projects. However the level of uncertainty is much higher within particular elements, with the focus being on ambiguity in the solution space and the problem space, respectively.

In contrast, the source of ambiguity in temporally complex projects relates neither to the ability to monitor multiple interdependencies, nor to the specification of project problems or solutions, but to constraints. The constraints in structurally, technically and directionally complex projects can be assumed to be predominantly stable once they are in place. This is not true for a temporally complex project. Instead, when dealing with temporal complexity it may be necessary to plan the project in terms of multiple potential constraints, with the exact nature of the constraints changing over the life of the project.

Both the problem and solution spaces may be relatively well defined for a temporally complex project, at least in the beginning. However they may change over time. All systems are in constant states of change and therefore complex systems do not reach static equilibrium points (Dooley and Van de Ven, 1999). In temporally complex projects this effect is most noticeable and increases when the duration of the project is long. The complexity derives from lack of clarity regarding which project elements will still be relevant and appropriate when the project is delivered and how to integrate information from different sub-systems which themselves may be subject to independent changes over time. Temporal complexity is represented in Figure 6.1, where potential constraints have been marked by grey areas.

In the figure, at the start of the project T(0) we have eight different interconnected project elements (A – H). In this case the majority of these project elements have been shown as potentially affected by constraints which have not yet become an actuality. These project elements can be thought of as different options which will contribute to project objectives.

At T(n-x), some point during the project, one of the constraints has become real. Option F has ceased to become a possibility, or is no longer considered relevant. However, work is still being progressed on the other options. By the end of the project T(n) the situation has changed again. One more constraint has become an actuality, invalidating options E and H. However, the potential constraint surrounding options B and C is no longer a possibility, leaving options B and C free for development. At the time of delivery, the project outputs are a combination of options A, B, C, D and G. The constraint around options A and D is still only potential, and has perhaps been classified as unable to be decided for the foreseeable future.

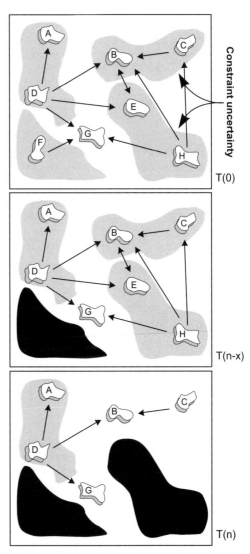

FITNESS LANDSCAPE AND TIME

One aspect which differentiates a temporally complex project from the three other kinds of complexity identified in this book can be explained in terms of the fitness landscape. For structural, technical and directional complexity, the fitness landscape can be assumed to be predominantly static. Changes may occur to the layout of the fitness landscape over time, but such change is slow and for the most part the landscape can be thought of as a stable

Figure 6.1   Uncertainty in temporally complex projects

geography which the complex project explores, looking for peaks of higher fitness.

In a temporally complex project, the fitness landscape is not at all stable. It moves, and can be thought of more as a rolling sea than as a static geography. As time passes, local peaks may become troughs, and troughs may become plateaus or peaks, while the project must navigate this changing scenery. Any solutions to a problem delivered by the project must be situated in time and delivered when the solution is on a peak. An exclusively technical focus will not necessarily guarantee success in a temporally complex project. A technically brilliant solution, which is delivered at the wrong time or addresses a politically inappropriate problem may just be ignored. At worst it could be a political catastrophe. By contrast, a well-timed but technically average solution which addresses the current issue is more likely to contribute towards success.

ORDER TO CHAOS

A temporally complex project is typically quite chaotic. A tightly structured and rigid project is unlikely to survive in a temporally complex context, as structured rigidity implies specialisation and commitment to a limited selection of capabilities. However, capabilities relevant at one point in time may lose their relevance as time passes. Until a definite opportunity for delivery presents itself, it is often a more successful strategy to pursue multiple options, with the project spread wide over the fitness landscape.

As the project is quite chaotic, it needs to be adaptable, capable of assuming new forms in relation to a changing environment. However, because of the highly chaotic nature of the project, control and maintenance of some sort of consistent form can be problematic. There is a strong danger that the project will fall apart if the environment changes too quickly.

COMMUNICATION

Communication is the key to maintaining some sort of internal integrity in a temporally complex project. Communication will have to be rich, frequent and mostly informal. It is important that stakeholders and the project team are all fully informed about changes to the context. Stakeholders will be able to provide insight into environmental changes that are not apparent to the project team. It is also important that members of the project team are well informed about environmental changes, so that any personal attachment to an option does not lead to resentment if the option must be abandoned because of emergent constraints.

Where there is little associated structural or directional complexity there is often one clear phase transition in temporally complex projects. For the most of the duration of the project gradual work will be progressed in parallel on different possible delivery options, with different options addressing different potential constraints. This phase will continue until relevant potential constraints have resolved themselves as real constraints, as not constraining the project further, or as delayed for the foreseeable future. When the situation has stabilised sufficiently, albeit momentarily, the project may undergo a phase transition. Parallel development of multiple options ceases and project resources are committed to delivering the option, or combination of options, considered most appropriate, as quickly as possible. Projects which are dependent on sensitive political decisions for approval often behave in this way. Project managers find themselves waiting in the wings until the time is right to progress the right option. Unlike traditional approaches to project management, it is more important to deliver the project at the right time, than to deliver the project on time. These kinds of temporally complex projects tend to defy attempts at scheduling, as the factors which dictate when might be an appropriate time to deliver the project are typically outside project control.

STRUCTURE

Structure and hierarchy in temporally complex projects is more like playing jazz than Beethoven. Players need to have multiple options running at the same time. This means lots of redundancy (Grant, 1996; LaPorte and Consolini, 1991; Perrow, 1984). Lots of parts of the project will be doing very similar things to other parts. Like a group of jazz musicians the project team explores their themes separately and together. The project team needs to communicate with each other constantly. Therefore it is often a good idea not to have separate groups working on the different parts, but to try to have as many people working on as many parts as possible. This means that if you have to kill one option then personal commitment is spread across multiple options, instead of solely attached to one. It is important that all solutions are kept open until definitely not required so that solutions are not owned. You don't want to end up with someone fighting for what they see as their solution.

For temporally complex projects which also have significant elements of structural, technical and directional complexity, phase changes can occur at any time during the project life cycle and there might be more than one phase change during which the project moves rapidly from being in control to running out of control. Typically these projects are large infrastructure projects and engineering projects, such as aerospace, transport and defence projects. The longer the duration the more certainly temporal complexity will be manifested.

Project management challenges

The major project management challenges include keeping as many options open and alive until the right time for a move towards delivering the project, and anticipating when and where issues will occur during the project life cycle. For large, structurally complex projects it is increasingly being recognised that managing ever expanding knowledge networks is also a major challenge (Ivory and Vaughan, 2004; Söderlund, 2002; Glynn et al., 1994).

Planning temporally complex projects is all about anticipation of what is coming and positioning yourself – knowing what is likely to happen and putting the pieces in place before it happens. If something which was anticipated doesn't happen then this leaves more options open. Options can be discarded at a later date as needed. Planning involves a combination of contingency planning and planning by options. The motto should be: 'Expect the unexpected and be ready to respond.' Project constraints will be likely to change during the life of the project. Developing a single option, as the only option, in a temporally complex project is equivalent to putting all your eggs in one basket. A single inopportune change in constraints could invalidate all work done on the project so far. By contrast, developing multiple different options provides the opportunity to hedge against changing constraints. With multiple options, when the right moment to deliver the project presents itself, the project team can be in a position to meet the needs of the time, at the right time.

On the other hand, in very large projects having many options available may be only one useful strategy. In an excellent analysis of the failure of three complex projects Ivory and Alderman (2005) argue that these kinds of projects might benefit from project teams 'mapping out the project as a series of interconnected nodes' in order to discover potential weaknesses. Project managers can then ask questions about whether the local ways of doing things in a given node are likely to support or undermine the goals of the project. They suggest that nodes with the potential to be problematic might require more intensive governance support or resources which could be identified early in the project (Ivory and Alderman, 2005, 14).

Temporal complexity is also intricately linked with managing project knowledge. It is particularly apparent in projects which require integration of many technical components. Successful integration is dependent upon efficient transfer of knowledge. Based on his studies of product development projects, Söderlund (2002, 429) argues that knowledge processes are dependent on time as 'knowledge is justified by local processes and thus dependent on the synchronisation of their activities'. He also argues that lead-time is a key component in temporal complexity, having a profound effect on the integration of the other parts of the project. This means that successful integration is less to do with compliance with pre-determined standards but rather that it fits with the efficiency criteria for the whole system at a given point in time. That is, the whole system reaches a satisficing position based on what is known and agreed at the time. This also implies that what satisfices in terms of solutions will change over time. Instead of reaching a final position at rest the project outcomes are in a state of flux.

CRITICAL PROJECT PHASES

All phases are critical in projects characterised by temporal complexity. In highly volatile environments the project teams could be expected to change tack at any time during the project life cycle. For example, an unexpected demand from a political leader might require the project team to temporarily drop the project mid-way, putting it on hold or shelving it permanently, and move on to something else, or to alter course in a radical way. People who work in the public sector are very familiar with these kinds of situation. In an engineering project, such as the Pendolino tilting train project (Ivory and Alderman, 2005; Williams, 2002), which involved many technological challenges and multiple design changes over time, the temporal complexity escalated as time progressed.

EXECUTIVE SUPPORT

Project senior executives should be very conscious of the organisation structure or structures, if more than one organisation is involved, and of how existing organisation structures might affect the project. Wheelwright and Clark (1992) emphasise the difficulties of managing projects involving innovation and change in mature organisations which have entrenched functional hierarchies. In an investigation of two very successful projects, one at Volvo and one at Eriksson, Söderlund (2002, 428) found tight coupling between sub-system teams and project phase teams. He attributes this to project management having to deal with '… problems that concerned both the relationship between sub-systems and the relationship between downstream and upstream activities'.

It is also very important that project teams are kept in touch with the whole of system requirements. As this meta-view is most easily obtained from the perspective of the organisation and the environment it is the responsibility of senior management to constantly provide the perspective. When interviewed about a successful project in the health sector, which was also temporally complex, the project manager reported that a valuable role performed by the project executive sponsor was as follows:

> *'[She would] continuously give me lots of information about context. She kept me grounded. Kept me heading in the right direction, kept dragging my head up from focusing on technical issues to paying attention to the environment, which was very useful.' (Interview L1: Helm and Remington, 2005)*

Selection of the right people to fulfil the management role is also a key executive responsibility. Having selected the right people the project executive needs to exhibit a great deal of trust in the manager and the project team. Because the project management team is likely to comprise highly experienced people, executive support tends to be most effective if it is ad hoc, when and if the manager needs it, hands-off day-to-day issues, but with frequent updates on relevant contextual issues (Helm and Remington, 2005).

Both in terms of mitigating risks and for the purpose of knowledge management, the executive sponsor must be aware that some redundancy in key areas will be necessary. This is required both when there is a need to develop and maintain several approaches and also because project knowledge must be able to travel freely across multiple boundaries and it is best taken by people. Redundancy has been shown to be vital for effective knowledge management (Grant, 1996; La Porte and Consolini, 1991; Perrow, 1984). This can appear to be very wasteful to auditors, and the senior executive must be prepared to defend the approach.

Project communication structures should support system-wide communication for information sharing, problem solving and maintaining the project vision. Information-sharing sessions should traverse as many system and sub-system boundaries as possible. Söderlund (2002) found that much effort was put into cross-boundary information sharing in the successful time-constrained projects which he studied. Information sharing, affecting knowledge management and therefore ability to learn from experience, was identified as an issue in each of the failed time-constrained projects studied by Ivory and Alderman (2005).

Unpredictable changes can be very demoralizing for project team members, who never seem to see their work finished before another change occurs, especially if such changes result in complete termination of their part of project. Leadership at the executive level is fundamental to morale. For instance, it is vital that any apparent rationale for the changes is communicated by the executive sponsor to the project team and that some kind of closure is affected. Communication should be in person, not via email! At the very least the executive sponsor should explain to the project team why the former project has been terminated or put on hold and what any new directives might involve. In these kinds of environments managers and project teams often complain that they are 'change weary'. This usually means that changes have occurred so rapidly that they overlap, resulting in people becoming not only confused but demotivated.

PROJECT MANAGER CAPABILITIES

Creating the climate for knowledge transfer is one of the key roles of the project manager in temporally complex projects. To do this the project manager must expand communication networks to encompass unfamiliar communities of practice (Garrety, Robertson and Badham, 2004). Flexibility and skill in managing multiple interfaces and multiple delivery options is also a distinct advantage. With multiple options, whatever happens there is a direction to take. It is important never to be in a position where all previous work is no longer valid. There should always be another option that can be developed. The project manager must be comfortable with keeping many options in play and also have the ability to pounce once the timing is right. In managing multiple sub-systems it is important to keep a focus on other teams, on other stakeholder groups and on external issues which might affect the project. This is a super-human task and cannot be done without collaboration between the executive team and the project team. Ability to foster a collaborative, problem-sharing attitude is particularly useful.

The project manager needs to assist the team to let go of options which are no longer relevant. The project manager must be able to motivate the project team and keep their spirits up during periods of rapid change. Team members should be kept informed of the rationale behind changes, even if that amounts to nothing more than 'the Ministry has changed its mind'. Motivating the team may involve constructing artificial end-points and handovers so that team members can have some sense of achievement. In our experience team members often complain that there is no formal closure of initiatives which have been overridden before completion by new imperatives. As a result project teams can exist in constant states of confusion regarding what initiative they are supposed to be working on. The old initiative needs to be formally put to bed before introducing the new one.

The role description above suggests that a project management team with linked and complimentary roles might be a viable option to fill the position in contrast to seeking a single super-human. However, team management can be problematic and the management team needs to be carefully built and maintained.

TEAM SUPPORT

Surviving temporally complex projects is truly a team effort. Clearly, these kinds of project teams may exist and change over considerable lengths of time, and the past and the potential future will influence present performance (Arrow, McGrath and Berdahl, 2000; McGrath, 1990; 1991). Arrow and McGrath (1993) have observed that teams whose members stayed together over several sessions experienced more conflict than teams with changing membership. In other studies Harrison et al. (1998; 2002) found that effects of cultural diversity on group cohesiveness were reduced over time, but behaviour differences became more important. Particularly as effective teamwork is crucial to project success these are important findings. Therefore it is reasonable to conclude that building and maintaining the teams should be priorities. Based on action research conducted over 15 years in a successful new product development unit comprising about 1000 engineers, Jokinen et. al (2006) argue that intensive and comprehensive training is essential to develop and maintain high-performing teams.

It is normal practice to compose a team from those with experience on the project or tasks at hand. Task experience clearly facilitates performance through the acquisition of task knowledge (Schmidt, Hunter and Outerbridge, 1986). However, membership based on expertise alone ignores other potentially influential member characteristics that affect how well such persons would work together (Colarelli and Boos, 1992). If the team must work together over an extended period of time, personality issues can affect knowledge sharing and transfer. There also is some evidence that familiarity with team members who have worked together on past projects will support knowledge transfer (Harrison et al., 2002) though this must be tempered by other research which emphasises the importance of behaviour.

FINANCIAL ISSUES

Temporally complex projects are financially challenging because of the degree of uncertainty which will, without doubt, increase with time. For this reason these projects must have adequate contingencies built into the budget. As discussed earlier, many financial failures have been approved on what could be described as very optimistic budgets (Flyvbjerg, 2006; Flyvbjerg et al., 2003).

Nevertheless, providing even partly realistic cost estimates for whole projects subject to temporal complexity is difficult. The bits that are able to be defined can be estimated accurately provided they are not subject to change. There is a need for substantial research in this area (Söderlund, 2002). In the public sector, budgets are tied to funding cycles, adding a further complication. It is important to clearly acknowledge that the project will be subject to temporal complexity when presenting any budget estimates for approval. Not only must cost estimation allow for sufficient contingency; it must also allow for sufficient redundancy to ensure knowledge transfer can occur at critical stages (Grant, 1996; La Porte and Consolini, 1991; Perrow, 1984).

SCHEDULING ISSUES

Projects which are subject to politically induced constraints may have long lead times. Miller and Hobbs (2002; 2005) analyzed projects that had front ends averaging seven years. Scheduling these kinds of projects other than with vague milestone targets would seem to be a waste of time. However, as Miller and Hobbs (2005) point out, large infrastructure projects are both highly visible and contestable. The visibility implies difficulty in managing public expectations with respect to governance and particularly with respect to expenditure and timing of delivery. In addition timing is often linked to political outcomes, such as elections. Often political promises are made which cannot be kept or can only be kept at considerable sacrifice, while project teams find that deadlines are brought forward dramatically or protracted for extended periods. One of our colleagues was looking particularly harassed one day. When asked why he responded by saying: 'Well as you know an election has just been called ahead of time and I have five major road projects to finish before it!'

Whether the project is delayed or accelerated there will be organisational and financial consequences that have practical and ethical implications for project governance.

During implementation of temporally complex projects some researchers have suggested that schedules should allow activities to synchronise with other key activities (Söderlund, 2002; Ancona and Chong, 1996; McGrath, 1990). Labelled 'entrainment', this kind of thinking has implications both for the project schedule and for the project life cycle. Entrainment was first observed by the seventeenth-century physicist Christian Huygens. It is defined as the tendency of two oscillating bodies to lock into phase so that they vibrate in harmony. Brown and Eisenhardt (1997) have noted this phenomenon in relation to market constraints. However, according to Letiche and Hagemeijer (2004) entrainment is not the same as consistency. In complex systems this linkage is dynamic, disharmonious and unpredictable. This suggests that traditional approaches to scheduling are not appropriate where there is temporal complexity. An additional role has been suggested, that of the 'pacer'. This is a dynamic role which sets a 'dominant temporal order or macrocycle' which Söderlund (2002: 428) suggests was played by project management in the case studies he investigated.

RISK ISSUES

The major sources of risk in temporally complex projects come from changes that are externally imposed and difficult, sometimes impossible, to predict in advance. Risks can include delivering the wrong option at the wrong time. This can be politically disastrous for all concerned, with career-limiting consequences. In large projects risks are often related to inadequate knowledge transfer across sub-systems resulting in re-work and subsequent escalation of costs and delays. These can be the result of poorly communicated changes imposed on isolated sub-systems, such as a local requirements change, which have implications for other sub-systems and the whole. Similar effects can result from misinterpretations occurring particularly in sub-systems when unfamiliar work or processes are involved.

The traditional approach to risk management involves decomposition into progressively smaller and more manageable sub-tasks, but Ivory and Alderman (2005: 23) argue that this may simply shift the focus from the complexity to integration of an 'ever-expanding project network', hiding the complexity from the immediate view of management. As mentioned earlier they see some benefit in a 'control room' approach in which interconnected nodes are mapped out to help identify weaknesses. However, the control room must recognise that 'much is occurring unchecked, out of sight and beyond their control'.

In projects which are not necessarily large but are politically sensitive to timing, risk mitigation can be greatly assisted by diligent options analysis. When the time is right the project team can find itself in the position where it has to move quickly to implement the most suitable option. In order to move quickly the project team must have a suitable range of very well-developed options. That means that the risks associated with the options must have been fully analyzed so that decisions quickly can be made to proceed or not to proceed, based on sound information. If the project team is unable to act quickly enough to seize opportune moments, it is likely that the environment will change again before the project is delivered, creating an endless series of partially complete projects. This is a demotivating cycle for a project team and highly wasteful of resources.

PROCUREMENT ISSUES

A shift in focus to improve long-term quality and maintenance of projects has promoted the adoption of Build Operate Transfer (BOT) and Refurbish Operate Transfer (ROT) contracts for major infrastructure projects. This effectively protects the customer and end user by shifting much of the risk to the project owner. However it adds enormously to the temporal complexity of the project. Projects which might have been one year in length now must be conceptualised as having a life cycle of five to ten years. This trend was well-established for the 2000 Sydney Olympics, the Government of the day wanting to ensure that the facilities would be operational for many years into the future. The approach aims at ensuring quality but it also increases temporal complexity for project management.

Procurement needs to allow for and anticipate change. In many cases a combination of procurement methods will be required. It is important to delay letting of contracts until the appropriate options have been selected and approved for delivery. Rapid deployment of the contract once an opportune moment has arrived can be problematic in organisations that have unwieldy procurement processes. This is often found in public sector organisations, where procurement may be tied to funding cycles which bear little connection to project phases, and approval processes are unwieldy. Approaching procurement as manageable chunks, linked to small deliverables might contribute to reducing costs of litigation in large, temporally complex projects.

Traps and consequences

In temporally complex projects there is often a belief that the situation will stabilise and that the temporal complexity will simply go away. It is true that parts will align at different points, allowing pursuit of one option or another to completion; however real stability is unlikely and it is best not to wait in vain. You have to be ready for the chance to implement one of your developed options, not waiting for the time when everything becomes stable. Waiting for the situation to stabilise before implementing anything may demotivate the project team.

It is easy to become locked in to early ideas or ideas which have taken time to develop – something that was appropriate for a past that no longer exists. Similarly, it is important to ensure that team members do not develop ego attachment to particular options. Having multiple team members working on multiple options helps to reduce this possibility.

Constant change can be highly demotivating to project managers and team members, who may rarely see an idea fully resolved and implemented because of the rapidity of externally provoked changes.

These projects are very difficult to manage in the public sector where budgets are tied to funding cycles. In order to retain budget allocation levels, money is sometimes spent on options which may soon become inappropriate.

Traps and consequences due to temporal complexity tend to escalate exponentially as the size and duration of the project increase due to the number of key project stakeholders and the extended duration during which risks have an increasing propensity to be triggered.

Reference and further reading

Alderman, N., McLoughlin, I., Ivory, C. J., Thwaites, A. T. and Vaughan, R. (2003), 'Trains, Cranes and Drains: Customer Requirements in Long-Term Engineering Projects as a Knowledge Management Problem', in von Zedtwitz, M., Haour, G., Khalil, T. and Lefebvre, L. (eds), *Management of Technology: Growth through Business, Innovation and Entrepreneurship.* (Oxford. UK: Pergamon Press), 331-48.

Ancona, D. and Chong, C.-L. (1996), 'Entrainment: Pace, Cycle and Rhythm in Organizational Behavior', *Research in Organizational Behavior* 18, 251-84.

Argyres, N. S., (1999), 'The Impact of Information Technology on Coordination: Evidence from The B-2 Stealth Bomber', *Organization Science* 10, 162-80.

Arrow, H. and McGrath, J. E. (1993), 'Membership Matters: How Member Change and Continuity Affect Small Group Structure, Process, and Performance', *Small Group Research* 24, 334-361.

Arrow, H., McGrath, J. E. and Berdahl, J. L. (2000), *Small Groups as Complex Systems: Formation, Development, and Adaptation.* (Thousand Oaks, CA: Sage).

Brown, S. and Eisenhardt, K. (1997), 'The Art of Continuous Change: Linking Complexity Theory and Time-Paced Evolution in Relentlessly Shifting Organizations', *Administrative Science Quarterly* 42:1, 1-35.

Clark, K., Chew, B. and Fujimoto, T. (1987), 'Product Development in the World Auto Industry', *Brookings Papers on Economic Activity* 3, 729-771.

Clark, K. and Fujimoto, T., (1991), *Product Development Performance: Strategy, Organization and Management in the World Auto Industry.* (Boston, MA: Harvard Business School Press).

Colarelli, S. M. and Boos A. L. (1992), 'Sociometric and Ability-based Assignment to Work Groups: Some Implications for Personnel Selection', *Journal of Organizational Behavior* 13, 187-196.

DeMaio, A., Verganti, R. and Corso, M. (1994), 'A Multi-project Framework for New Product Development', *European Journal of Operational Research* 78, 178-191.

Dooley, K. and Van de Ven, A. (1999), 'Explaining Complex Organizational Dynamics', *Organization Science* 10:3, 358-372.

Flyvbjerg, B. (2006), 'From Nobel Prize to Project Management: Getting Risks Right', *Project Management Journal* 37:3, 5-15.

Flyvbjerg, B., Bruzelius, N. and Rothengatter, W. (2003), *Megaprojects and Risk. An Anatomy of Ambition.* (Cambridge, UK: Cambridge University Press).

Garrety, K., Robertson, P. L. and Badham, R. (2004), 'Integrating Communities of Practice in Technology Development Projects', *International Journal of Project Management* 22:5, 351-358.

Glynn, M. A., Lant, T. K. and Milliken, F. J. (1994), 'Mapping Learning Processes in Organizations: A Multi-Level Framework Linking Learning and Organizing', in Garud, R. and Porac, J. (eds), *Advances in Managerial Cognition and Organizational Information Processing*, 5. (Greenwich, CT: JAI Press), 43–83.

Grant, R.M. (1996), 'Toward a Knowledge-Based Theory of the Firm', *Strategic Management Journal* 17 - Special Issue, 109-122.

Harrison, D. A., Price, K. H., Gavin, J. H. and Florey, A. T. (2002), 'Time, Teams, and Task Performance: Changing Effects of Surface- and Deep-Level Diversity on Group Functioning', *Academy of Management Journal* 45, 1029-45.

Harrison, D. A., Price, K. H. and Bell, M. (1998), 'Beyond Relational Demography: Time and the Effects of Surface- and Deep-Level Diversity on Work Group Cohesion', *Academy of Management Journal* 41, 96-107.

Helm, J. and Remington, K. (2005), 'Effective Sponsorship, Project Managers' Perceptions of the Role of the Project Sponsor', *Project Management Journal* 36:3, 36-51.

Hobday, M. (1998), 'Product Complexity, Innovation and Industrial Organization', *Research Policy* 26, 689-710.

Hoffman, E., 1997, 'NASA Project Management: Modern Strategies For Maximizing Project Performance', *Project Management Journal* 28:3, 4–6.

Horwitch, M., 1982. *Clipped Wings: The American SST Conflict*. (Cambridge, MA.: MIT Press).

Ivory, C. and Alderman, N. (2005), 'Can Project Management Learn Anything from Studies of Failure in Complex Systems?', *Project Management Journal* 36:3, 5-16.

Ivory, C. and Vaughan, R. (2004), 'Managing Projects Through Making Sense of Project Discourses: The Case of Long Term Service-Led Engineering Projects', in *Conference Proceedings of EURAM 2004 Conference*. (Governance of Projects Track), 5-7 May.

Jokinen, T., Muhos, M. and Peltoniemi, M. (2006), 'Project Teams and High Performance Culture', *Proceedings of IRNOP VII Conference*, (Xi'an, China: Northwestern Polytechnical University) 176-85.

La Porte, T. R. (1994), 'Large Technical Systems, Institutional Surprises, and Challenges to Political Legitimacy', *Technology in Society* 16:3, 269-88.

LaPorte, T. R. and Consolini, P. M. (1991), 'Working in Practice but Not in Theory: Theoretical Challenges of "High-Reliability Organizations"', *Journal of Public Administration Research and Theory: J-PART* 1:1, 19-48

Letiche, H. and Hagemeijer, R. E. (2004), 'Linkages and Entrainment', *Journal of Organizational Change Management* 17:4, 1032-48.

Lindkvist, L., Söderlund, J. and Tell, F. (2004), 'Managing Product Development Projects: On the Significance of Fountains and Deadlines', *Organization Studies* 19:6, 931-951.

Loch, C.H. and Terwiesch, C. (1998), 'Communication and Uncertainty in Concurrent Engineering', *Management Science* 44, 1032–48.

McGrath, J. E. (1990), 'Time Matters in Groups', in Galagher, J. (ed.), *Intellectual Teamwork: Social and Technological Foundations of Cooperative Work*. (Hillsdale, NJ: Erlbaum) 23-61.

McGrath, J. E. (1991), 'Time, Interaction and Performance (TIP): A Theory of Groups', *Small Group Research* 22, 147-74.

Miller, R. and Hobbs, B. (2005), 'Governance Regimes for Large Complex Projects', *Project Management Journal* 36:3, 42-50.

Miller, R. and Hobbs, B. (2002), 'A Framework for Analyzing the Development and Delivery of Large Capital Projects', in Slevin, D., Cleland, D. and Pinto, J. (eds.) *The Frontiers of Project Management Research*. (Newtown Square, PA: Project Management Institute) 201-10.

Perrow, C. (1984), *Normal Accidents: Living with High Risk Technologies*. (NY: Basic Books).

Quinn, J. B. and Pacquette, P. (1988), *Ford: Team Taurus*. (Dartmouth, USA: Amos Tuck School, Dartmouth College).

Sabbagh, K. (1996), *Twenty-First-Century Jet: The Making and Marketing of the Boeing 777*. (NY: Scribner).

Schmidt, F. L., Hunter, J. E. and Outerbridge, A. N. (1986), 'Impact of Job Experience and Ability on Job Knowledge, Work Sample, Performance and Supervisory Ratings of Job Performance', *Journal of Applied Psychology* 71, 432-9.

Scudder, G. D., Schroeder, R. G., Van de Ven, A. H., Seiler, G. R. and Wiseman, R. M. (1989), 'Managing Complex Innovations: The Case of Defense Contracting', in Van de Ven, A. H., Angle, H. L. and Poole, M. S. (eds), *Research on the Management of Innovation*. (NY: Harper & Row) 401–38.

Söderlund, J. (2002), 'Managing Complex Development Projects: Arenas, Knowledge Processes and Time', *R&D Management* 32:5, 419-30.

Uddin, S. and Tsamenyi, M. (2005), 'Public Sector Reforms and the Public Interest: A Case Study of Accounting Changes and Performance in a Ghanaian State-Owned Enterprise', *Accounting, Auditing and Accountability Journal* 18:5, 648-57.

Wheelwright, S. C. and Clark, K. B. (1992), *Revolutionizing Product Development*. (NY: McGraw-Hill).

Williams, T. (2002), *Modelling Complex Projects*. (Sussex, UK: John Wiley & Sons).

Tools and Techniques

CHAPTER

7 *Guide to the Tools*

This chapter provides a link between the theory in the preceding chapters and the practical approaches which follow. As we stated in Chapter 1, managing complex projects requires approaches to management that extend beyond those traditional methods used to manage discrete, stable projects. Managing a complex project is a higher-order management activity and should be treated and resourced accordingly. Project managers who manage these projects successfully are more like artists, selecting the most appropriate tools and approaches from their very large palettes and working with those tools to produce the colour, form and texture appropriate to the work in hand. They tend to develop their own methodologies and vary these considerably from project to project. For this reason and because projects vary so much in size, value and context, we have resisted recommending one methodology. A methodology should be developed by the project team to fit the explicit requirements of each project (see Payne and Turner, 1999; Shenhar, 2001).

The tools and approaches to follow this chapter have been drawn from our own experience and the experience of other practitioners who have struggled with complex projects, from our experience in teaching post-graduate project management courses, from our research projects and our observations of expert project managers at work. Experience from senior project managers who have been kind enough to contribute their own insights has added many dimensions and insights, especially in industry sectors with which we are not personally familiar. In addition, in the very recent past, project management research in this field has expanded in the recognition that traditional approaches were not always delivering the best results.

Some tools we have developed ourselves to help manage particular challenges or to help our post-graduate students explore difficult issues. Other tools and approaches have been found to be successful by other experienced practitioners working in various industries. It is important to stress, however that it is the purpose of the tool or approach which is more important than the actual tool itself. The tools presented below are by no means exhaustive. There will be many cases in which other tools can be substituted. Also other excellent tools and methods have been referred to in the discussion but not described in detail. The intention is that each tool and the associated discussion will provide its own insights to be adapted by practitioners as they wish. The art of project management is in selecting the right combination of tools at the right time to create the right methodology for the situation.

Relationship between theory, methodology and tools

In this book, we address theory, methodology and tools. One popular way of looking at the relationship between theory, methodology and tools is to think of them as a hierarchy. In this kind of hierarchy, theory is usually thought of as sitting at the top, with methodology below that, and tools sitting at the bottom of the hierarchy (see Figure 7.1). In this kind of hierarchy,

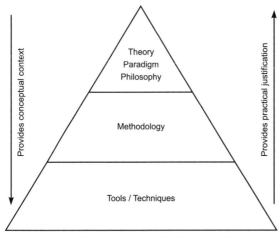

Figure 7.1   Hierarchical relationship between the theoretical and practical

the upper layers can be thought of as more philosophical or theoretical and distanced from the mess of practical application. By contrast, the lower levels are never as clean, requiring actual engagement with pragmatic necessity and providing a context where theoretical claims can be tested. Many different practitioners and researchers have found it useful to view this relationship as a hierarchy with different levels of abstraction (see for example Mingers and Brocklesby, 1997; Fitzgerald and Howcroft, 1998; Ragsdell, 2000).

The upper levels in this hierarchy constitute the conceptual basis and intellectual context for the increasing practicalities in the lower layers. The upper layers provide a basis against which consistency can be judged. These philosophical and theoretical aspects provide the 'why' for methodology. Methodology can be thought of as specifying 'what', while tools and technique specify 'how' (Mingers, 1997b, 429–30). More can be learnt about the application of the lower layers by reflecting upon their links to upper layers. One can '… learn more about these tools by reflecting on their links to methodologies, or about methodologies by reflecting on their links to theory' (Jackson, 1999: 19).

The practical world of the lower layers plays a different role in this hierarchy. A theory which bears no relationship to the real world of practice is not of much practical value. For theory to be valuable it must enable action; it has to be applied and tested in the real world. Testing the real-world efficacy of the practice provides justification for statements made in the realms of theory and philosophy. Practical application of the lower layers can be used to test the validity of claims made in the upper layers, resulting in either validation of claims or the need to reassess and rework statements about the nature of the world. The lower layers can be thought of as a feedback system for the upper layers.

WHAT ARE THEORY, METHODOLOGY AND TOOLS?

Clearly and simply defining theory and philosophy is a difficult matter as the words are used in different ways in different contexts. Perhaps the most appropriate approach is to define these terms on a functional basis. As such, for the purposes of this discussion philosophy and theory are seen as providing a formal conceptual framework for examining the world; an explicit perspective through which the world can be viewed. Likewise, 'paradigm' is broadly defined as '… a world view, spanning ontology, epistemology and methodology …' (Healy and Perry, 2000: 121), '… based on a set of fundamental philosophical assumptions that define the nature of possible research and intervention.' (Mingers, 1997b: 429–30). Readers interested in a more thorough exploration of the ontology of paradigms should refer to Kuhn (1962). Complexity Theory, a broad group of ideas, models and predictive descriptions about how complex systems behave, has been used in the role of theory for the majority of this book. However, other theories have been appealed to, where we believed them to be appropriate.

A methodology is a structured set of guidelines for the improvement of the effectiveness of a project (Mingers, 1997a). It develops within a particular paradigm and embodies particular philosophical and theoretical principles (Mingers and Brocklesby, 1997; Mingers, 1997b). However, methodology differs from theory and philosophy in that it contains practical guidelines. Checkland (1981: 162) places methodology as the middle ground between philosophy and technique, containing elements of both, as while '... a technique tells you "how" and a philosophy tells you "what"', a methodology will contain elements of both "how" and "what".' Methodology is here considered to be '... the logos of method ...' (Checkland, 1999: S36). It provides the principles on which method is based (Checkland, 2002), and can be considered '... a higher-order term than method and, indeed, than procedures, models, tools, and techniques, the use of all of which can be facilitated, organised and reflected upon in methodology' (Jackson, 2000: 11).

Tools, approaches and techniques are the most directly practical part of the hierarchy, and they tend to make little direct reference to theory or philosophy. However, they are often created under, or associated with, particular theories or philosophies. For instance PERT and Gantt charts are both associated with the way of thinking embodied in project management and can be linked to positivist and realist philosophies.

Tools, approaches and techniques generally involve a series of clearly delineated steps. Because of this, it is possible to create clear standards for their use, while this is significantly more difficult for methodologies. According to Mingers (1997b) and Mingers and Brocklesby (1997) tools are specific activities with well-defined purposes. A tool can also be an artifact, such as computer software, that can be used to perform a particular technique; it can '... lead to an end point without the need for reflective intervention ...' (Rosenhead, 1997: xiii). However, reflection on tools, in relation to theory and methodology, can be useful in learning from past mistakes and improving future performance.

NON-HIERARCHICAL RELATIONSHIP

It is not universally accepted within the systems thinking and project management communities that the best way to think of the relationship between theory, methodology and tools is as a hierarchy. To Midgley (2000), thinking of this relationship as a hierarchy suggests that theory and philosophy are given special value and thought of as incontestable. He suggests that the '... idea that encountering a problem in practice may signal a philosophical inadequacy is not conceivable from the point of view of those who believe in this hierarchical relationship' (Midgley, 2000: 21). However, it is clear that in practice, theory and philosophy are often challenged by practical experience. Midgley argues that philosophy, methodology and tools should be viewed as mutually supportive.

Alternatives to thinking of this relationship as a hierarchy exist. One useful alternative model applicable to managing complex projects is described by Paton (2001). Paton's model was developed as a generalization of the cycle between investigation and action found in many different systems methodologies. This model shifts the focus off theory and philosophy, to examine how methods are created in practice. Paton builds on previous work on the creative design of methods by Midgley (1990; 1997), who found that it is often necessary to synthesize a method that is specific to a situation from the elements of many different methodologies.

Methods can generally be thought of as an interrelated series of tools, used in practice to achieve a specific purpose (Midgley et. al., 1998). Methods may include representational guidelines, such as modelling techniques, and procedural guidelines, which describe how work is to be conducted (Lind and Goldkuhl, 2002). To Paton (2001) a method is constructed to deal with an individual situation. It is particular and individual. Methodologies '... provide us with logic to help us construct a method from a given set of tools and techniques' (Paton, 2001: 99). Methods can be thought of as the practical output of the combination of methodologies and tools (see Figure 7.2).

Methodology provides a context for, and principles for, creating a whole of project process, within which we can select and combine particular tools to meet particular ends. Tools are selected to meet the daily situation-specific needs of the project, and applied as part of a method in practice. Methodology, and subsequently theory,

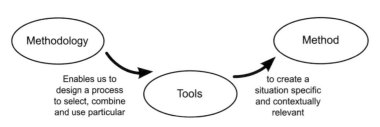

Figure 7.2   Derivation and design of methods

Source: Adapted from Paton, 2001: 99

become embodied in practice, through informing both the selection of tools and how they are applied in the project. 'The task of the user of a systems methodology is to embody the principles of the methodology in a *method* suitable for the specific situation addressed' (Checkland, 2002: 105 – original italics).

Although the emphasis has been taken off theory, this model does not advocate abandoning theory and becoming purely pragmatic. Rather, Paton emphasises that it is necessary to reflect on the results of practice in relation to theory, as a way of learning. By paying attention to theory, '... we can move beyond simply using methods which merely work in the short term to understanding why and how they do so, and this enhances our ability both to communicate between practitioners and to evolve better methods' (Paton, 2001: 100). This opinion is not isolated, with many others in the systems field sharing similar views regarding the relevance of theory and methodology to reflective learning (see for example, Checkland and Holwell, 1998; Checkland and Scholes, 1990; Jackson, 1999; 2000).

As such, in this book we have taken an approach to providing assistance to the project manager faced with a complex project which is based on a combination of theory, methodology and tools. In the preceding chapters we have looked at how insight from Complexity Theory can be applied to develop an understanding of different kinds of complex projects. In the following chapters we take a more practical focus, first looking at a selection of methodologies and a whole set of project approaches which can be of assistance in managing complex projects. Following that we provide a selection of tools to meet specific needs in complex projects.

How to select the tools

Many standard project management methodologies assume that you will use a particular set of tools in a particular order, and that all tools in the methodology will be used in all projects. This book does not offer one standard methodology to be used unvaryingly in all contexts. Instead the tools are there for the manager to select from, alter and add to, as the situation requires, in whatever order suits the project. When dealing with complex projects we argue that the most productive management approaches are based on the concept of systemic pluralism, introduced in Chapter 1. In implementing a systemic and pluralistic approach the manager must first identify the type or types of complexity, and then, like an artist, select from the palette of tools those which will provide a variety of perspectives, reveal the layers of complexity and make the project manageable.

Chapters 8 to 16 in Part II describe ways of thinking and conceptualising whole projects or groups of projects. These whole-of-project approaches act more like a methodology, informing how the project as a whole can be thought about or structured. Some incorporate techniques which can be useful throughout the project, while others place more emphasis on how the project is conceptualised.

Chapters 17 to 21 describe more specific tools, which can be used by the project manager to help with the particular aspects of complexity which may become apparent during the project life cycle. These tools might be used in conjunction with either traditional or non-traditional approaches to project management. In some cases they may complement traditional project management tools. In others they may replace traditional project management tools.

How the tools are set out

Where possible an estimate of the time required for using the tool is indicated, though for tools and approaches that are really thinking strategies to guide the project as a whole, this is impossible as it depends very greatly on the size and complexity of the project.

The level of difficulty is indicated as follows:

Relatively easy to use

Some experience needed to use

For use by an experienced practitioner

There is also an indication of the number of people involved in using the tool: for instance, if you can use it by yourself or if the tool is best used with a group.

Chapter	Title	Type of complexity				When to use	
		Structural	Technical	Directional	Temporal	Life cycle	Ad hoc
8	**Mapping the Complexity**– a simple way to illustrate where the sources of complexity are likely to occur and how they change throughout the project life cycle.	■	■	■	■	X	
9	**System Anatomy** – an approach developed for the telecommunications industry which involves simple graphic means of coordination between international centres.	■	■	■	■	X	
10	**TOC (Target Outturn Cost)** – an approach developed for construction projects based on collaborative working agreements.	■				X	
11	**Programme Tool** – a concept which uses the programme to help define differential strategies for managing projects within the programme according to their type and level of complexity.	■	■	■	■	X	X
12	**Role Definition** – a checklist for use when defining role capabilities for managing different types of complex projects.	■	■	■	■	X	X
13	**Jazz (Time-linked Semi-structures)** – a way of thinking about the organisational structure for a complex project in order to balance creativity and output.		■	■	■	X	

Table 7.1   Summary of tools chapters

Chapter	Title	Type of complexity				When to use	
14	**Multimethodology in Series** – an approach which grafts soft systems thinking to the front end of a project or project phase.					X	
15	**Multimethodology in Parallel** – an approach which embeds soft systems thinking into the entire project life cycle.					X	
16	**Virtual Gates** – an approach which utilizes the idea of variable control gates to help manage project risk.	▨	▨	▨	▨	X	
17	**Risk Interdependencies** – a quick tool to help identify emergent risk patterns in small- to medium-sized projects.	▨	▨	▨	▨		X
18	**TCTC (Temporal Cost-Time Comparison)** – an approach to preparing realistic ranges of estimates during uncertainty.	▨	▨	▨			X
19	**Kokotovich Triad** – a group of tools to assist in stimulating creative solution finding.	▨	▨				X
20	**Stanislavski's 'Method'** – a tool to help expand personal perspectives in a given situation.						X
21	**Discursive Universe** – a tool to help with communication and managing difficult stakeholder relationships.	▨	▨				X

Table 7.1 *Continued*

Just as all categories are artificial boundaries and many sources of complexity can be present in any one project, strict categorisation of tools is not really possible. An indication of the type of complexity for which the tool is suggested as follows:

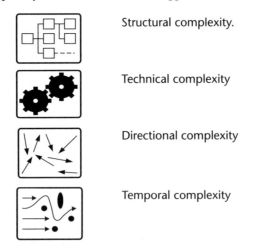

Structural complexity.

Technical complexity

Directional complexity

Temporal complexity

Discussion of the tool itself starts with a short description of the problems the tool addresses, how it relates to complexity theory and any theoretical background which might be of interest. A detailed discussion of how to use the tool is followed by a step-by-step guide to its application, cautionary notes, and examples of the use of the tool in practice.

References and further reading

Checkland, P. (1981), *Systems Thinking, Systems Practice*. (Chichester, UK: John Wiley & Sons).

Checkland, P. (1999), 'Soft Systems Methodology: A 30-Year Retrospective" in Checkland, P. and Scholes, J. (eds), *Soft Systems Methodology in Action*, A1–A65 (Chichester, UK: John Wiley & Sons).

Checkland, (2002), 'Thirty Years in the Systems Movement: Disappointments I have Known, and a Way Forward', *Systemist* 24:2, 99-112.

Checkland P. and Holwell, S. (1998), *Information, Systems and Information Systems – Making Sense of the Field*. (West Sussex, UK: John Wiley & Sons).

Checkland P. and Scholes, J. (1990), *Soft Systems Methodology in Action*. (Chichester, UK: John Wiley & Sons).

Fitzgerald, B. and Howcroft, D. (1998), 'Towards Dissolution of the IS Research Debate: From Polarization to Polarity, *Journal of Information Technology* 13, 313-26.

Healy, M. and Perry, C. (2000), 'Comprehensive Criteria to Judge the Validity and Reliability of Qualitative Research within the Realism Paradigm', *Qualitative Market Research: An International Journal* 3, 118-26.

Jackson, M. (1999), 'Towards Coherent Pluralism in Management Science', *Journal of the Operational Research Society* 50, 12-22.

Jackson, M. (2000), *Systems Approaches to Management*. (NY: Plenum).

Kuhn, T. (1962), *The Structure of Scientific Revolutions*. (Chicago, USA: University of Chicago Press).

Lind, M. and Goldkuhl, G. (2002), 'Grounding of Methods or Business Change: Altering Between Empirical, Theoretical and Internal Grounding' *Proceedings of the European Conference on Research Methodology for Business and Management Studies*. Remenyi, D. (ed.), (Reading, UK: MCIL).

Midgley, G. (1990), 'Creative Methodology Design, *Systemist* 12, 108-13.

Midgley, G. (1997), 'Mixing Methods: Developing Systemic Intervention' in Mingers, J. & Gill, A. (eds.) *Multimethodology: The Theory and Practice of Combining Management Science Methodologies*. (Chichester, UK: John Wiley & Sons).

Midgley, G. (2000), *Systemic Intervention: Philosophy, Methodology, and Practice*. (NY: Plenum).

Midgley, G., Munlo, I. and Brown, M. (1998), 'The Theory and Practice of Boundary Critique: Developing Housing Services for Older People', *Journal of the Operational Research Society* 49, 467-78.

Mingers, J. (1997a), 'Multi-paradigm Multimethodology', in *Multimethodology: The Theory and Practice of Combining Management Science Methodologies,* Mingers, J. and Gill, A. (eds.) 1-20. (Chichester, UK: John Wiley & Sons).

Mingers, J. (1997b), 'Towards Critical Pluralism', in *Multimethodology: The Theory and Practice of Combining Management Science Methodologies,* Mingers, J. and Gill, A. (eds.) 407-40. (Chichester, UK: John Wiley & Sons).

Mingers, J. and Brocklesby, J. (1997), 'Multimethodology: Towards a Framework for Mixing Methodologies', *Omega, International Journal of Management Science* 25, 489-509.

Paton, G. (2001), 'A Systemic Action Learning Cycle as the Key Element of an Ongoing Spiral of Analyses', *Systemic Practice and Action Research* 14:1, 95-111.

Payne, J. H. and Turner, J. R. (1999), 'Company-Wide Project Management: The Planning and Control of Programmes of Projects of Different Type', *International Journal of Project Management* , 17:1, 55-59.

Ragsdell, G. (2000), 'Engineering a Paradigm Shift? An Holistic Approach to Organizational Change Management', *Journal of Organizational Change Management* 13, 104-20.

Rosenhead, J. (1997), 'Foreword', in *Multimethodology: The Theory and Practice of Combining Management Science Methodologies,* Mingers, J. and Gill, A. (eds.) xii - xiv. (Chichester, UK: John Wiley & Sons).

Shenhar, A. J. (2001), 'One Size Does Not Fit All Projects: Exploring Classical Contingency Domains', *Management Studies* 47:3 394–414.

8 *Mapping the Complexity*

Time to use:	Approximately 60 minutes per session.
Level of difficulty:	
Group:	Key decision makers should be present accompanied by experts from the various sectors covered by the project.
Types of complexity suited for:	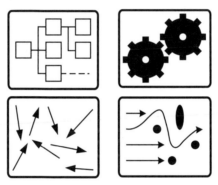

Problem

Too often complex projects fail because key decision makers do not identify that the project is complex until it is too late and the project is out of control and beyond help. This tool can be used first at the inception of the project when you have a sense that a level of complexity is present which should be attended to and you need to communicate this to the project decision makers. It can be used again at the start of each project phase or at each project control gate.

Purpose

It will help achieve an understanding of the types of complexity which the project will face so that appropriate decisions can be made regarding budget, schedule and resources. Using the tool at the beginning of each project phase will also help map the change in the type of complexity expected over time.

Types of complexity

The tool is used to discover patterns of complexity and is therefore appropriate to all types of complexity.

Theoretical background

Earlier seminal work by Turner and Cochrane (1993) produced an excellent tool known as the Goals and Methods matrix which simply asks the question are the goals clear or unclear and are the methods well defined. Using a 2x2 matrix Turner and Cochrane were able to show that projects fit into at least four categories. According to their classification, Type 1 projects had clear goals and known methods. These were straightforward projects which could be managed using standard project management processes. Type 2 projects were projects for which goals were clear but methods were not well defined. Type 3 projects had unclear (or non-static) goals and Type 4 projects, had both unclear goals and undefined methods. Turner and Cochrane's matrix indicated that the chance of project failure increased dramatically with decrease in clarity in either goal definition or known methods for delivery.

This is still an excellent tool to help establish whether the potential for complexity exists and whether it derives from technical or directional sources.

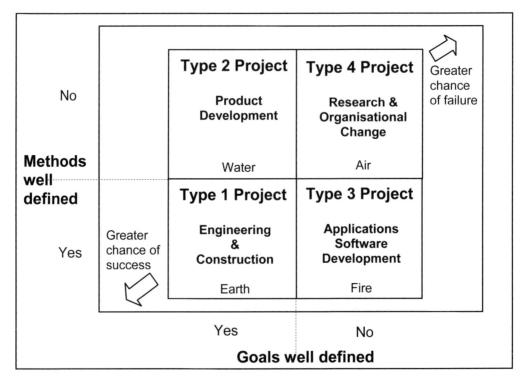

Figure 8.1   Goals-and-methods matrix: coping with projects with ill-defined goals and/or methods of achieving them

Source: Turner and Cochrane (1993) – reprinted with kind permission of Professor J. Rodney Turner

Discussion

Several authors, including Turner, have identified the value in using a multi-methodological approach to address different projects using different methodological approaches (Payne and Turner, 1999; Shenhar, 2001; Engwall et al., 2005). The Mapping Complexity Tool is a simple way of helping a group of decision makers to identify the sources of complexity expected in the project. It is useful when you need to raise the awareness of key decision makers about the sources of complexity so that appropriate courses of action can be taken. Commitments in terms of finance, governance structure and resources need to be made early before non-linear patterns of risks have emerged.

The tool

The tool is simple to use and can be reproduced with flip charts or a white board and markers. It can be used as a quick workshop. Key decision makers should be present accompanied by experts from the various sectors covered by the project who can advise on expected levels of complexity on the basis of their expert knowledge.

STEP 1

Draw a diagram like the one in Figure 8.2.

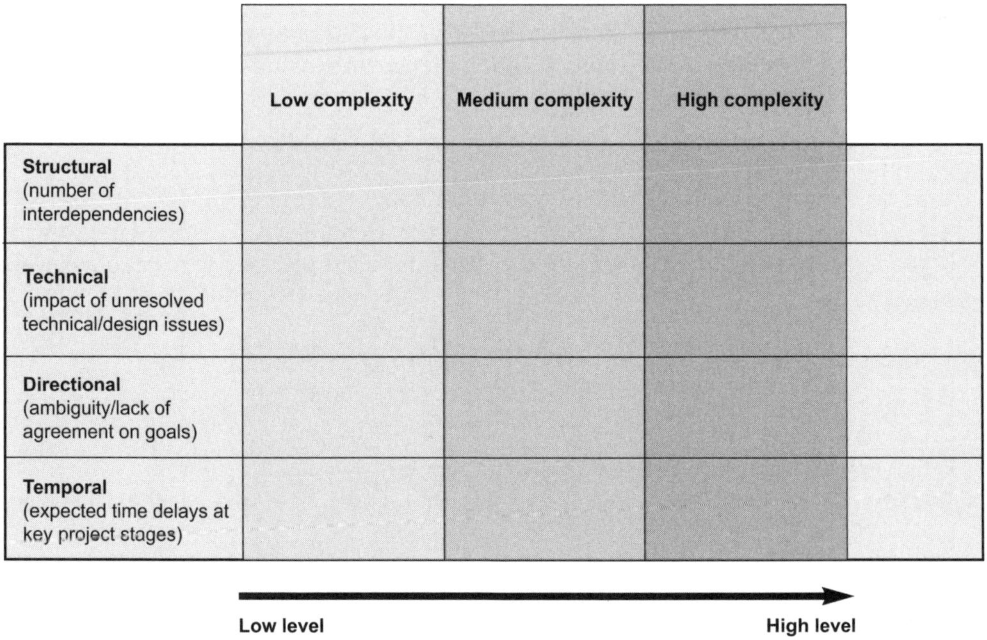

	Low complexity	Medium complexity	High complexity	
Structural (number of interdependencies)				
Technical (impact of unresolved technical/design issues)				
Directional (ambiguity/lack of agreement on goals)				
Temporal (expected time delays at key project stages)				

Low level → High level

Figure 8.2   Base for mapping the project complexity

Discuss each of the types of complexity separately. This needs to be done initially for each major phase as the pattern of complexity will change over time. Ask individuals around the table questions such as:

For structural complexity

- How big is the project?
- How many contractors, sub-contractors, suppliers will be involved?
- Do we expect many interdependent activities in this phase?
- Do we expect to have many interdependent activities in later phases?
- Is time to delivery a key success factor? (This can affect the Structural complexity because it requires very tight planning and a project manager/director who can exercise tight control over hundreds or even thousands of activities during the implementation phase of the project.)

For technical complexity

- Do we expect many new or unsolved technical or design issues?
- Do we know how to build/make it?
- Is time to delivery a key success factor? (This is important for Technical complexity because time constraints will make achievement of a satisficing solution more difficult to manage.)

For directional complexity

- What are the objectives from your point of view? (It is very important to get each person to respond to this individually – it is common for people to assume that 'if it is clear to me it is clear to everyone else'.)
- Are we all agreed on the project objectives? (The answer to this question will give a sense of the level of Directional complexity.)
- How many stakeholders with differing positions do we expect to find?
- Are there time constraints? (This can add to Directional complexity because of the difficulty of reaching agreed solutions under time constraints, when there are very disparate needs/desires.)

For temporal complexity

- Do we have a firm start/go-live date?
- Is the project dependent on political/environmental issues being resolved?
- Is it likely that issues will arise during project implementation that could delay the project?
- Do any major sub-contractors/suppliers have monopolies that might affect supply?

Once you have the answers, map the complexity as shown in the IT development project example in Figure 8.3. Complexities mapped early in the project life cycle of the IT development project indicate that there was general agreement on goals and therefore a relatively low level of directional complexity. There was a medium to high level of structural complexity due to the size of the project. As the technology was breaking new ground a high level of technical

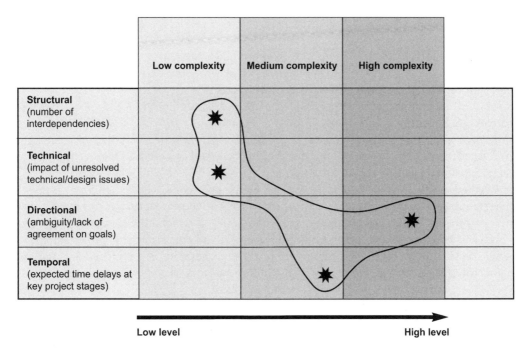

Figure 8.3 Mapping complexities for an IT development project

complexity was anticipated. Additionally, a medium–high level of temporal complexity was expected due to rapid developments in the wider technical field which might impose changes on design and scope.

Repeat the process for each major phase to get an overall picture of the expected project complexity throughout the entire life cycle.

Do this again at each major decision point or control gate. The map should change as the project progresses.

Based on the complexity map decisions can be made about the governance structure, roles and responsibilities, and other management strategies, such as levels of contingency for budget and schedule, appropriate resource allocation and procurement methods.

Step by step

1. Gather together decision makers and key subject-matter experts.
2. Draw the base map.
3. Explain the different types of complexity.
4. Ask questions to get agreement about the level of complexity for each type.
5. Plot the levels and draw the map.
6. Repeat the process at the beginning of each major phase or at major decision points.
7. Use the map to help make decisions about governance structure, roles and responsibilities, and other management strategies, such as levels of contingency for budget and schedule, appropriate resource allocation and procurement methods.

Caution

The mapping process will only reach its maximum potential benefit if enough expertise can be gathered around the table and the key decision makers are there to experience the levels of complexity expected from different aspects of the project.

The process must be repeated regularly at the end or beginning of each phase to make changes and review the implications on project processes.

Bear in mind that initial estimates of the degree of complexity at various phases of the project are based on the information to hand at the time and can often be wrong. That is why it is essential to repeat the process frequently.

Estimating the levels of complexity is highly contextual. It is based on people's understanding of what constitutes complexity which in turn is based on experience with complex projects. For instance, a project might be viewed as structurally complex by a project manager who is used to managing small infrastructure roll-outs. The same project might be seen as merely complicated by a seasoned project manager who is used to managing large engineering projects. This emphasises that finding the right person with the right kind of experience to manage each project is vital to its success.

Example in practice

At the beginning of a large project to implement new regional hospital services the potential complexity was mapped out as in Figure 8.4.

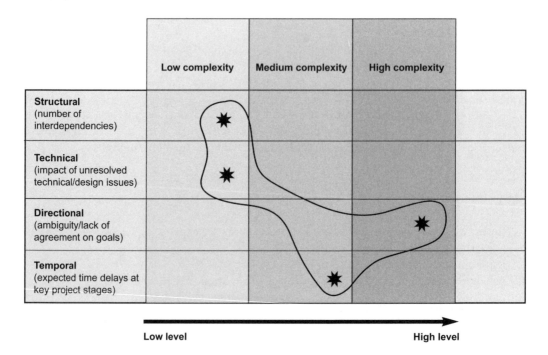

Figure 8.4   Complexity map at the definition phase for the hospital service project

The key stakeholders anticipated that the structural complexity and technical complexity would be low. At that stage they were not intending to build any large infrastructures based on the assumption that existing regional facilities could be used by some minimal upgrading. However directional complexity was rated as high because on further analysis the goals were unclear and certainly not agreed by all key stakeholders. There were also conflicting viewpoints about what was inferred from the promises by the politicians. Most of the rhetoric was cast in very vague terms. Temporal complexity was judged to be relatively high also because the project was initiated during an election year.

By the planning phase the picture had changed. Based on the perceived directional complexity a number of workshops were held using Appreciative Inquiry techniques, followed by Value Management workshops to establish the best value for money of the solutions proposed.

By the beginning of the planning phase the complexity map looked like the one shown in Figure 8.5.

Most of the directional complexity issues had been resolved and because the election had come and gone many of the sources of temporal complexity had been removed. However, detailed planning revealed sources of structural complexity that had not been anticipated in the early stages of the project. This was to do with coordinating the myriad of interdependencies and differences between the various facilities involved and the new infrastructure that was found to be necessary to support the regional service. The agreed solution also offered sources of technical complexity, relating to design of the software needed to integrate the various disparate services.

By the implementation phase the complexity map had changed again to Figure 8.6.

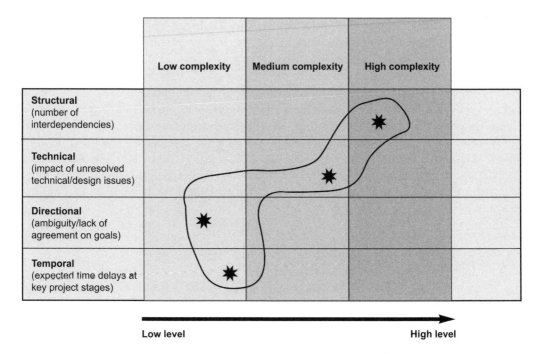

Figure 8.5 Evolution of the map at the beginning of the planning phase

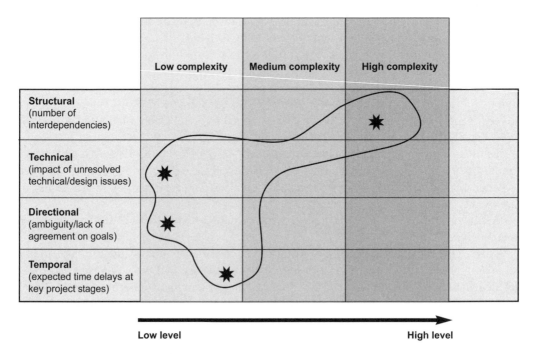

	Low complexity	Medium complexity	High complexity
Structural (number of interdependencies)			
Technical (impact of unresolved technical/design issues)			
Directional (ambiguity/lack of agreement on goals)			
Temporal (expected time delays at key project stages)			

Low level ➜ High level

Figure 8.6   Evolution of the map at the beginning of the implementation phase

By this phase most of the technical and directional sources of complexity had been removed with only some sources of temporal complexity remaining. This time the temporal complexity was due to service monopolies which caused delays to the project as supplies were held up with no viable alternatives available. However the structural complexity remained relatively high until the end of the project.

As is often the case, reducing the complexity was highly dependent on getting the key stakeholders to agree on the project objectives and then on a solution which would deliver those objectives. Initial rhetoric was based on an incomplete analysis of the problem. It was not until all key stakeholders were brought together that the real nature and scale of the problem was revealed based on the disparate needs of the regional population. The initial concept suggested that structural complexity would not be an issue in this project. However the final agreed solution involved a significant level of structural complexity which persisted in varying degrees until handover. The participants found the mapping process useful in determining appropriate management strategies.

References and further reading

Engwall, M., Kling, R. and Werr, A. (2005), 'Models in Action: How Management Models are Interpreted in New Product Development', *R & D Management* 35:4, 427-39.

Payne, J. H. and Turner, J. R. (1999), 'Company-Wide Project Management: The Planning and Control of Programmes of Projects of Different Type', *International Journal of Project Management* 17:1, 55-59.

Shenhar, A. J. (2001), 'One Size Does Not Fit All Projects: Exploring Classical Contingency Domains', *Management Studies* 47:3, 394-414.

Turner, J. R. and Cochrane, R. A. (1993), 'Goals-And-Methods Matrix: Coping with Projects with Ill-Defined Goals and/or Methods of Achieving Them', *International Journal of Project Management* 11, 93.

CHAPTER

9 *System Anatomy*

Time to use:	This approach is a whole of project approach.
Level of difficulty:	
Group:	Key stakeholders involved at every stage.
Types of complexity suited for:	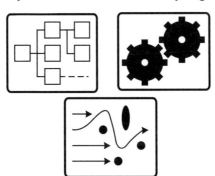

Problem

The coordination of large, multi-site, international projects represents a high level of complexity for the project managers and project team members. This approach, developed by practitioners at Ericsson, originated in response to the challenge of managing the development of complex telecommunications systems, such as third-generation mobile telecommunications networks. These projects are usually carried out in global development environments that include many different organisations. The coordination of these very large projects involves a huge number of technical, market-related and organisational interdependencies. In addition these projects are challenged by the high rate of technical development in the field, evolving standards and customer demands.

Any project management approach must provide the flexibility to incorporate new solutions or functionalities during the development process. New circumstances and opportunities that arise throughout the project must be dealt with dynamically to meet both fixed and emerging targets.

Purpose

The purpose of the approach is to assist key stakeholders to plan and communicate the interdependent activities in specific, large, international, multi-site development projects in the telecommunications industry. However the basic approach could be extended for use in any industry in which development and implementation are characterised by similar constraints.

The System Anatomy addresses the problem by effectively containing the master planning and communication documents to a one-page 'anatomy' which is constructed by key stakeholders. In the process of defining the anatomy, key stakeholders develop a common understanding of the interdependencies involved in these huge global projects. The containment of the key documentation to the single page anatomy allows stakeholders to keep a grasp on the complexity of the project, and therefore the consequences of any changes on the rest of the system.

The System Anatomy is a whole-of-project approach. However, the mapping between the decision model (how you take decisions regarding economy, resources, business opportunities and so on) and the work model (where you define how to develop the system) is different as compared to more traditional project models. Usually, the decision model and work model proceed in a linear fashion where certain documents shall be ready at a certain decision point. In the approach suggested here, the decision model still proceeds linearly while the work model is based on the functional dependencies given by the anatomy and its associated plans (the increment plan and the integration plan, see below).

Types of complexity

The System Anatomy approach addresses three types of complexity: structural complexity, technical complexity and temporal complexity. It assists in managing structural complexity by creating a common understanding of the multitude of interdependencies. It facilitates monitoring of progress of the myriad of elements by providing a clear and simple way of communicating the consequences of any changes on dependent elements in the network. In very large design and development projects complexity stems from the number of interdependent elements and the difficulties associated with understanding and communicating the interdependencies and the effects of any changes on design changes anywhere in the system.

Technical complexity is addressed in that the approach was specifically constructed for development projects in the telecommunications industry. These projects are characterised by multiple design problems to be solved, tested for quality, revised and adjusted before any part of the system can 'go live'.

Temporal complexity is also addressed because it allows for change to be communicated rapidly to all stakeholders. The key to managing temporal complexity is flexibility. The System Anatomy makes the consequences of change immediately obvious to all key stakeholders so that rapid replanning can take place. In politically charged environments, such as global telecommunications, flexibility and the ability to respond rapidly to change are essential.

Additionally, with many internationally distributed teams, and many local work practices, there is a need to keep everyone informed of the interdependencies and consequences to all parts of the system and of change in any one part of the system; therefore structural complexity is addressed in this way.

Theoretical background

The most difficult task in this kind of context is to establish and communicate a common meaning amongst the people concerned about what should be coordinated and how (Taxén, 2003; Lilliesköld, 2003). In large international projects people working on the project and project teams may be geographically dispersed, have different roles, come from different traditions and speak different languages (Taxén, 2004; Eriksson et al., 2002). The nature of the coordination will change according to new insights, new market demands and so on.

People become proficient in particular areas such as system analysis, design of software or hardware and so on. Lilliesköld and Taxén (2004) refer to the way a particular person or group goes about their work, which is influenced by the discipline area, location or culture as a 'workpractice'. Each workpractice has its own way of thinking, specific tools and methods, rules, norms and so on. Most actions carried out in a workpractice remain local to that particular practice. However, actions may influence other workpractices which will affect management of the project.

Due to the complexity of the project it is difficult to anticipate the consequences of any action on the development task as a whole. For instance an action which might seem to be perfectly logical in a certain workpractice may result in unmanageable consequences for other workpractices.

Therefore, in complex systems development there is a need for ways in which the actions in different work practices can be reconciled. Any approach must have at least two qualities. It must be meaningful in each workpractice and across all workpractices and it should enable the people within the workpractices to recognise what actions are possible and anticipate the consequences of those actions for other workpractices.

Discussion

The telecommunications network is a truly complex system. It has been called the world's largest machine. It comprises interacting nodes, each of which performs some kind of function, such as keeping track of a cellular phone or charges to individual phones and so on. A multitude of technologies is used, including radio, optical, software, hardware and mechanical technologies. Old legacy systems exist alongside new state-of-the-art systems. The interest in developing these systems using an approach called Distributed Software Development (DSD), also known as Global Software Development and Offshore development, is motivated by the need to reduce costs, the possibility of twenty-four-hour development and associated access to customers worldwide. A project to develop a node in third-generation mobile systems networks, which vastly extends the capabilities for data transfer, can take more than a year to implement and may involve several thousand participants. Development is usually carried out at many different sites around the globe, each of which may have some degree of autonomy in workpractice.

The particular approach to DSD developed by Lars Taxén and his colleagues at Ericsson during the 1990s is now referred to as the Integration Centric Development (ICD) approach. It is based on two foundations. The first, which Taxén calls the 'anatomy-based engineering process' (ABEP), aims at managing critical functional dependencies in the projects. The second, the 'domain construction process' (DCP), operationalises coordination of the engineering processes in order to provide global support for coordination, and to achieve common understanding about what should be coordinated and how.

The motivation for the ABEP came from the need in complex projects to understand, at any time, how activities and outcomes depend on each other. It was found that traditional project management processes did not address this problem satisfactorily. The beauty of the anatomy is that it provides an illustration, preferably on one page, showing the functional dependencies in the system from start-up to operation. Functional dependencies describe the property of certain elements in the system providing capabilities needed by other elements in the system. The idea is to design and test the system in the same order that the functions are effectuated, hence the reference to anatomy.

For example, in order for a car engine to function properly, you first have to turn the start key. If the battery is charged, the starter motor starts to turn. The crankshaft starts to revolve, providing lubrication and the basic turn cycle of the four-stroke engine. Next, the carburettor provides fuel to the engine from air and gas. The generator provides electricity to the spark plugs, which ignites the fuel and the engine starts to run in idle state, ready for doing its job in the car.

The motivation for the DCP came from the need to provide tool support for managing the multitude of items needed to coordinate the ABEP. Such items are, for example, requirements, engineering change orders, products and documents describing the system, test cases by which the system functionalities are tested, deliveries to customers, milestones and baselines by which the progress in the project is planned and controlled and so on. It is a far from trivial task to provide such a tool support, since there has to be a workable consensus about how all these items should be characterised and related to each other. The term 'construction' is used in order to indicate that a common meaning about the coordination has to be actively developed, or constructed by the people involved. Obviously, this group cannot comprise the entire organisation; this has to be confined to a smaller group, or 'domain', that has the responsibility to implement the tool support for coordination.

The tool

THE ANATOMY BASED ENGINEERING PROCESS (ABEP)

Taxén and Lilliesköld (2005) describe the process of creating the anatomy as:

1. anatomy definition
2. increment planning
3. increment definition

1. ANATOMY DEFINITION

The boxes in the anatomy indicate functions and the lines indicate dependencies (see Figure 9.1). The anatomy is read from the bottom to the top and grows like a tree as it is developed. It is created in several meetings and pathways are developed in answer to the question: 'if you power-on what happens then and then'. This question is repeated until the end functionality is reached. When deciding upon which functions to include, the emphasis should be on integration and testability as the anatomy will be used not only to plan but also to monitor the project as well. The final form of the anatomy is specific to the people who produce it.

This is important in order to achieve a joint ownership of the anatomy. Therefore it is also important that all key stakeholders are included in the creation of the anatomy.

2. INCREMENT PLANNING

The purpose of the second step is to define how the system will be implemented. The functions are grouped incrementally into development and integration steps in such a way that the additional functionality achieved after each increment is executable and verifiable. The intention is to run design and testing in parallel as much as possible in order to reduce lead-times. Decisions about how the development work is distributed are based on available resources, customer feedback such as priorities of functions delivered, degree of difficulty of the function, geographical distribution of resources, functions that can be tested jointly or those that must be tested separately and so on. For example, in Figure 9.2 it makes sense to allocate both the 'Reset SPU' function and the 'I-test SPU' function to the same increment, since these functions would most likely be developed at an organisational unit where people are knowledgeable about signal processors (SPUs). Another example would be the functions 'Power on', 'Clock MAI' and 'Reset MAI'. These are all needed in order to provide a tested and solid platform for the rest of the system (four functions are dependent on 'Reset MAI'). Thus, it makes sense to allocate these basic functions to one 'platform' increment.

In this step the emphasis is on the dependencies between increments, rather than functional dependencies. However, it must be remembered that the anatomy is the basis for increment dependencies.

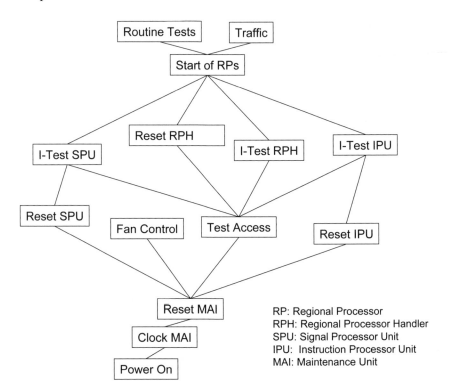

Figure 9.1 Example of the anatomy diagram developed for a telecommunications development project

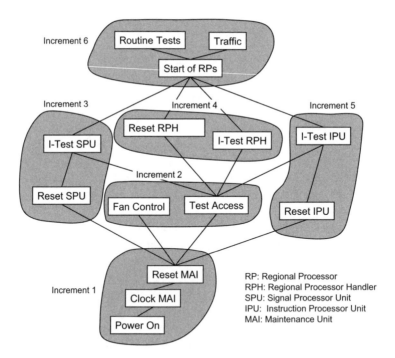

Figure 9.2   Diagram showing the increments defined in terms of interdependencies in the Anatomy

3. INTEGRATION PLANNING

The purpose of the third step is to divide the work between sub-projects and to establish a common understanding about what is to be delivered by whom and when. At this stage traditional project management time and resource plans are used to assign resources and determine dates for deliveries of the increments once they have been negotiated with key stakeholders.

During project implementation the integration plan is used as a communication tool to indicate the progress of the project at any time. Traffic light cues (Green = On, Yellow = Warning, Red = Off Track) for impacts of delays are clearly shown, giving the project management team time to take corrective actions.

At first glance, the integration plan looks like a traditional precedence diagram (such as a PERT chart) in that it shows dependencies between tasks. However, the integration plan and the precedence diagram are created in quite different ways. The integration plan focuses on dependencies between functions and increments, while the traditional precedence network diagram focuses on dependencies between activities. The precedence network diagram is derived from a strict precedence relationship between individual elements and is based on the assumption that once an activity is completed it is always possible to go on to the next dependent activity. In this kind of project the functional dependencies, which restrict the dependencies between activities, are usually not in focus. These projects involve cyclical development and testing of elements and groups of elements, before the next functional unit can be developed. Therefore it is often not possible to continue in such a linear fashion and the technical complexity will be likely to yield surprises which cannot easily be anticipated.

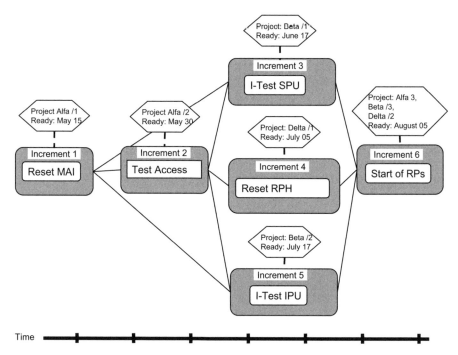

Figure 9.3   Integration plan

Furthermore, the integration plan focuses on significance, clarity and ease of use in order to create common understanding of what functionality has to be delivered to integrate the system. This is less emphasised in precedence diagrams which were originally developed to schedule the implementation of projects for which the design problems had already been resolved. Where multiple design decisions are being made in tandem with development the large amount of information created when focusing on detailed sequential activities aggravates the enactment of common understanding about the project. The anatomy-based engineering process uses a simple illustration – the anatomy – to achieve common understanding amongst different stakeholders about the coordination of the project. In a project which is being implemented in a volatile environment frequent replanning of the project is needed in response to external and internal changes. The need to replan any one element may affect all other steps in the process. Keeping the anatomy to one single diagram allows the key stakeholders to grasp the situation as a whole at any one time and visualise the effects of change on interdependencies.

DOMAIN CONSTRUCTION PROCESS (DCP)

The second part of the approach is the operationalisation of the engineering processes, that is, providing concrete support for managing the coordination of the ABEP. Taxén's approach (2006) is to focus on how to achieve a sufficient degree of common understanding about coordination, since this by experience is a very burdensome task. The central idea in the DCP is to develop tool support for coordination simultaneously with the development, or construction, of the common understanding about the tool support. Such support may include, for example, requirement traceability, milestone monitoring, status accounting, managing engineering change orders, test progress follow up and so on. In order to achieve this, a conceptual model (the so-called 'context' model) is suggested by a team responsible for defining coordination. The context model shows what items the team consider relevant for managing the ABEP. An example of a context model is given in Figure 9.4, where the anatomy can be seen in the centre of the figure (encircled).

By continually iterating between modifications of the context model, implementing this and evaluating the usefulness of the support in realistic project environments, a gradual, useful development and construction takes place of the model, the tool support and common understanding of these elements.

Step by step

These steps include both the ABEP (steps 1–3) and the DCP (step 4):
1. *Anatomy definition* Use sticky notes and involve relevant key stakeholders in order to define the anatomy. Start from the bottom and ask questions of the key stakeholders such as 'if you power on what happens then and then?' The boxes or sticky notes are the functions and the lines in the anatomy indicate the dependencies. (See Figure 9.1).
2. *Increment Planning* Group the functions incrementally into development and integration steps in such a way that the additional functionality achieved after each increment is

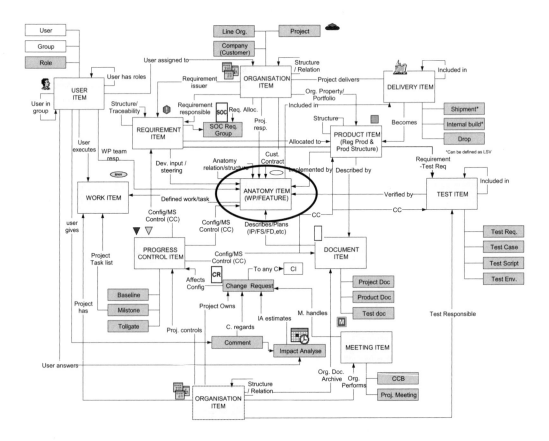

Figure 9.4 Context model with the System Anatomy shown circled in the centre

executable and verifiable. The emphasis is on the functional dependencies between the increments, rather than within each increment. (See Figure 9.2).

3. *Integration planning* With the involvement of key stakeholders divide the work between subprojects to establish a common understanding about what is to be delivered by whom and when. Use traditional project management time and resource plans to assign resources and determine dates for deliveries of the increments. (See Figure 9.3).

4. *Define a context model* showing which items are relevant for coordination (see Figure 9.4 above). This can be done, for example, in PowerPoint or Visio. Implement the model in a tool. This requires a tool in which it is easy to change the implementation. A good example of such a tool is Matrix from Matrix-One, Inc. (www.matrixone.com). Load the tool with relevant project data such as requirements, functions, increments, deliveries and so on. Evaluate the result by, for example, generating reports. If not satisfactory, modify the context model, implement the modifications and evaluate the results anew. Continue in this way until the support for coordination is found useful by the project.

Examples in practice

One of the early projects to use the System Anatomy approach was conducted between 1995 and 1999 (Lilliesköld et al., 2005). The goal of the project was to develop a new central processor for the main Ericsson switching system, the AXE System. Due to a number of factors, such as new technology, many sub-projects distributed around the world, new customer relations, cultural differences, newly appointed project managers and so on, the project was exhibiting extreme disorder bordering on chaos. The anatomy was introduced to the project team as a way to help bring the project back on track. The observers reported that the use of the anatomy promoted the following:

Everyone's part in the project was made visible to everyone else at the same time. This helped the people involved to understand the project/system and to anticipate the consequences of their actions. Planning of the project was enhanced as the use of the anatomy allowed many of the design and verification activities to be conducted in parallel with control since the dependencies between the activities were clearly visible. This enabled early integration of functions and early start to production if necessary. The margins in the project could therefore be controlled more easily than if all the integrations had been done towards the end of the project. Monitoring of the progress of the project was also improved through the 'push and pull' effect that the anatomy has as a result of a receiver being identified for every delivery in the project. The use of the traffic-light cues made progress visible to all.

Another example comes from the development of the third-generation mobile systems between approximately 1999 and 2003 (Taxén, 2003; 2006). Around 140 main projects and sub-projects were involved. One node in this system, the so-called Mobile Switching Centre, was developed by 27 sub-projects distributed over 22 development units in altogether 18 countries. This project was a major challenge for Ericsson. The requirements were unclear, the 3G standard was not settled, the project was very large and globally distributed, the technology was at the cutting edge and so on. This situation was expressed by the total project manager as follows in 1999:

'The total technical changes being implemented in this project are enormous. Such changes are needed in order for Ericsson to get a world-leading product first to market. Using traditional

methods then the scope of change implemented in single steps will be too large and can not be managed.'

The combined effects of applying the ABEP and the DCP had a profound effect. This was formulated by a project manager in the following way:

'Especially for the execution part I think we would not have been able to run this project without the tool. I think if you simply look at the number of increments, the number of products that we have delivered, the number of deliveries that we have had, if we would have to maintain that manually, that would have been a sheer disaster.'

References and further reading

Eriksson, M., Lilliesköld, J., Jonsson, N. and Novosel, D. (2002), 'How to Manage Complex, Multinational R&D Projects Successfully', *Engineering Management Journal* 14:2, 53-60.

Lilliesköld, J. (2003), 'Coordinating Dependencies in Complex System Development Projects', *Proceedings of the IEEE Engineering Management Conference, IEMC'03*, Nov., 400-4.

Lilliesköld, J. and Taxén, L. (2004), 'Coordinating Dependencies in Global System Development Projects – The Use of Dependency Diagrams', *Engineering Management Conference, 2004*, IEEE International 2, 755-759.

Lilliesköld, J. and Taxén, L. (2006), 'Operationalizing Coordination of Mega-projects – A Workpractice Perspective', *Proceedings of IRNOP VII Conference*, Oct., (Xi'an, China: Northwestern Polytechnical University), 574-87.

Lilliesköld, J., Taxén, L. and Klasson, M. (2005), 'Managing Complex Development Projects – Using the System Anatomy', *Proceedings of the Portland International Conference on Management of Technology and Engineering, PICMET'05*, July-Aug.

Taxén, L. (2003), 'A Framework for the Coordination of Complex Systems' Development, Dissertation No. 800'. *Linköping University, Dept. of Computer and Information Science*. Available at: www.eliu.se/diss/science/08/00/index/html, accessed Oct. 2006.

Taxén, L. (2004), 'Articulating Co-ordination of Human Activity – the Activity Domain Theory', *Proceedings of ALOIS, Second International Conference*, March 17-18, Linköping, Sweden. Available at: www.vits.org/konverenser/alois2004/proceedings.asp, accessed Nov 2004.

Taxén, L. (2005), 'Categorizing Objective Meaning in Interacting Activity Systems', in Whymark, G. and Hasan, H. (Eds), *Activity as the Focus of Information Systems Research*. (Everleigh, Australia: Knowledge Creation Press).

Taxén, L. (2006), 'An integration centric approach for the coordination of distributed software development projects', *Information and Software Technology* 48, 767-780.

Taxén, L. and Lilliesköld, J. (2005), 'Manifesting Shared Affordances in System Development – The System Anatomy', *Proceedings of ALOIS, Second International Conference*, March 15-16, Limerick, Ireland. Available at www.alois2005.ul.ie, accessed Feb. 2006.

Taxén L., and Svensson, D. (2005), 'Towards an Alternative Foundation for Managing Product Life-Cycles in Turbulent Environments', *International Journal of Product Development* 2:1/2, 24-46.

10 *Target Outturn Cost*

Time to use:	The tool is whole-of-project approach which is used throughout the project life cycle.
Level of difficulty:	
	Use by an experienced construction or engineering project manager
Group:	The management group is governed under a Collaborative Working Arrangement (CWA) comprising the project manager, client, design consultants, contractors, sub-contractors and vendors, as one team, with incentives to establish a structure to ensure that everyone works together to achieve agreed shared targets.
Types of complexity suited for:	
	Target Outturn Cost (TOC) implementation is a good example of a combination of new and old approaches. Collaborative procurement methods are combined with some of the more powerful tools from construction/ engineering project management.

Problem

Many major construction projects have failed to meet targeted costs over recent years. A number of contributing factors have been cited, including high interest rates, inflation, competition for fewer projects, margin slashing and out-of-control speculation. Certainly poor project organisation, fee-bidding for architectural services resulting in reduced attention to the detail in design, poor project structure, communication, and the flow on effect from the US of ever-increasing litigation may be identified anecdotally as key factors in many claim-ridden projects.

Very large construction and engineering projects all exhibit characteristics of structural complexity. Due to circumstances out of the direct control of the project manager, a series of apparently minor risks can be triggered causing rapid escalation of otherwise unconnected risk events. If the risks are not identified and dealt with very, very promptly this can be disastrous for the project. In complexity terms this is like a phase change, which can have a landslide effect, causing the project to quickly plummet out of control.

Purpose

Most traditional procurement systems result in an adversarial rather than a collaborative approach to resolution of project challenges. The purpose of *this* approach is to create a collaborative working arrangement between the key parties to the contract. At the same time tight control over quality, budget and schedule is maintained using traditional project management tools. The rationale behind this approach simply exploits the fact that the key parties all want to obtain the maximum benefits from the project: the client wants a good quality product, delivered on schedule and within budget; to optimise return on investment, the contractors, sub-contractors and suppliers want to maximize their profit; and the project manager wants to conduct a tightly controlled project which can deliver maximum benefits to all.

The benefits of a CWA are intended to include the following:

* improved predictability of cost, time and quality;
* minimised risk;
* reduced costs;
* all parties enabled in a team environment to make maximum contribution;
* innovation promoted with additional benefits as to 'best for project' attitude;
* understanding of other parties' issues;
* continuous improvement of process as it is in the interest of all parties;
* development of long-term relationships and highly efficient vendor supply chains;
* improved trade performance and better schedule control;
* workarounds to reduce delays when things go wrong;
* acceptance of an agreed project management approach.

Type of complexity

This tool is particularly suited to managing the structural complexity commonly found in large engineering and construction projects. The structural complexity comes from the difficulty in controlling delivery times, cost and quality for the vast number of activities needed to complete the project. Each activity may involve a separate sub-contract or supplier contract and the interdependencies are time related through the schedule. An accumulation of small changes or slippages in the schedule can result in a phase change with an effect not unlike an avalanche, the project becoming rapidly out of control.

In addition these large projects may also experience other types of complexity, particularly technical complexity and temporal complexity. Large public construction and engineering projects are particularly vulnerable to the latter. However, this approach is particularly useful for structurally complex projects that are able to be delivered within a reasonably short time, say less than twelve months (though some have been running for much longer) and for which technical challenges can be solved early in the project life cycle with the major design decisions being made before the bulk of the work begins. The relatively short time frame reduces the possibility of temporal complexity and by solving the technical problems first, technical complexity is reduced.

Theoretical background

The report, entitled 'Constructing The Team', *Final Report of the Government/Industry Review of Procurement and Contractual Arrangements in the UK Construction Industry* (now known as 'the Latham Report'), was seen by many as a turning point for the construction industry, dramatically reforming relationships between clients and contractors. It recommended that building contracts should be based upon principles of fairness, mutual trust and teamwork, rather than the usual adversarial and confrontational lump-sum tender (Latham, 1994).

Collaborative working or partnering was seen as the solution: the process by which the project parties and individuals operate in a mutual manner to align their interests for the successful outcome of the project. Partnering is a subset of collaborative working usually with a more formal type of arrangement or contract. Without exception, project team members who had experienced partnering on a CWA stated that they would use it again on future projects. The process evolves as the CWA partners learn and work together rather than against each other; basically, keeping the high costs of the legal profession at bay.

According to Rix (2004) a CWA may be defined as follows:

- It is an alternative procurement/project delivery methodology to a traditional master/servant model.
- It is designed to build a unity of purpose between all principals and other stakeholders.
- It aligns commercial drivers and incentives in such ways as to facilitate a win-win outcome.
- The CWA operates with a 'no claim, no blame' culture such that the team owns and manages the risks to the best of its ability.
- Through better control of scope, joint costs and risk management and the promotion of innovative and 'best for project' solutions, all stakeholders in the CWA will benefit.

In order to have a CWA:

- There should be equitable benefit for all parties in the arrangement.
- A correct attitude of openness and trust is required to make collaborative working successful.
- Encourage team attitude and 'What is best for the project'.
- Ensure adequate time is spent at the pre-planning stage; it is worthwhile in the long run.
- Include all the organisations and sub-contractors from as far down the supply chain as possible, as it is they who do the work.
- Make long-term arrangements to eliminate the need to start from scratch on each project.
- Do not underestimate the cultural shift involved and the time that could take.

The main purpose of CWAs is to engage the client, design consultants, contractors, sub-contractors and vendors into one team, with incentives to establish a structure to ensure that everyone works together to achieve agreed shared targets. The idea is the building of a unified team with the purpose of creating an environment whereby outstanding results can be achieved. The incentives are developed into a 'gain share/pain share' arrangement. If the project is successful there will be gain share, if it is not then there may well be pain share. There cannot be a win-lose result because of the way gain share and pain share are structured. The most important aspect is that there are no adversarial contracts as in the normal lump-sum tender process.

Discussion

This approach utilizing Earned Value Performance Measurement, developed by Raf Dua for large-scale construction projects for the New Zealand government, integrates a partnering approach to management of large construction and engineering projects with standard project management tools and techniques in a new and innovative manner. It relies on careful and collaborative estimation and control of costs, which are defined in terms of Targeted Outturn Cost (TOC) hours negotiated with each sub-contractor in the partnership. Earned Value Management is essential to monitor and control costs and is an integral part of this approach because it calculates the actual value of the work performed in relation to schedule and budgeted cost. (For more information on Earned Value Management the Australian Standard AS4817:2006 is particularly useful).

Because all parties are partners in the project and share in any gain or any loss they each have a vested interest in helping other sub-contractor partners to achieve what they have agreed to achieve in the time available. Thus the motivation for adversarial behaviour that plagues most large-scale construction and engineering projects is removed.

The approach

MANAGEMENT STRUCTURE

The management of the CWA is usually undertaken by two groups. The first is the principals group which is made up of the most senior manager (e.g. the CEO) of each of the various major partners in the arrangement. They oversee and are responsible for the strategic guidance of the project. The second group manages the day-to-day aspects of the project, is usually known as the project executive group, and takes direction from the principals group

ESTABLISHING TARGET OUTTURN COST

The basis of managing the project is through the development of 'Target Outturn Cost', more commonly known as TOC. With the exception of those costs specifically excluded, the TOC embraces the entire cost of the project. Actual costs are used rather than prices, which include other values such as the sub-contractor's profit margin, so it is simple to see how the cost of an activity is arrived at.

The components of the TOC include design costs, costs to set up and maintain the CWA, cost of permanent and temporary works, on-site management, establishment costs, off-site management, off-site overheads, profit and margins as well as a risk contingency.

Any cost components which do not make up the TOC must be specifically excluded by the CWA management. In fact the CWA is responsible for all cost management from the initiation of the project as part of the original negotiations to the final handover to the client of any component of the scope of works and the final settlement of all accounts for the work carried out by the partners.

Detailed designs need to be in place before any serious attempt can be made at determining the TOC. The time taken to develop the TOC once detailed designs are completed will depend on the size and complexity of the project. The process of arriving at the TOC is very rigorous and it can be expected to take at least 2 to 3 months to work through the process of arriving at the expected actual costs, risks and so on.

Because the TOC is established and conducted under a partnership agreement, the process of determining the TOC relies on achieving transparency of financial and other data and on independent scrutiny of the numbers, assumptions and calculations. Given that in a CWA there is no market testing of the cost estimates through traditional tender processes, transparency and independent scrutiny are the mechanisms through which assurance is gained that costs are the most efficient.

During the process of arriving at the TOC the accuracy of the cost estimates by the sub-contractors is examined rigorously and must continue to be improved during their development. This may be achieved by firming up and reducing scope uncertainty and removing cost uncertainties as shown in Figure 10.1.

The process is iterative. For each sub-contract partner the TOC is compiled based on the actual base cost and on-site overheads. According to Francis (2005) the CWA must work on removing all external influences on the labour cost hours in order to get its actual base costs to the real minimum and then identify other cost components to establish the TOC.

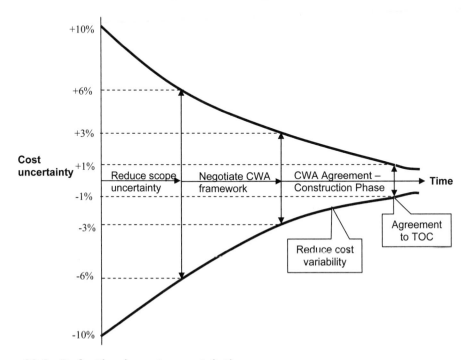

Figure 10.1 Reduction in cost uncertainties

Source: Stewart Rix CMS Ltd.

Often the initial estimates of TOC will exceed the client's budget expectations. Value management and quantitative risk assessment are applied to obtain the most cost-effective ways of matching client expectations with budget. Value management is a group problem-solving process which seeks to develop value for money through collaboration and divergent thinking processes. For the best results it should be facilitated by a professional facilitator.

Under strict probity guidelines agreed between the principals at the outset, a facilitator from the CWA works with each sub-contractor to determine actual costs, off-site overhead costs and normalised profit. A centralised estimating software package is used to achieve single-point control, flexibility and mathematical consistency and reliability, and everyone must be trained in its use.

A great deal depends on getting the TOC in place as soon as possible. Until the TOC is agreed, the CWA partners are remunerated according to the actual costs they incur. Until the process of independent scrutiny of direct costs, audit of margin, overhead and burdening calculations and Value Management is completed, the client does not have final assurance that the estimated costs represent an efficient level of costs. Moreover, until the TOC is in place, the gain/pain share arrangements cannot be finalised. The gain/pain share provides an important and further spur to efficiency and delivery of a project meeting, or in excess of, client expectations.

The principals group is responsible for establishing the partnership as a legal entity and setting up agreed rules of probity. The most important role for the principals group is to agree to the actual terms which will be used to manage the scope of the project.

During implementation the measurement of work performed is quantified using a Critical Path Network, with a tool that imports the schedule TOC hours into the program from the estimating software. Measurement is done either by CWA members in-house or by professional quantity surveyors.

Costing is based on 'first principles'. Schedules are costed in conjunction with TOC coordinators who assist sub-contractor partners with the costing techniques. Costs comprise actual costs (labour, materials and plant) plus profit margins and overheads. An independent quantity surveyor reviews costs. Profit margins and overheads are normalised to ensure equity between sub-contracts. This provides a first level of review and builds a high level of confidence and a robust model.

Value Management is used as an on-going process throughout to optimise the value of the design solution, to deliver fitness for purpose and de-risk the project and project costs. Negotiated savings through Value Management exercises are included in the risk register. This reduces the overall risk and allows potential participation in gain share to be achieved on the items of saving included in the TOC.

Quantitative Risk Assessment involves analysis of all commercial risk and compilation of risk schedules. Each risk is given a value and rated for probability and consequence using Monte Carlo analysis.

IMPLEMENTING THE PROJECT USING TOC

Scope is controlled in the following way. TOC coordinators manage all trades and ensure the scope between trades has been covered, such as builders' work, mechanical or electrical work which is associated with the particular trade. The control documents are maintained by the TOC manager. Estimators mark up their own drawings/specifications and cross reference with the control set in conjunction with the TOC coordinator.

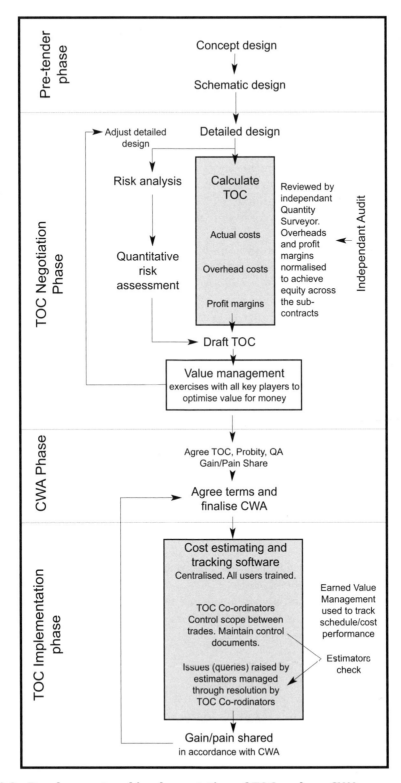

Figure 10.2 Development and implementation of TOC under a CWA

Any issues, known as queries, are raised by estimators to TOC coordinators and maintained on the master schedule. Queries are managed through to resolution by TOC coordinators.

Step by step

1. Finalise schematic design.
2. Establish the principals group (refer references for information on establishing a CWA) which is made up of the most senior manager (for example the CEO) of each of the various major partners in the arrangement. They are responsible for negotiating the terms of the CWA, establishing probity rules and maintenance and they oversee and are responsible for the strategic guidance of the project.
3. Agree on rules and conditions of probity to achieve the level of transparency needed to create and manage the TOC.
4. Establish the project executive group. This is the second group which manages the day-to-day aspects of the project and takes direction from the principals group.
5. Complete, detailed design subject to changes based on Value Management and Risk Quantification exercises.
6. Establish the TOC with each sub-contract partner, using trained TOC coordinators. The components of the TOC include design costs, CWA costs, permanent and temporary works, on site management, establishment costs, off-site management, off-site overheads, profit and margins as well as a risk contingency. Use Value Management as a key tool to optimise approaches and costs and quantitative risk assessment.
7. Principals finalise agreement on terms and conditions of CWA and distribution of gain and pain to be shared equally by the partners.
8. Implement centralised cost estimating and tracking software to control project, including training.
9. During implementation, control scope and cost through TOC coordinators who manage all trades and ensure the scope between trades has been covered, such as builder's work, mechanical or electrical work which is associated with the particular trade. The control documents are maintained by the TOC manager. Estimators mark up their own drawings/specifications and cross-reference with the control set in conjunction with the TOC Coordinators.
10. Use Earned Value Management to keep control of cost by integrating the scope of work performed to the schedule and cost.
11. Estimators raise any issues, known as queries, to TOC coordinators, who manage them through to resolution and maintain them on master schedule.
12. Share gain and pain in accordance with the agreement.

Caution

Partnering arrangements are 'not a substitute for strong and effective governance and decision making by government, which continues to be responsible and accountable for the project or service in a way that protects the public benefit' (Phillips Fox, Public Private Partnerships).

Partnering is often a challenge for organisations that are used to framing contracts in terms of fully specified processes and technical requirements. Accounting practice has not really caught up with the concept of partnering and alliances. Consequently there might be resistance from auditors who are not familiar with the approach.

Audit controls must be robust in order to maintain transparency and assure all parties that decision making and selection processes are within the agreement of the partnership or alliance and will stand up to public scrutiny. Auditing will need to include both financial and performance measures.

For long-term projects, assessing value for money can be particularly difficult. Assumptions will have to be made.

In the case of a project alliance, the private sector participants are usually selected solely on their technical and quality attributes. The budget is usually not agreed between the parties until after the selection process has been completed. This means uncertainty about the budget for a long period, and a risk that the whole process could be aborted after significant resources have already been committed. Recently some project alliances have introduced price competition. There is much debate about whether this runs counter to the philosophy of alliancing.

Under a project alliance, participants collectively assume all risks associated with the project, regardless of whether these risks are within the control of the alliance and whether participants have considered them in advance. The exceptions are any risks that the alliance participants specifically agree to retain individually. In allocating risks it is important to determine not only the most appropriate party to accept the risks financially but whether political or moral constraints allow transfer of the risks to another party. For instance, in the case of a public hospital, even though it may be possible to transfer financial risks to another participant, in certain circumstances the project owner might be forced to take responsibility for the risks. Typically this might occur if continued provision of ongoing hospital services to the public is at risk.

Establishing and maintaining trust between the parties through transparent and sound processes can be difficult. A comprehensive probity plan helps ensure that transparent and sound processes are in place and being adhered to. The plan should address the means of ensuring that selection processes are consistent and fair and that conflicts of interest are declared and managed. It also needs to define how commercially sensitive information is managed. An independent probity auditor is usually appointed to ensure that agreed issues of probity are followed.

Examples in practice

At the time of writing the government projects to which this approach has been applied are not able to be identified. However, now that the projects have been running for almost twenty months, the benefits outlined above are beginning to make themselves felt, in spite of some severe weather at one of the project sites. Because of the collaborative, rather than adversarial working arrangement, some of the unavoidable delays have been minimised and have not led to the usual adversarial posturing that goes on in the typical lump-sum contract process. It has been quite gratifying to see the different construction companies (who normally would not be very cooperative) helping each other out to sort out unforeseen problems when for example materials fail to perform according to specification.

The programme of projects, into its third year at the time of writing, has delivered two out of the four construction sites within the budget and on time. An outstanding element of the CWA process has been that there have been no labour disputes; the major and minor partners in the CWA have all been cooperative. All partners agree that the process delivered nearly of all their expectations and there was gain share in both the projects. The remaining two are also proceeding well and will finish on time and budget and they too have had no labour problems.

Existing experience in construction shows that most construction companies will only do the absolute minimum amount of project management: the CWA however embraced the full range of traditional project management processes and tools. The extensive use of resources management as well the use of Earned Value Management delivered considerable benefits in client management decision making.

Although the government projects in question cannot be named, the project manager, Raf Dua, can be contacted for more detailed information at Decisive Tools t/a Micro Planning International Pty Ltd., e-mail: rafd1@attglobal.net.

References and further reading

AS 4817-2006, *Project Performance Measurement Using Earned Value.* (Sydney, Australia: Standards Australia).

Budd, C. I. and Budd, C. S. (2005), *A Practical Guide To Earned Value Project Management.* (Vienna, VA: Management Concepts).

Dua, R. (2006), 'Making Performance Happen Using Collaborative Working Arrangements in the Construction Industry', *Proceedings of the IRNOP VII Conference* (Xi'an, China: Northwestern Technical University), 119-32.

Egan, J. (1998), 'Rethinking Construction', *Report from the Construction Taskforce* (London, UK: HMSO).

Francis, D. (2005), Presentation on CWA Techniques to Hawkins Construction Ltd. (Christchurch, NZ.)

Rix, S. (2004), *Target Outturn Cost and Payment Mechanism Workshop.* (Remuera, Auckland, NZ: Collaborative Management Services).

Latham, M. (1994), 'Constructing the Team', *Final Report of the Government / Industry Review of Procurement and Contractual Arrangements in the UK Construction Industry* (London, UK: HMSO).

Project Management Institute (2005), *Practice Standard For Earned Value Management,* (Newtown Square, PA: Project Management Institute, Inc.).

Webb, A. (2003), *Using Earned Value: A Project Manager's Guide.* (Aldershot, UK; Burlington, VT, USA: Gower Publishing).

CHAPTER **11** *Programme Tool*

Time to use:	An approach which informs the entire project
Level of difficulty:	
	Use by an experienced practitioner
Group:	Involves the whole project team and key senior stakeholders
Types of complexity suited for:	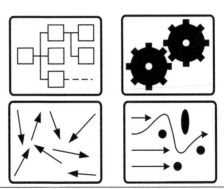

Problem

Most large projects are too big to be managed as a single project by a single person or group.

Purpose

The aim is to break down the large project into smaller manageable units to make it possible to address the source and level of complexity of each unit separately. By monitoring the whole group of units in relation to the environment and the strategic goals of the programme, systemic responses may be made in relation to the whole programme. The tool is based on standard approaches to programme management informed by complexity sources as a management strategy.

Types of complexity

Where the project is large, the approach can apply to all types of complexity. In very large projects it is likely that all types of complexity will occur.

Structural complexity will arise from the enormous number of activities to be completed and the resulting interdependencies between activities. Breaking down the whole into an interrelated group of smaller groupings, each with discrete deliverables, makes it easier to visualise and manage the interdependencies.

Technical complexity is more likely to be found in large projects because of the increased possibility for technical and design problems to emerge, either because of risks being triggered or because of design issues that were not anticipated at the beginning of the project. Breaking down the whole into smaller projects can allow you to isolate technical problems specific to particular projects which can be managed using specialised approaches.

Directional complexity is commonly found in very large projects as the propensity for disagreement between the many key stakeholders is high. A programme approach allows you to organise delivery of key outcomes in ways which can accommodate key decision-making processes more effectively.

Temporal complexity is more likely to occur in projects with long time frames. Just because of the length of time to delivery, these projects are very sensitive to political and environmental changes and key stakeholders who simply change their priorities during the project life cycle. A programme of smaller projects helps you clarify what has been delivered and assists in the management of disputes over what is to be paid for by the client or customer.

Theoretical background

Project complexity is not a single, unvarying attribute. The nature of complexity can vary in different parts within the project. It is helpful therefore to think of any large project as a group of related smaller projects, commonly referred to as a programme. There is now a substantial body of literature on programme management (see for example Reiss et al., 2006; Thiry, 2004). Generally speaking large initiatives are too large to be managed by one person as a single project. In order to manage systemically, which implies taking both an overview and detailed views of the individual initiatives, large projects are best conceptualised as an integrated group of projects, known as a programme in project management terminology. Each project within the programme is small enough to be the responsibility of a single manager or management team.

Within a programme, the projects are typically interconnected. Their impacts on each other, in terms of risks and resource use, can be tracked at a programme level and appropriate action can be taken to manage risks and distribute resources effectively. Most importantly, the environment, including organisational strategy and external impacts, can be tracked and the impact on any project within the programme assessed and action taken to continue with change or eliminate projects from the programme. Impacts of projects on each other, in terms of risks and resource use, can be tracked at the programme level and appropriate action can be taken to manage risks and distribute resources effectively. This model for management requires a manager or management team responsible for managing the programme. It also requires that the programme management team be in direct contact with senior players.

Decisions about how best to implement the projects within the programme relate specifically to the nature of project complexity expected. One piece of compelling evidence for a tailored approach rather than a single unified approach across the organisation or programme comes from the work of Payne and Turner (1999). They found that respondents, on average, reported better results if they tailored their procedures to the type of project and increased failure if common procedures were used across all projects.

We argue that this thinking can be extended to consider not only the size of the project but also the type of complexity. For instance there might be some projects within the programme that exhibit very little complexity. On a spectrum from control to chaos they exist at the control end. They have relatively few parts, objectives can be clearly defined and agreed, there are few technological surprises and they will be unlikely to be affected by political or environmental change during implementation. These projects are most efficiently managed using standard project management methods based on hard-systems thinking. Other projects within the same programme may exhibit varying aspects of complexity. Understanding the nature of the complexity that characterises each project has important implications for a number of key decisions to be made about the projects, such as the project governance structure, role capabilities and the selection of key personnel, approaches to risk management, finance and procurement.

Governing complex programs and projects may offer challenges that are quite different from those found in functional organisations (Hobbs and Miller, 2002). The organisational structure for the programme and each project within defines how information is exchanged formally and authority is allocated. Recent research (Helm and Remington, 2005) strongly indicates that the capabilities needed for the role of the executive sponsor in complex projects may not be sufficiently understood. Evidence is also mounting about the importance of the role of the executive sponsor and the governing board which are now considered to be fundamental to project success in any large complex project (Crawford et al., 2006).

Appropriate selection of key personnel is critical for complex projects. Lack of appropriate resources and divided loyalties of project personnel are well recognised sources of project failure (Dinsmore, 1993). Project teams are often expected to work much longer hours than required by functional roles. Many personnel suffer from stress-related symptoms as a result (Birch and Paul, 2003). Finding appropriate personnel who have the ability to work with complex issues while under pressure is not easy. We often assume that a project manager's role is generic. However a person who is able to cope with political uncertainty and ambiguity may not be able to protect and motivate designers and technical experts to deliver within a timeframe, or may not be sufficiently hard-nosed to manage multiple contracts and ensure strict time deadlines. Being able to identify the source and nature of the complexity may assist the programme director to fit the nature of the complexity with available capabilities.

Discussion

In order to manage systemically, which implies taking both an overview and detailed views of the individual initiatives, large projects are best conceptualised as an integrated group of projects or programme. The word 'programme' is problematic in some organisational settings so any other terms might be substituted, such as set, group, cluster or assemblage. It is the concept rather than the title that matters.

The model draws upon the programme management literature which is essentially based on hard-systems approaches to control based on decomposition from a top-down perspective with feedback and response iterating between local level and overall strategy level. We have added to this the concept of individualised project management methodologies at the local level based on identified sources of complexity.

The tool

The model in Figure 11.1 illustrates an approach to managing complex projects that demands a systemic perspective and accommodates a pluralistic approach to methodologies selected for implementation. As mentioned above, it combines traditional project management approaches to control, based on decomposition from a top-down perspective, with individualised project management methodologies at the local level, oscillating between local levels and strategic levels in response to feedback.

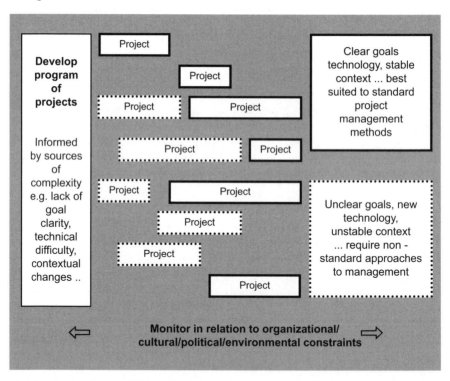

Figure 11.1 Systemic model for thinking about complex infrastructure projects

The model is dynamic in that it allows for rapid response to changes at the level of the environment, the organisation and the project. The structure of the model acknowledges that there are status review points at which key decisions must be made.

A programme management team (programme directorate) is established comprising senior representatives of the key functions responsible for delivering the project and users/client. The programme directorate must be in direct contact with those who set and monitor the organisational strategy because the programme directorate is responsible for ensuring that organisational strategy is translated into a group of interrelated projects that can be implemented. The programme directorate should appoint a programme director who chairs meetings of the programme directorate and has responsibility for the following:

- meaning-making activities, including dialogue with those who have set the goals to clarify goals as much as possible. This is an essential step in reducing directional complexity. It will not necessarily remove directional complexity but will assist greatly with project definition;
- analyzing and anticipating the types and levels of complexity which are likely to be encountered during the life cycle of the project/programme;
- decomposing the project as a series of sub-projects or projects within a larger programme;
- deciding upon project/programme organisational structure;
- appointing and monitoring key personnel;
- analyzing complex relationships between sub-projects or projects within the programme;
- managing inter-dependencies between sub-projects or projects;
- monitoring emergent issues and risks resulting from non-linearity;
- liaising with the senior executive in relation to environmental changes or project outcomes which require executive response and approval;
- discontinuing projects which are no longer relevant due to strategic or environmental changes;
- introducing new projects in order to respond to emergent characteristics;
- making adjustments to individual project objectives in response to changes.

IMPLEMENTATION

Management of the programme is iterative (see Figure 11.2). Information from individual projects or the environment is captured by the programme directorate/manager and decisions are made about the programme. This gives an opportunity for terminating projects within the programme if necessary, redefining them or adding others in order to deliver the strategic goals of the programme.

Decisions about how best to implement the projects within the programme relate specifically to the types of complexity expected. At this stage it should be emphasised that there might be some projects within the programme that exhibit little complexity. On a spectrum from control to chaos they exist at the control end. They have relatively few parts, objectives that can be clearly defined and agreed, few technological surprises and they will be unlikely to be affected by political or environmental change during their lifecycle. Other projects within the same programme may exhibit one or more types of complexity.

For instance a project which involves design and implementation of new IT inventory and a warehousing function that has never been implemented in this kind of setting before may exhibit aspects of structural, technical, directional and temporal complexity. Structural complexity will be related to the size of the project and how many activities, sub-contracts, supplier contracts, are involved and how many of those activities are interdependent. Technical complexity will be related to the difficulty in designing the code to support the new processes. Managing technical complexity presents many difficulties. For instance how much time do we allow in the schedule for the design and development component and how will that impact on commitments to key stakeholders and budget? How do we decide when the design is good enough? How do we select procurement systems which will also allow us to take advantage of

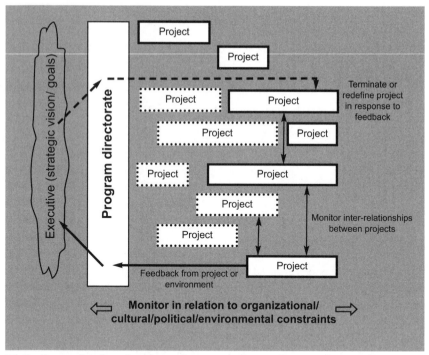

Figure 11.2 Example showing how the programme changes in response to changing constraints and feedback

emergent characteristics commonly found during the design phase? Directional complexity will be apparent when attempting to get agreement on objectives and shared understanding about what the final deliverable will actually deliver. The longer the time span of the project the more likely it is to encounter temporal complexity as the environment moves on. How do we manage stakeholders, risk, finance and procurement in such circumstances?

Step by step

1. Appoint programme directorate (or programme manager plus appropriate committee support).
2. Programme directorate to engage in dialogue with executive to reduce directional complexity.
3. Analyze project from the perspective of potential cause of complexity associated with each area of the work.
4. Divide the programme into a series of projects based on the level of complexity anticipated.
5. Select personnel to manage individual projects matching capabilities with type of complexity expected.
6. Select procurement/risk/finance management strategies for each project based on the type of complexity.
7. Monitor progress and environmental shifts.
8. Communicate regularly with the executive to ascertain impact of changes from a bottom-up, top-down and environmental perspectives.

9. Make regular adjustments to programme, terminating, redefining and adding projects in response to feedback.
10. Key to decision making is knowledge of the cultures and constraints inherent in the organisations involved together with a detailed understanding of the roles and capabilities of the key people associated with the project. Refer to the tool dealing with role capabilities for further discussion about selection of project personnel.

Caution

To use this tool successfully there must be commitment from the executive and adequate resources committed at the programme and the project level.

The role of the programme directorate is the key role as it is the conduit through which information from the executive, the individual projects and the environment is transmitted and acted upon.

Individual project managers also occupy key roles and the capabilities of the people to fill the roles must be carefully considered (refer tool dealing with role capabilities).

Dialogue with the executive must be open and frequent so that changes in strategic direction can be communicated to the programme directorate and outcomes, risks and local environmental impacts can be communicated through the programme directorate to the executive.

With large projects it is commonly assumed that standard project management processes, methods and role capabilities which have been used successfully for small implementation projects can simply be scaled up for use on large projects. This is not the case! Large projects are of a totally different order to small implementation projects. The size of the project alone means that there is an increased risk of encountering any or all of the four types of complexity discussed in this book.

Examples in practice

Figure 11.3 illustrates a project organisational structure which was designed to address both the known characteristics of key personnel and the anticipated complexity of the project. It is not a general model, however, and may not work in a different organisational culture. The main point to note is that the senior executive, in acknowledging the importance of project to the organisation, took

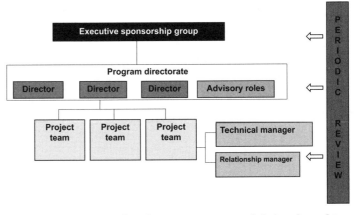

Figure 11.3 Example of programme model developed to meet particular organisational needs

some key decisions based on a thorough analysis of the situation. First they acknowledged the complexity of the challenge, recognised the abilities and shortcomings of the managers available for the project and were prepared to increase personnel levels so that they were commensurate with the anticipated complexity. Too often personnel levels are increased only when the project goes wrong, and that is invariably too late!

Figure 11.3 was developed specifically to address the following aspects of organisational culture:

- a risk-averse culture which did not support rapid decision making;
- technical complexity associated with the new systems to be installed;
- personnel who were largely inexperienced in delivering large complex projects;
- directional complexity due to volatile organisational politics and lack of clarity or agreement about the key project objectives;
- a restrictive deadline which meant that rapid decision making was essential in order to deliver the project milestones.

The senior executive recognised that the project was large enough to be treated as a programme of projects, allowing it to be divided and managed as smaller discrete entities. With appropriate support the discrete parts or projects within the programme were small enough and short enough in duration to be managed by project managers who had only managed simple projects in the past. The project managers or team leaders were supported by technical managers to address the technical complexity and relationship managers who were able to identify and manage the key stakeholders and the organisational politics. Project team leaders were selected according to their ability to manage the dominant type of complexity associated with their particular project or sub-project. The programme directorate managed the interfaces. However, acknowledging the predominantly risk-averse nature of the organisation which had supported a culture of avoidance of sign-off by some senior managers, it was necessary to design a structure that prevented delays due to slow decision making by senior management. The programme directorate met weekly. Their decisions were informed by an appropriate team of experts. Decisions not taken or issues unresolved at each weekly meeting which might result in a delay to the project were escalated immediately to the executive. Any lack of progress drew the immediate attention of the senior executive.

In addition the project was reviewed regularly by an external team of highly experienced people whose task was to mentor the project teams and the programme directorate by providing advice and independent assessment of progress and processes. The mentoring was regular and ad hoc. Mentors were available for telephone consultations as needed by project team leaders, managers and directors. This mentoring was in addition to and in support of formal auditing processes.

References and further reading

Birch, C. and Paul, D. (2003), *Life and work: Challenging Economic Man.* (Sydney, Australia: University of New South Wales Press).

Crawford, L., Cooke-Davies, T., Labuschagne, L., Hobbs, B. and Remington, K. (2006), 'Exploring the Role of the Project Sponsor', *PMI Research Conference*, 18 July, Montreal.

Dinsmore, C. (1993), *Human Factors in Project Management.* (NY: Amacon).

Helm, J. and Remington, K. (2005), 'Effective Sponsorship, Project Managers' Perceptions of the Role of the Project Sponsor', *Project Management Journal* 36:3, 51-62.

Hobbs, B. and Miller, R. (2002), 'The Strategic Front End of Large Infrastructure Projects: A Process of Nesting Governance,' *Proceedings of the PMI Research Conference* (Seattle, USA: Project Management Institute) 14-7.

Payne, J. H. and Turner, J. R. (1999), 'Company-wide Project Management: The Planning and Control of Programmes of Projects of Different Type', *International Journal of Project Management* 17:1, 55-9.

Reiss, G., Anthony, M., Chapman, J., Leigh, G., Pyne, A. and Rayner, P. (Eds) (2006), *Gower Book of Programme Management*. (Aldershot, UK: Gower Publishing).

Shenhar, A. J. (2001), 'One Size Does Not Fit All Projects: Exploring Classical Contingency Domains', *Management Studies* 47:3, 394–414.

Thiry, M. (2004), 'Programme Management', Ch. 12 in Morris, P. and Pinto, J. (Eds.) *The Wiley Guide to Managing Projects*. (Sussex, UK: John Wiley and Sons).

Turner J. R. and Cochrane, R. A. (1993), 'Goals-and-Methods Matrix: Coping with Projects with Ill-Defined Goals and/or Methods of Achieving Them', *International Journal of Project Management* 11, 93.

Williams T. (1999), 'The Need for New Paradigms for Complex Projects', *International Journal of Project Management* 17, 269-73.

Williams, T. (2002), *Modelling Complex Projects*. (Sussex, UK: John Wiley & Sons).

12 *Role Definition*

Time to use:	This is an ongoing process that must be revisited at the beginning of any major project phase and be continually monitored throughout the project
Level of difficulty:	
Group:	Usually managed with consultation and involvement of key stakeholders
Types of complexity suited for:	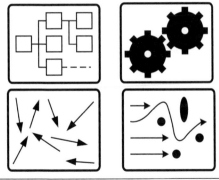

Problem

Defining the role capabilities needed in managing a complex project can be very challenging. Role definitions really need to be revisited and redefined at the beginning of every phase of the project when team and personnel changes may be expected as a result of the different nature of the activities in each project phase.

Purpose

There is a qualitative difference between the role capability requirements for a complex project in comparison to a simple project. Managing complex projects is a higher-order management activity. This tool is designed to inform thinking about the specialised role capabilities for complex projects at management and senior management levels.

Types of complexity

The tool is relevant for each type of complexity. It is based on research by the authors and others and can be easily adjusted to suit the needs of special projects.

We recognise that the degree to which this approach can be successfully implemented is contextually dependent. It is conditioned by the culture of the organisation or organisations involved and by who is available to manage the projects or provide the governance for the project.

Theoretical background

Recent research has revealed that in complex projects role capabilities needed by project managers and executive sponsors are substantially different from those required for simple projects.

PROJECT MANAGER ROLE

Twenty-six senior project managers from Australia, New Zealand and the UK were selected on the basis of having managed high-risk, complex projects that were deemed by all key stakeholders to be a success. Subjects participated in in-depth interviews designed to capture their 'lived experience'. A grounded theory approach was then used to analyse the data and develop further questionnaires (Helm and Remington, 2005; Remington and Pollack, 2006). When asked to describe their behaviour and the attributes that they valued most when managing complex projects, only two out of twenty-six project managers mentioned scheduling ability (an activity traditionally associated with project management) as one of their valued attributes. This doesn't mean that ability to schedule was unimportant. It was simply seen as less important than other attributes needed for managing complexity. Thematic analysis software was used to analyse the behaviours which were used most often in managing complex projects. All rated the following aspects very highly:

- ability to develop creative ways forward – to 'think out of the box';
- high-level communication abilities with all levels of the organisation or community;
- ability to be comfortable with ambiguity and ability to communicate ambiguity to other levels in appropriate ways – that often meant simplifying the issues in different ways;
- political savvy in order to negotiate the politics of the organisation(s) involved;
- ability to select from a multitude of methodologies or paradigms in order to manage the projects successfully – flexible in their approach, bottom-up/top-down and so on;
- ability to take multi-perspective viewpoints – constantly moving their focus back and forth from individual elements to the whole system – respecting individual approaches while keeping the whole in perspective;
- ability to facilitate information exchange, fostering dialogue between key stakeholders, including project teams, specialist consultants and so on, in order to help solve problems;
- opportunistic to take advantage of ideas from unexpected places and people – made space available for groups to explore and develop issues in their own ways;
- treating the project as many interrelated projects, each with its own idiosyncrasies.

It is clear from this research that the role capabilities of project managers who have successfully delivered complex projects differ substantially from capabilities centring on planning, monitoring and reporting. All interviewees recognised that they did these things as well but that these activities were seen as less important to the ultimate success of the project than the attributes noted above. It is also apparent that the attributes listed above are complex behaviours and attitudes rather than simple skills.

EXECUTIVE SPONSOR ROLE

Until recently it was commonly believed that the role of the project executive sponsor was essentially responsibility for finance; however initial research suggested that the role was much more wide reaching (Curry, 1995; Crawford and Brett, 2001). Recent research (Hall et al., 2003; Cooke-Davies, 2005; Helm and Remington, 2005; Crawford et al., 2006) has changed the understanding of the role of project executive sponsor, attributing a great deal of responsibility for the success or failure of projects on the successful performance of this key role. This research has been supported by anecdotal evidence found in the practitioner literature (Kay, 1997; Melymuka, 2004a; 2004b).

Essentially research indicates that the project executive sponsor role is responsible for providing good governance for the project. This includes the following:

- maintaining a focus on the broader issues on behalf of the project – informing the project manager and team of organisational and environmental changes which might impact the project;
- establishing connections on behalf of the project, and supporting interfaces between the project team and the wider organisation and external environment;
- advocating on behalf of the project with the senior executive and other key senior stakeholders;
- clearing pathways so that key resources can be obtained for the project;
- motivating the project team when times are difficult;
- objectively criticising project performance;
- providing ad hoc support to the project manager and project team, including mentoring;
- approving finance.

This list of capabilities goes well beyond the commonly held understanding of the role of the project sponsor. For a complex project the role of project sponsor requires significant time commitment.

Discussion

The fundamental difference in the role capability requirements for a complex project is often misunderstood and executive managers often make the mistake of assuming that a person who has managed a small project well will be able to manage a complex project equally well. Managing a complex project is a higher-order management activity and should be treated and resourced accordingly.

This confusion stems from the perception commonly held in the business community that a project is simply implementation of an idea fully resolved by the executive or other senior body. However, this may not always be the case, or the project objectives may be inadequately communicated to those who must implement them. As a result any sensible project manager should carefully check that the project has really been properly defined and the business case has been tested before proceeding to detailed planning and implementation.

With the exception of dedicated post-graduate degrees which focus entirely on project management, project management is usually taught as a single unit within a business degree such as an MBA. Consequently the focus is on small implementation projects with the emphasis on the tasks listed below. In the context of implementation of a standard project, management activities include planning the scope in detail, scheduling, project specific budgeting, quality assurance, selection of suppliers, tendering and so on. Once the project is underway the management activities involve tracking, measuring, monitoring, reporting and managing any contracts for delivery of goods or services. At closure the activities include collating records, resolving accounting differences, organising training packages and knowledge management activities, such as archiving records, recording lessons learned, conducting post-implementation reviews and so on.

People are discovering, however, that there is a quantum leap from a small implementation project to a complex project. Therefore it is a mistake to assume that the person who is adept at monitoring, tracking and reporting in a simple project is the right choice for project manager when the project is large or complex or both.

Equally, as our research and that of others is indicating, the governance of such projects is vital to project success and is not an easy task.

The tool

The tool is essentially a checklist to assist planners in making decisions about who should fill the roles of executive project sponsor and project manager.

The checklist is based on our research and therefore there is an emphasis on behaviours and attitudes as well as thinking skills.

EXECUTIVE SPONSOR ROLE

Step 1: Ideal role definition   Place ticks in the columns to the right of each attribute in Table 12.1 according to your knowledge of the level of project complexity (refer Chapters 3–6) and the importance of the project to the organisation. This will provide an *ideal* role definition based on the research. Add any other categories that you require. In this first assessment *do not* take into account cultural aspects or availability of resources to fill the role. This will be addressed later in the tool. Experience suggests that people tend to compensate for limitations through compromise when deciding to allocate resources. This is not desirable particularly if the project is both complex and very important to the organisation.

Step 2: Cultural/organisational fit   Having established an *ideal* role definition the checklist in Table 12.2 can assist in making decisions about whether to resource the position internally or externally, whether the role is best filled by one person or a group and whether external mentoring is required.

Table 12.1 Executive sponsor – ideal role definition

Attribute	Not essential 1	Useful 2	Essential 3	Notes from the research on sponsorship of complex projects.
Foster high-level connections within the organisation and communicate relevant issues to the project team.				Being essentially involved with day-to-day issues of project delivery it is important that the project manager is kept abreast of events that might affect the project
Foster high-level connections outside the organisation and communicate relevant issues to the project team.				As above
Holds senior position within the organisation				This attribute relates to the degree of formal power the sponsor holds within the organisation which might be important for escalation and rapid decision to issues, especially where the project is time dependent
Demonstrates high-level communication skills				This attribute is linked with most others and refers to communication skills with a wide range of stakeholders
Exhibits courage to support the project team in delivery of the project objectives				This refers to the willingness to go into battle with other key stakeholders to smooth the way for the project team, for resources and so on
Can provide motivational support for the project team to deliver the vision when the going gets tough				If risks are triggered team members often work very long hours and morale can be very difficult to maintain; the executive sponsor must be able to assist the project manager in providing motivational support during difficult times
Compatible with a broad range of people				Compatibility with the project manager and project team was important in establishing mutual respect, necessary especially if the project is particularly difficult and long term
Willingness to partner the project manager and team to deliver the project objectives				Senior project managers found that sponsors who were willing to take a partnership approach, rather than those who exerted authority in a formal manner, engaged more collaboratively in problem solving. Where formal power was exerted sponsors were often excluded from the decision-making processes by project managers and teams
Provide ad hoc support to the project team				Support should be available when needed. The level should vary according to the experience of the project manager.
Provide objectivity to the project team and challenge assumptions				Senior project managers interviewed appreciated being challenged by the executive sponsor. Objectivity did not require the sponsor to have a detailed knowledge of the project processes
Detailed technical knowledge of the project				Very few project managers reported that a detailed knowledge of the project was required by the sponsor. In some cases detailed technical knowledge led to micro-management of the project processes with less attention to the other attributes required of the sponsor

Table 12.2 Executive sponsor – cultural/organisational fit

Question	No	Yes	Discussion based on the research findings	Action/options if YES
Is the project of high priority?			High-priority projects must be resourced appropriately; under-expenditure on key resources from the beginning of a project is widely recognized as a key contributor to project failure	Increase the project budget if necessary to allow for adequate resources
Is the project time dependent?			Time-dependent projects require rapid escalation and decision-making processes at a senior level so that risks can be addressed and the project can proceed within the approved schedule	Assign an executive sponsor or sponsorship board who has a mandate and the capability to take responsibility for rapid decision making. Decisions can be taken by a majority
Is there a shortage of resources who can match the required role definition?			Based on the answers to the questions above a decision must be made whether to resource internally or through an external contract. Several senior project managers interviewed mentioned that the best executive sponsors on very large projects had been retired executives or executives nearing retirement because they had very good connections, a great deal of experience and few personal agendas.	Consider engaging external resources to fill the role
Is the organizational culture risk averse? Does the dominant culture make it difficult to exercise personal courage in support of projects?			The influence of organizational culture on behaviour is enormous. For instance in a risk-averse culture it is may be difficult for individuals to exercise the courage needed to battle for the support and resources needed to deliver the project	Consider establishing a sponsorship board comprising at least three senior people representing the owner, user and client. Decisions can be taken by any two
Is there sufficient expertise within the organization to take on the project?			The role of external mentor, usually undertaken by a highly experienced retired senior executive has been shown to be very useful in enhancing and retaining knowledge within the organization	Consider appointing an external mentor or mentoring panel to the project to give regular but ad hoc advice to the project executive and project team Note: This role is additional to the role of external auditor

PROJECT MANAGER ROLE

Step 1: Role capability definition   Place ticks in the columns to the right of each attribute in Table 12.3 according to your knowledge of the level of project complexity and the importance of the project to the organisation.

The first assessment should *not* take into account cultural aspects or any limitation of resources available to fill the role. This will be addressed later in the tool. As mentioned above, experience suggests that people tend to compensate for limitations through compromise when allocating resources.

Step 2: Cultural/organisational Fit   Having established an *ideal* role definition the checklist in Table 12.4 can assist in making decisions about whether to resource the position internally or externally, whether the role is best filled by one person or a group and whether external mentoring is required.

Table 12.3 Manager role – capability definition

Attribute	Not essential 1	Useful 2	Essential 3	Notes from the research
Uses high-level communication skills in ways appropriate to individual stakeholders and groups.				Senior project managers valued the ability to communicate informally as well as formally with a broad range of people from senior executives to specialist team members and different stakeholders within and outside the organisation
Manages the interfaces within the organisation to achieve project outcomes.				Awareness and ability to work with the internal politics of the organisation to achieve project goals is highly valued by senior project managers working on complex projects
Accepts and works with ambiguity.				A project manager working on a project which is likely to exhibit characteristics of technical, directional or temporal complexity needs to be comfortable with uncertainty as the project may seem to be out of control at times. This kind of project is unsuited to managers who prefer strict adherence to rules ir order to maintain a sense of control
Translates ambiguity in ways appropriate to the needs of various stakeholders so that they can participate effectively.				It is part of the project manager's task to communicate those aspects of the complexity that are relevant to the needs of particular senior managers, team members, specialist consultants, clients, customers and interested parties, so that they can contribute most productively
Views the project from an holistic perspective.				Often only some people will have a true sense of the complexity and the associated uncertainty. The project manager must be able to view the project from multiple perspectives so as to be able to move around the project and intervene as required and at the appropriate level of detail
Uses a flexible, multi-paradigm approach to management, suiting the style of management to the purpose and the group				Particularly where the project involved technical, directional and temporal complexity successful project mangers reported that they used a multitude of approaches from traditional (control-based) project management methods to approaches deriving from soft-systems thinking which are people-centred
Able to motivate the teams to deliver the project milestones while allowing them space to work effectively				This involves achieving a balance between maintaining focus on milestones while resisting the temptation to micro-manage. This is especially important in projects that exhibit technical complexity as design or research teams must have the space to do their creative work.
Uses divergent thinking to solve problems and negotiate obstacles.				Ability to think outside the box to find imaginative ways around obstacles was one of the attributes most highly valued by senior project managers
Employs high-level holistic, analytical and organising skills.				This ability is particularly relevant to projects exhibiting structural complexity. The project manager must be able to see the complex picture of interrelationships in order to manipulate the interdependencies to achieve optimum time and cost outcomes and respond to emergent risk patterns
Uses high-level scheduling skills.				Scheduling large numbers of activities and being able to analyse the relationships between interdependent activities is particularly relevant to projects exhibiting structural complexity. The project manager should be able to use advanced scheduling software
Uses advanced cost management and analysis skills.				Projects exhibiting structural complexity would require high-level cost analysis and management skills, such as Earned Value Management, which tracks scope, schedule and cost and can be used to predict final project costs

Table 12.4 Project manager – cultural/organisational fit

Question	No	Yes	Discussion based on the research findings	Action/options if YES
Is the project of high priority?			High-priority projects must be resourced appropriately. Under-expenditure on key resources from the beginning of a project is widely recognised as a key contributor to project failure	Carefully analyse the project for sources of complexity. Increase the project budget if necessary to allow for adequate resources. Load resources in the early phases of the project to increase organisational capability and build a reserve of people with knowledge about the project who can contribute later if needed
Is the project time dependent?			Time dependent projects require rapid escalation and decision-making processes at a senior level so that risks can be addressed and the project can proceed within the approved schedule	Appoint a project manager with high skills in detecting and managing emergent risks to the schedule. Assign to the project manager delegated authority to manage risks at a project level (within agreed schedule and budget contingencies) and direct access to the executive sponsor for rapid escalation of emergent risks. *Caution*: Particularly with technically and directionally complex projects this ability must be balanced with ability to manage relationships
Does the project have very stringent cost constraints?			Highly cost-constrained projects require rapid escalation and decision-making processes at a senior level so that risks can be addressed and the project can proceed within the approved budget	Appoint a project manager with high skills in detecting and managing emergent risks. If the project is structurally complex the project manager should be able to use tools such as Earned Value Management. Provide direct access to the executive sponsor for rapid escalation of emergent risks
Is there a shortage of resources who can match the required role definition?			Based on the answers to the questions above a decision must be made whether to resource internally or through an external contract. Issues such as lack of cultural fit can often impede the effectiveness of external contractors. A common source of project failure is engagement of external contractors late in the project life cycle. It is usually more cost effective to load resources in the early stages of the project so that project personnel have time to develop the necessary knowledge before dangerous risk scenarios occur	Consider engaging external resources to fill the role. However, this decision must be made early and there must be a cultural fit between the contracted personnel and the organisation. Consider engaging an experienced mentor to support internal personnel

Table 12.4 *Continued*

Question	No	Yes	Discussion based on the research findings	Action/options if YES
Do available resources match some but not all of the attributes defined?			It is rare to find personnel who can match all requirements of a role definition. People who are very skilled at monitoring and control may not also be highly skilled at managing relationships and political issues or they may be unable to motivate the team. On a large or fast-tracked project a project management partnership often provides a more effective way of providing the management support at the project level	Consider appointing a project management team; for example a functional project manager (to manage schedule, cost, quality, risk and reporting) and a relationship project manager to look after managing the internal relationships between team members, senior management and other stakeholders
Is the organisational culture risk averse? Does the dominant culture make it difficult to exercise personal responsibility?			The influence of organisational culture on behaviour is enormous. For instance in a risk-averse culture it may be difficult for individuals to exercise the courage needed to battle for the support and resources needed to deliver the project	Consider supporting the project manager through appointment of a strong executive sponsor (or board) to encourage responsibility. Consider appointing a senior project manager to mentor and support the project manager or project management team
Is there sufficient expertise within the organisation to take on the project?			The role of external mentor, usually undertaken by a highly experienced retired senior project manager has been shown to be very useful in enhancing and retaining knowledge within the organisation	Consider appointing an external mentor or mentoring panel to the project to give regular but ad hoc advice to the project manager and project team

Step by step

1. Analyse project for potential sources of complexity.
2. Use checklist to help build the role definition for the project executive sponsor.
3. Based on organisational culture, the project size and availability of key personnel decide whether to:
   (a) appoint a single person or establish a sponsorship board;
   (b) resource internally or engage an external person to fill the role;
   (c) introduce an external mentor.
4. Use checklist to help define the role definition for the project manager.
5. Based on organisational culture, the project size and availability of key personnel decide whether to:
   (d) appoint a single person or establish a project management team;
   (e) resource internally or engage an external people to fill the role;
   (f) introduce an external mentor.

Caution

This tool focuses on role definition attributes for the key roles of project executive sponsor and project manager. However it can also be adapted to the role of programme director if the project is large and should be managed as a programme. The programme director is usually a very senior project manager who possesses the ability to design and appraise the programme from a holistic perspective, distributing resources across many projects to optimise their effectiveness. At the same time, the role requires the ability to manage the organisational politics and senior stakeholders. The role requires a level of seniority and authority which allows direct access to and influence with the senior executive.

The ability to perform key roles is intrinsically linked to the project governance structure. Our research indicates that experienced project managers are able to deliver the project outcomes in spite of unwieldy governance structures and uncooperative or unsupportive project executive sponsors. However with the rapid expansion of the numbers of projects being undertaken there is an increasing lack of experienced project managers. Inexperienced project managers may need significant mentoring and support in order to negotiate the politics of many organisations.

References and further reading

Cooke-Davies, T. J. (2005), 'The Executive Sponsor – The Hinge Upon Which Organizational Maturity Turns?', *PMI Global Congress Europe*, May 2005, Edinburgh, UK.

Crawford, L. H. and Brett, C. (2001), 'Exploring the Role of the Project Sponsor', *Proceedings of the PMI New Zealand Annual Conference 2001 – Project Success: Putting it all Together*. (Wellington, New Zealand: PMINZ).

Crawford, L. H. and Cooke-Davies, T. J. (2005), 'Project Governance – The Pivotal Role of the Executive Sponsor', *PMI Global Congress*, North America, September 2005, Toronto, Canada.

Crawford, L., Cooke-Davies, T., Labuschagne, L., Hobbs, B. and Remington, K. (2006), 'Exploring the Role of the Project Sponsor,' *PMI Research Conference*, July, Montreal.

Curry, H. (1995), 'Project Sponsorship', *PM Network* IX:3, 7.

Hall, M., Halt, R. and Purchase, D. (2003), 'Project Sponsors under New Public Management; Lessons From The Frontline', *International Journal of Project Management* 21, 495-502.

Helm, J. and Remington, K. (2005), 'Effective Sponsorship, Project Managers' Perceptions of the Role of the Project Sponsor', *Project Management Journal* 36:3, 36-51.

Helm, J. and Remington, K. (2005), 'Adaptive Habitus – Project Managers' Perceptions of the Role of the Project Sponsor', *Proceedings of EURAM Conference*, May. (Munich: TUT University).

Kay, B. J. (1997), 'Who Needs a Project Sponsor? You Do', *Proceedings of 28th PMI Annual Seminar and Symposium*. (Chicago, Illinois: Project Management Institute).

Melymuka, K. (2004a), 'Surviving the Sponsor Exit' , *Computerworld*, 00104841, 38:7.

Melymuka, K. (2004b), 'Firing your Project Sponsor', *Computerworld*, 00104841, 38:8.

Remington, K. and Paul, D. (2006), 'Organizational Change as a Complex Project or Program: A Systemic Approach to Managing Complex Change Projects in the Public Sector', *ANZSOG Conference*, Canberra, February (copy may be obtained from the authors at kaye.remington@uts.edu.au.

Remington, K. and Pollack, J. (2006), 'Complex Infrastructure Projects: A Systemic Model for Management', *ANZSYS Conference*, Sydney, December (due for publication in 2007 on the web at http://isce.edu/ISCE_Group_Site/web-content/ISCEPublishing/ISCE_Publishing_index.html.

Remington, K., Paul, D. and Pollack, J. (2006), 'Projects or Programs? Characteristics of Complex Projects' *Proceedings of the IQPQC Conference*, Sydney, February (copy may be obtained from the authors at kaye. remington@uts.edu.au..

Thomas, J., Delisle, C., Juqdev, K. and Buckle, P. (2002), 'Selling Project Management to Senior Executives: The Case for Avoiding Crisis Sales', *Project Management Journal* 33:2, 19-29.

13 Jazz (Time-Linked Semi-Structures)

Time to use:	A whole of project approach
Level of difficulty:	
Group:	Best used with the whole project team and senior stakeholders involved
Types of complexity suited for:	

Problem

One of the major challenges in managing complex projects involving high levels of innovation is finding the right kind of project organisational structure to support the delivery.

Purpose

The aim of this approach is to help the senior executive and management to select a structure which will produce the most effective results. Although we recognise that the project structure chosen will be highly influenced by the culture and structure of the organisation in which the project is being managed it is important that the project structure also suits the nature of the project. This approach is designed for managing the project and is not suitable for planning or budget development.

Types of complexity

The approach is particularly relevant for technical and temporal complexity but might also be applicable to projects involving directional complexity.

Research and development projects, design projects and theatrical projects are all potentially confronted by technical and temporal complexity. Managing the technical complexity in the context of rapid turn-around of projects can be challenging. The apparent chaos which often characterises these workplaces may persist up to the final delivery date by which time the project team is often starting to engage with the next project.

Theoretical background

Jazz improvisation involves creating music on the spot without a prescribed score or plan. However, jazz is guided by a non-negotiable framework that constrains what the soloist can play. This structure provides the necessary backdrop to coordinate action and sequences of notes. To quote the bassist Charles Mingus:

'You can't improvise on nothin'. You gotta have somethin'.'

The 'somethings' that provide the resources players draw upon are songs that are made up of chords and corresponding scales:

'Jazz is a rule-bound activity. What jazz improvisers do when they're playing is to follow those chord changes like they're a road map. To play outside of those chord changes is to break a rule. You can't do that.' (Barrett and Peplowski, 1998, 558)

In 1998 an entire issue of *Organization Science* was devoted to jazz as a metaphor for improvisation in organisations. The 'overture' was by Meyer, Frost and Weick (1998). Earlier scholars such as Bastien and Hostager (1988) and Hatch (1997) had also used the theme to illustrate how improvisation seems to takes place most effectively within a loose structure. Jazz is an example of improvisation which to outsiders might be referred to as 'doing your own thing and making it up as you go along'. However more detailed analysis shows that jazz really involves performers communicating intensively with one another in real-time but within a loose structure comprising specific rules, such as order of soloist and accepted chord sequences. In the context of a jazz performance the players can innovate and explore new possibilities within a loose structure. Without any kind of framework, or basic rules, the performance would be chaotic and nonsense to the audience and players alike.

Some researchers (Burns and Stalker, 1961; March, 1981; Peters, 1994) have concluded that innovation is more likely to be found in organisations with organic structures – fluid job descriptions, vague organisation charts, few rules and high levels of informal communication. The lack of constraints was thought to free developers so that they could respond flexibly and create new ideas.

However, other evidence, especially that from a very deep study of high-velocity computer technology firms by Brown and Eisenhardt (1997), suggests that some limited structure is preferable. This limited structure can be provided by role definitions and responsibilities. It seems to be very effective when coupled with high levels of communication, within and across projects, and proactive future probing activities. More particularly they found that:

'... managers combine limited structure (for example priorities, responsibilities) with extensive interaction and freedom to improvise current products. This combination is neither so rigid as

to control the process nor so chaotic that the process falls apart. Second, successful managers explore the future by experimenting with a wide variety of low-cost probes.' (p. 3)

They also found that the less successful firms employed rigid management processes which seemed to get in the way of both innovation and rapid delivery times.

In addition they concluded that time-linked delivery of products seemed to be another feature in common with those organisations which managed successful design projects. They found that:

'... rather than ignoring change or never changing, they link products together over time through rhythmic transition processes from present projects to future ones, creating a relentless pace of change.' (p. 3)

Our observations of successful drama and industrial design projects suggest patterns similar to those observed by Moorman and Miner (1998) in the arts, the military and manufacturing. In most of these fields the structure is defined through very tight role definitions and responsibilities and regular meetings which everyone attends. In between these meetings apparent chaotic activity and a great deal of informal communication may take place. The meetings act as milestones where the creative effort is coordinated and teams are motivated to explore or close. They also promote cross-organisational information exchange and problem-solving sessions. In addition, especially in relation to the drama projects, a schedule of new plays is developed annually, or even on a much longer time frame when key international directors, performers or designers are to be involved. This maintains a rhythmic pace which keeps up the pressure on the various teams, and helps create a future-oriented focus. It also means that there is always work to do if the pace on one project slows down temporarily, effects also noted by Gersick (1994).

Discussion

The approach is more of a theoretical model than a tool which supports management of projects experiencing technical or temporal complexity.

In terms of Complexity Theory the situation described above resembles the concept of 'edge of chaos' as it is understood in the organisational literature (Crutchfield and Young, 1990; Beinhoffer, 1997; Stacey, 1996). In the organisational literature this concept has been applied to organisations attempting to maintain a dynamic position between a rigid structure at one extreme and chaos at the other. The dynamic edge implies that the organisation is able to create just enough order to maintain the system and balance this with enough chaos to permit the unexpected connections and ideas necessary for innovation and development. The approach described below attempts to guide managers in the direction of establishing such a dynamic equilibrium to help manage technical and temporal complexity in projects.

Regular meetings used by design teams allow for structured information exchange. The meetings focus and integrate thinking and communication which has occurred informally during the period in between meetings. In this way they function as information nodes.

Two of the major challenges in managing temporally complex projects are continuity of information during long periods of inactivity and sustaining motivation as team members become distracted by other work and lose interest in the project. However, it is important that the project team is ready to act with a number of options in hand. Regular meetings encouraging exchange of information on the current status of the environment would also provide the link and continuity missing in this kind of project. If the meetings were structured to include future probing and creative scenario planning they would have a purpose beyond simple information exchange and would become the mechanism by which readiness to act is ensured.

The tool

This is a management approach. When building a project plan, for the purpose of estimating the budget and time, methods relying on decomposition techniques, such as work-breakdown structures and precedence networks, which use historical data and case scenarios, are preferable. However a highly structured framework is unlikely to be best for managing the project overall.

The approach relies on finding the right mix of order and chaos to support innovation within the culture. However, it should be expected that the right mix will take a while to hone. Just as the edge of chaos is a dynamic concept, any structure to support innovation will be dynamically dependent upon the organisational culture, the people available to fill the key roles and environmental changes. We will utilise the term 'semi-structure', which was also used by Brown and Eisenhardt (1997) to describe the loose organisational structure which seems to produce the most successful results in this kind of complex setting.

The semi-structure involves setting milestones, roles and responsibilities, and managing through regular meetings and informal communication. Bearing in mind that adjustments will be made over time we suggest that once the project objectives have been defined and agreed the key milestones should be determined. Milestones are preferable to detailed time schedules, as Turner (1999) explains. In this kind of project there is no reliable way, at this stage of the proceedings, to determine a really meaningful detailed schedule and therefore, other than for the purpose of estimating overall project time and cost, there is no sense in spending time doing so.

The key roles are determined next. For the same reason that milestones rather than detailed schedules are used, role descriptions would have a broad definition such as 'lead design team to produce X component by 2 August' with clear responsibility to do just that and clear financial delegation.

Next, regular meeting dates need to be communicated. It is very important that the meetings are seen by all as important. They should involve a quick assessment of progress from each team but meetings should focus on problem solving. Therefore meetings need to be facilitated to promote dynamic interchange of ideas. Teams should be encouraged to share ideas and knowledge. It is also helpful to invite radical innovators to the meetings so that new ideas are introduced to the project teams. Finally the meetings should be closed with clear objectives set for teams to achieve by the next meeting. This is not very different from a description of any good project team meeting. However, as the meetings form the only means of control, apart from earlier definitions of milestones and responsibilities, they must be managed with great expertise.

In between the meetings apparently chaotic activity will occur which is largely self-managed by the teams. It is vital to avoid micro-managing the teams in between meetings or bogging them down with project related paperwork. The project manager can do a great deal to support the teams in between the meetings. The project manager can observe the status (without appearing to spy or be too intrusive), prepare and keep reports on behalf of the teams and facilitate the informal dialogue and knowledge exchange that must occur to stimulate innovation and integration of ideas. The project manager can also advocate on behalf of the teams and keep senior management updated on progress.

Eventually alignment will occur and the earlier chaos between meetings will be less apparent. This might sound too vague for comfort but generally speaking, unless the problem is extraordinarily difficult, design teams are very good at responding to milestone dates, providing they have the freedom to manage their own time in between. Therefore

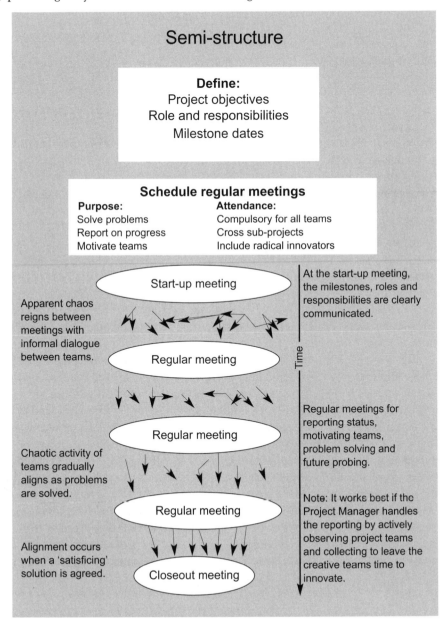

Figure 13.1 Example of a project semi-structure model

micro-management by the project manager will be likely to be counter-productive, causing a breakdown in cooperation. However the milestone dates must be communicated firmly and re-emphasised so that teams can come to a satisficing solution which may not be the optimum solution but is the best solution given the constraints imposed.

Step by step

1. Determine project objectives.
2. Determine project milestones.
3. Determine roles and responsibilities in broad terms.
4. Set compulsory regular meeting dates.
5. At the first meeting communicate roles, responsibilities and milestones.
6. Between meetings resist the desire to micro-manage. Allow the teams to communicate and explore in an apparently chaotic manner. Support the teams as necessary, particularly with project paperwork, which they generally detest as it keeps them away from their creative work or other responsibilities.
7. Use meetings to focus on problem solving, innovation and future probing. Status reports should be given as they have a motivating influence but they should not dominate the meeting. End each meeting with clear objectives for the next meeting.
8. When alignment starts to occur, as it will towards the deadline when the teams come to agreement on solutions, management activities should include collecting and collating project records.

Caution

This is a management tool not a predictive tool. To predict or estimate schedules or budget you must use tools based on decomposition supported by historical data with clearly stated assumptions.

For Project Managers who are unused to managing technically and temporally complex projects there is a tendency to panic because of the apparent chaos between the meetings and the reluctance of project teams to cooperate on reporting activities. By focusing on milestones and less on what happens in between or how the teams get there, the Project Manager can be a real catalyst and assist teams by taking away the burden of reporting which is seen as interfering with innovative processes.

The dividing line between structure and chaos is very thin in these kinds of projects and the danger of going too far in either direction is high. Managers are often inclined to panic when they see apparent chaos and there may be a tendency to tighten control by attempting to apply micro-management. Often this is the least effective tactic because it is generally resisted vigorously, especially by research and design personnel, who tend to value a high level of autonomy as part of their sense of professionalism. It is better to keep reinforcing those areas in the semi-structure which provide the control, such as milestones, roles and responsibilities and then back off.

Examples in practice

Research has focused on how organisations cope with product development projects. Some of the most relevant research in this field has been conducted by Brown and Eisenhardt (1997) who reported in detail on how six high-velocity IT development companies managed projects within an environment of continuous change. Three of those firms had successful product portfolios. These firms had managers that combined limited structure (clear and agreed project priorities, milestones, roles and responsibilities) with extensive communication, future probing and time-linked projects which effected continuous change rather than sporadic or incremental change. The other three, less successful firms, had management approaches which varied from highly structured processes, using traditional project-planning techniques, to the other extreme, very unstructured, almost laissez-faire, processes in which rules played little or no part.

The major lesson to learn from this research is that achieving the right balance to determine the edge of chaos between rule-bound processes, at one end of the spectrum, and totally free-form, unstructured management, at the other, is vital for managing product development projects and possibly also other projects of a similar kind of complexity.

References and further reading

Ashmos, D. P., Duchon, D. and McDaniel, R. R. Jr. (2000), 'Organizational Responses to Complexity: the Effect on Organizational Performance', *Journal of Organizational Change Management*, 13:6, 577-95.

Bastien, D. T. and Hostager, T. J. (1988), 'Jazz as a Process of Organizational Innovation', *Communication Research* 15, 582-602.

Barrett, F. J. and Peplowski, K. (1998), 'Minimal Structures Within a Song: An Analysis of "All of Me"', *Organization Science* 9:5, 558-60.

Beinhoffer, E. (1997), 'Strategy at the Edge of Chaos', *McKinsey Quarterly* 1.

Brown, S. L. and Eisenhardt, K. M. (1997), 'The Art of Continuous Change: Linking Complexity Theory and Time-paced Evolution', *Administrative Science Quarterly* 42:1, 1-34.

Brown, S. L. and Eisenhardt, K. M. (1998) *Competing on the Edge: Strategy as Structured Chaos*. (Boston, MA: Harvard Business School Press).

Burns, T. and Stalker, G.M. (1961), *The Management of Innovation*. (London, UK: Tavistock).

Crutchfield, J. and Young, K. (1990), 'Computation at the Onset of Chaos', in *Entropy, Complexity, and the Physics of Information*, W. Zurek, (ed.), SFI Studies in the Sciences of Complexity, VIII, (Reading, MA: Addison-Wesley) 223-69.

Eisenhardt, K. M. (2004), 'Chapter 42. Speed and Strategic Choice: How Managers Accelerate Decision Making', in Katz, R. (Ed.) *The Human Side of Managing Technological Innovation : A Collection of Readings*. (NY: Oxford University Press).

Eisenhardt, K. M. (2002), 'Has Strategy Changed?', *Sloan Management Review*, MIT, Winter, 88-91.

Eisenhardt, K. M. and Martin, J. A. (2000), 'Dynamic Capabilities. What are they?', *Strategic Management Journal* 21:10-11, 1105-1121.

Eisenhardt, K. M. and Brown, S. L. (1999), 'Time Pacing: Competing in Markets That Won't Stand Still', reprinted in *Harvard Business Review on Managing Uncertainty*. (Boston, MA: Harvard Business School Press).

Gersick, C. (1994), 'Pacing Strategic Change: The Case of a New Venture', *Academy of Management Journal* 32, 274-309.

Hatch, J. (1997), 'Exploring the Empty Spaces of Organizing. How Jazz Can Help Us Understand Organizational Structure', Working paper. (Cranfield, UK: Cranfield School of Management).

Langton, C. G. (1990), 'Computation at the Edge of Chaos', *Physica* D, 42.

March, J. G. (1981), 'Footnotes to Organizational Change', *Administrative Science Quarterly* 26, 563-77.

Meyer, A., Frost, P. J. and Weick, K. E. (1998), 'The Organization Science Jazz Festival: Improvisation as a Metaphor for Organizing: Overture', *Organization Science* 9: 5, Special Issue: Jazz Improvisation and Organizing (Sept.-Oct.), 540-42.

Moorman, C. and Miner, A. S. (1998), 'Organizational Improvisation and Organizational Working Memory', *The Academy of Management Review*, 23, 698-743.

Peters, T. (1994), *The Tom Peters Seminar: Crazy Times Call for Crazy Organizations*. (NY: Vintage Books).

Stacey, R. (1996), *Complexity and Creativity in Organizations*. (San Francisco, CA: Berrett-Koehler Publishers, Inc.).

Tatikonda, M. V. and Rosenthal, S. R. (2000), 'Technology Novelty, Project Complexity, and Product Development Project Execution Success: A Deeper Look at Task Uncertainty in Product Innovation,' *Engineering Management, IEEE Transactions* 47:1, 74-87.

Turner, J. R. (1999), *The Handbook of Project-Based Management*. (London, UK: McGraw-Hill).

Weick, K. E. (1998), 'Improvisation as a Mindset for Organizational Analysis', *Organization Science* 9:5, 543-55.

14 *Multimethodology in Series*

Time to use: Throughout the early stages in the project

Level of difficulty:

Group: Usually facilitated with a group of key stakeholders

Types of complexity suited for:

Problem

Projects can start with goals so ambiguous that they are not amenable to traditional project management breakdown techniques.

Purpose

The majority of traditional project management tools and techniques are based on the assumption that goals can be broken into constituent elements. In cases where goals are not yet defined, it may be necessary to use separate problem structuring techniques before traditional project management techniques are used. This tool describes how the relationship between these two separate sets of techniques can be managed.

Types of complexity

This is particularly suitable for *directionally complex* projects. In directionally complex projects the complexity is often a result of a lack of clear definition of the goals, objectives or purpose of a project. This can be a result of a number of factors, all of which make use of reductionist techniques problematic. This kind of complexity could be the result of intangible goals, which different people are apt to interpret in different ways. In this case, goals are often only qualitatively defined. Another contributing factor can be the implicit and unexpressed goals of significant stakeholders, such as the sponsor. Directional complexity can also be a result of contentious goals, which are being politically debated.

Theoretical background

Two distinct theoretical traditions can be seen influencing the development of a variety of theoretical and practical disciplines, such as project management, systems thinking, operations research and management science. The more common and arguably more respected tradition is based on realist and positivist philosophies, which consider the world to be open, unambiguous and equally accessible to everyone. From this perspective the discovery of objective knowledge and examination of 'facts' is of prime concern. An alternative perspective is based on interpretivist and social constructivist philosophies, and considers our knowledge of the world to be socially contingent, based on a continual process of meaning negotiation. From this perspective, examination of 'interpretation' is of significance.

These two philosophical traditions have given rise to a wide variety of different practical techniques and methodologies. Practical approaches based on the former position can generally be termed problem-solving approaches, while those based on the latter position can be termed problem-structuring approaches. As these names imply, approaches based on these different philosophical positions have different emphases, are suitable for reaching different ends, and tend to produce different kinds of results.

Problem-solving methods tend to emphasise efficiency of delivery and control to predetermined goals. In these approaches, the models that are produced are generally for simulation, to model the real world so that optimal decisions can be made. There tends to be an emphasis on quantitative techniques, and when research is done from this perspective it tends to be distanced from the subject and focused on testing hypotheses. Traditional approaches to project management share these tendencies.

Problem-structuring methods tend to focus on learning and exploration in ambiguous situations. In these approaches, models are produced as aids to discussion, and are used to facilitate debate so that an accommodated position can be reached. There tends to be an emphasis on qualitative techniques. Research based on this kind of perspective generally directly engages with research subjects as participants in the research. These kinds of methods sometimes result in the generation of hypotheses, rather than in testing them, although hypotheses can be explored using these approaches.

A great deal of research has been conducted in the systems-thinking community on the practice of methodological and theoretical pluralism. This branch of research is referred to as Critical Systems Thinking (CST). This field has developed out of the understanding that there is no one best methodology or theory. Rather, theories and methodologies can be considered more or less suited to reaching particular ends.

Many authors have contributed both practical and theoretical insight to this ongoing debate, with a variety of methodologies, models and frameworks for mixing methods populating the literature. Many of the approaches developed as part of CST address practical problems of defining which methods are appropriate for which situations. Jackson and Keys' (1984) System of Systems Methodologies and Flood and Jackson's' (1991) Total Systems Intervention address these issues and continue to have a strong influence on the field today. Other authors focus more on the practicalities of combining approaches. For example, Mingers (1997) categorised nine separate ways in which methods can be combined. Some focus almost exclusively on the practical side of combining methodologies (for example Ormerod, 1997).

However, combining methodologies based on different philosophical perspectives, as in this tool, involves conceptual difficulties that combining methodologies from within a single philosophy does not. When working with multiple philosophical perspectives in a single project, care must be taken to ensure that tools and techniques are used in a way which is consistent with the ideas on which they are based.

Discussion

This tool is a complement to the Multimethodology in Parallel Tool (see next chapter). While the Multimethodology in Parallel Tool is specifically suited to temporal complexity, this tool is designed to address directional complexity.

In situations where the level of directional complexity is too high and where project goals have not been sufficiently defined, it may be possible to separately address the complexity and simplify the situation so that it can then be managed using standard project management techniques. Directional complexity often occurs as a result of not spending sufficient time exploring the project with relevant stakeholders.

In some situations, application of appropriate techniques can resolve directional complexity. A directionally complex project can become a straightforward project if conflicting stakeholder interpretations of key issues are resolved, if tacit stakeholder goals are uncovered and addressed, or if ill-defined goals are clarified.

This tool involves adding a stage to the front of project management, and is often referred to as 'front-ending'. A variety of examples of this kind of practice can be found in the literature. Turner (1999) recommends that in situations where neither the goals for a project nor the methods that will be used to achieve them are well defined, then it may be best to use separate methods to structure the project before traditional project management techniques are used. Miles (1988) recommends something similar, and refers to this kind of practice as 'grafting'.

The tool

At its most basic, this tool involves using a problem-structuring approach to clarify contentious aspects of the project or programme, before traditional project or programme management techniques are used (see Figure 14.1). In this tool, we are resolving the complexity, turning what was once a directionally complex project into a simpler project which is now amenable to standard techniques.

However, this tool is not as simple as it may seem. First, this tool requires someone available to the project that can facilitate a problem-structuring approach. Examples of approaches which may be suitable include Strategic Options Development and Analysis (SODA) (Eden and Ackerman, 2001) and Soft Systems Methodology (SSM) (Checkland, 1999). These are not tools which can be picked up and competently used in a lunch hour. They are methodologies which require practice and possibly even training before they can be used effectively.

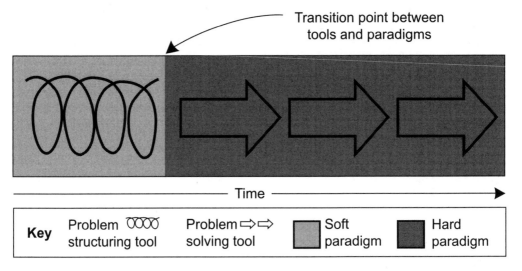

Figure 14.1 Multimethodology in Series process

These different phases of the project or programme will actually require quite different skill sets and ways of thinking. Not everyone is either suited to or comfortable with both problem-structuring and problem-solving methodologies. It may be necessary to engage an outside facilitator, someone from outside the project who will define the goals with you.

In being based on separate philosophical foundations, problem-solving methodologies such as traditional project management, and problem-structuring methodologies such as SODA and SSM embody different perspectives on the world, what is considered valid or useful action, and even what is considered valid or useful knowledge.

The result of this is that you will actively be seeking different goals at different points during the project. One way of thinking about it is to picture the use of problem-structuring methodologies as a mini-project at the start of the standard project. You will need to treat this mini-project as you would any other. You will need to carefully define what you want to achieve out of the mini-project. In this case, this will usually be some variant on developing an adequately, consensually agreed understanding of the context with stakeholders and defining an accommodated position and direction forward.

Evaluation criteria will also need to be defined, so that you know when you have achieved the goals for the use of the problem-structuring methodologies. Evaluation criteria for these kinds of methodologies are often best expressed qualitatively and assessed subjectively. For instance, it might be sufficient to have stated satisfaction by stakeholders with agreed project goals as the main evaluation criteria for the problem-structuring approach used.

It is more important for the project as a whole that the problem-structuring methodology is used well than evaluated positively. Pay attention to what you are trying to achieve in using the problem-structuring methodology. You will have used this methodology to help resolve issues that were preventing you from moving forward with the project. Make sure that the issues are resolved before using traditional project management techniques.

Many projects are delivered under considerable time pressure, and there will likely be a push, either from within or outside the project team, to stop exploring the situation and to get on with delivery. Resist this. Jumping into implementation will only result in costly rework and frustration, and inadequacies with goal definition will become apparent in later stages in the project. It is important that sufficient time is spent to make sure that the complexity has been resolved, before leaving this phase of the project or programme.

Step by step

1. Select a problem-structuring methodology and personnel who will facilitate its use in the project or programme.
2. Be clear about what you want out of the use of the problem-structuring methodology and how this will be assessed.
3. Use the problem-structuring methodology to clarify goals, reach accommodated positions or develop a deeper understanding of the context, as required.
4. Do not rush the process.
5. When the situation has been simplified, and the directional complexity has been resolved, end this project phase and use the insight developed in this phase as the basis for subsequent work using traditional project management techniques.

Caution

This tool is appropriate for directionally complex projects that stay relatively stable, once defined. If the project experiences temporal complexity as well, or instead, then initial exploration may be rendered invalid in later stages of the project; the Multimethodology in Parallel tool is more appropriate for these contexts.

It is important to manage the transition between phases, when using this tool. Problem-structuring and problem-solving methodologies have considerably different practical emphases. In order to gain maximum benefit from this tool, it is necessary to ensure that the problem-solving methodologies are underpinned by a positivist emphasis on control and learning, while the problem-structuring methodologies are underpinned by an emphasis on learning, exploration and facilitation. Using problem-structuring methodologies, while keeping the positivist emphases, will limit the effectiveness of the problem-structuring methodologies in this tool.

Examples in practice

There are many examples in the academic literature describing projects which could be considered examples of the use of this tool. For instance, Neal (1995) provides an example where SSM was used with traditional project management practice. SSM was used as a requirements definition phase for the project, to help clients define what it was they were looking for and to help avoid rework later in the project.

Lai (2000) also provides an example of SSM being used before project management techniques. This example is set in an information systems development project in the Hong Kong public sector. In this instance, SSM was used to develop the project team's understanding of stakeholder needs in the light of the then recent transfer of Hong Kong from a British colony to a Special Administrative Region of the People's Republic of China.

References and further reading

Checkland, P. (1999), 'Soft Systems Methodology: A 30-year Retrospective', in Checkland, P. and Scholes, J. (eds) *Soft Systems Methodology in Action*, A1-A65. (Chichester, UK: John Wiley & Sons).

Eden, C. and Ackerman, F. (2001), 'SODA – The Principles', in: Rosenhead, J. and Mingers, J. (eds) *Rational Analysis for a Problematic World Revisited: Problem Structuring Methods for Complexity, Uncertainty and Conflict.* (Chichester, UK: John Wiley & Sons).

Flood, R. and Jackson, M. (1991), *Creative Problem Solving: Total Systems Intervention.* (NY: John Wiley & Sons).

Jackson, M. and Keys, P. (1984), 'Towards a System of Systems Methodologies', *Journal of the Operational Research* Society 35, 473-486.

Lai, L. (2000), 'An Integration of Systems Science Methods and Object-oriented Analysis for Determining Organizational Information Requirements', *Systems Research and Behavioral Science* 17, 205-228.

Miles, R. (1988), 'Combining "Soft" and "Hard" Systems Practice: Grafting or Embedding?' *Journal of Applied Systems Analysis* 15, 55-60.

Mingers, J. (1997), 'Multi-paradigm Multimethodology', in Mingers, J. and Gill, A. (eds.) *Multimethodology: The Theory and Practice of Combining Management Science Methodologies.* (Chichester, UK: John Wiley & Sons), 1-20.

Neal, R. A. (1995), 'Project Definition: The Soft-systems Approach', *International Journal of Project Management* 13, 5-9.

Ormerod, R. (1997), 'The Design of Organizational Intervention', *International Journal of Management Science* 25, 415-435.

Turner, J. R. (1999), *The Handbook of Project-based Management.* (London, UK: McGraw-Hill).

15 *Multimethodology in Parallel*

Time to use:	For the duration of the project
Level of difficulty:	
Group:	Single person or group
Types of complexity suited for:	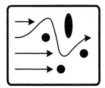

Problem

In some projects, goals are continuously changing in response to contextual influence outside project control, or when multiple persistent uncertainties threaten the project.

Purpose

This tool aids in ongoing learning about the environment in response to regular contextual change. The tool is particularly relevant to the process of continually re-defining project goals, and risk management. Traditional approaches to project management tend to work on the assumptions that goals and risks are defined once during the project, then monitored. In many cases these assumptions are not met and these needs can be better addressed using separate problem-structuring techniques. This tool describes a way in which the relationship between project management techniques and problem-structuring techniques can be managed in a project.

Types of complexity

Temporally complex projects face ongoing contextual change throughout the life of the project. The fitness landscape changes, but this change is neither constant nor predictable.

As a result of this, where the edge of chaos lies for the project also changes. When the project context changes, it will be more effective for the project team to be more exploratory and open to input from the environment. The edge of chaos will be closer to chaos, and the boundary for the system will be diffuse. At other points, when the context is relatively stable, it may be more effective for the project team to focus on delivery, efficiency and control. At these times, the edge of chaos will be closer to order, and the boundary for the system will be closer and less permeable. This tool provides a way to consciously adapt the focus of the project team in relation to ongoing change within the project environment.

Theoretical background

As discussed in the Multimethodology in Series Tool, two distinct theoretical traditions can be seen influencing the development of a variety of theoretical and practical disciplines, such as project management, systems thinking, operations research and management science. These traditions have given rise to two groups of approaches: problem-solving approaches, and problem-structuring approaches.

Problem-solving approaches, such as traditional project management, are based on realist and positivist philosophies. These approaches emphasise efficiency of delivery, control and objectivity, and tend to involve quantitative and reductionist techniques. Problem-structuring approaches are based on interpretive and social constructivist philosophies. These approaches emphasise learning, exploration and negotiation. Knowledge is viewed as intersubjective, where subjective views about the world are tempered by social processes.

The differences between these traditions are discussed in greater depth in the Multimethodology in Series chapter. Midgley (2000) and Jackson (2000) also provide excellent discussion of how these traditions have influenced a variety of practical disciplines.

Most of the research on the combination of interpretivist and positivist philosophies, and problem-solving and problem-structuring methodologies, has involved sequential combination, where methodologies or philosophies are used one after the other, in clearly defined phases. The Multimethodology in Series Tool is an example of this. The thinking behind this is that different methodologies and philosophies provide different benefits that are appropriate to different project phases.

However, evidence from practice is suggesting that in some projects, it is not feasible to divide the project into neat phases. Indeed, in temporally complex projects forcing a division into clear phases can cause problems when external factors change and a change in direction is required. It can be more beneficial to use multiple methodologies and philosophies in parallel throughout the project, instead of limiting them to separate phases. In this way benefits from different approaches can be gained at any stage of the project. The approach taken can be fluidly adapted to meet the needs of the situation.

This tool builds upon the work of Miles (1988), who investigated the possibility of using Checkland's (1981) Soft Systems Methodology (SSM) in combination with information systems modelling techniques. In Miles' research it was assumed that interpretivist philosophies governed the entire project. Research by the authors has shown that a positivist perspective can also be of benefit to temporally complex projects, and that both philosophies and methodologies can be used in parallel within a single project.

Discussion

This approach is a complement to the Multimethodology in Series Tool. While the Multimethodology in Series Tool is specifically suited to *directional* complexity, this tool is designed to address *temporal* complexity.

Traditional approaches to project management tend to assume that goals and risks are easily definable. In the case of goals, it is then often assumed that they can be easily decomposed into their constituent elements. In the case of risks, it is generally assumed that once defined, tracking risks is unproblematic. In many projects involving temporal complexity, these assumptions do not hold.

Many projects are subject to substantial environmental uncertainty and change. These changes can affect everything from the rationale behind the project, to the political support afforded the project, to the minutiae of goal specification. In extreme cases the uncertainty may rise to the point where the project team is expected to deliver even though it is unclear whether the project, or even the organisation, will exist in a week's time. As a general rule, the more political the project, the more likely it is to be subject to temporal complexity.

Working on a temporally complex project is a balancing act between investigating options and development of solutions. It is important not to commit too much effort to developing one particular solution, as there is too great a risk that early commitment to one development option will result in later rework. At the same time, it is important not to spend too much time exploring options and waiting for the situation to stabilise. The project context may never stabilise, but it will always be necessary to deliver.

In temporally complex projects, it is often necessary to work on multiple fronts, where multiple aspects of the project may be concurrently developed. The key to doing this successfully is to focus development work on aspects of the project which are relatively stable, while focusing exploratory work on aspects of the project subject to uncertainty. Which aspects are subject to which states will vary throughout the life of the project.

Particular care must be taken when the project also exhibits structural, technical or directional complexity. Temporal complexity will make management of these other kinds of complexity more problematic, as the temporal element will add persistence through time, potentially preventing these other kinds of complexity from being resolved. What will instead be required is ongoing monitoring and management.

The tool

This tool involves using two (or possibly more) methodologies, and their associated philosophical bases, in parallel throughout a project. One methodology should be a problem-structuring methodology, and one should be a problem-solving methodology. Use of the two methodologies is then alternated in a dynamic way, responding to change and anticipating needs.

The traditional approaches to project management provide many examples of problem-solving tools. They are used to solve a predefined problem as effectively and efficiently as possible. Examples of problem-structuring tools include SSM, Strategic Options Development and Analysis (SODA) (Eden and Ackerman, 2001) and Cognitive Mapping (Ackerman & Eden, 2001), discussed in the Multimethodology in Series chapter.

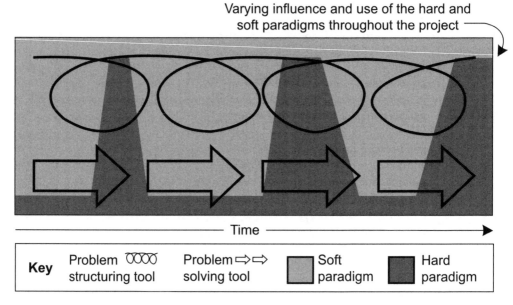

Figure 15.1 Multimethodology in Parallel process

In the Multimethodology in Series Tool, because the process of problem structuring can be treated as a separate phase of the project, it is possible and desirable to bring in an outside facilitator with competence in a problem-structuring methodology to help with a finite area of work – structuring the problem. In the Multimethodology in Parallel Tool however, members of the project team will require competence in a problem-structuring methodology, as it will be used throughout the project, at irregular intervals. This will require training the project team in the use of selected problem-structuring methodologies and action learning approaches.

As the project or programme is subject to temporal complexity, it will be necessary to remain constantly aware of changes in the environment. Changes can provide both threats and opportunities, and if the project is to be successful, it is necessary to stay abreast of these. Using a problem-structuring methodology will aid this process, as such methodologies are designed to encourage learning and exploration.

Insight gained from use of the problem-structuring methodology will help direct the use of the problem-solving methodology. The problem-structuring methodology will help develop understanding within the project team of which aspects of the project are uncertain and cannot yet be defined, and which aspects of the project are stable at that time, and are thus amenable to problem-solving approaches.

The project team should alternate between these two kinds of methodologies, progressing some aspects of the project, then checking the environment for changes. If the situation has changed, then it may be necessary to pause work on the aspects of the project that were previously being progressed until the contextual uncertainty has stabilised, and to work on another aspect of the project.

There are a variety of ways in which this can be managed. It is possible to formally change between methodologies at structured and predetermined intervals. However, as the project is temporally complex it is difficult to tell beforehand what an appropriate interval for changes would be. It is more effective if the change between methodologies is dynamic, in response to emergent needs. In order to do this, you will need to stay actively aware of changes within the project, using problem-solving methodologies when, and in places where, the situation is stable; and using problem-structuring methodologies when, and in situations where, the project is uncertain.

When working with a group, it can be useful to set up protocols for how and in which circumstances the project team will change between methodologies. It will also be necessary to explain to the group the purpose behind using problem-structuring methodologies throughout the project, so that team members do not feel that time which could better be spent on delivery is being wasted on further exploration. Depending on personality and the aspects of the project on which different team members are working, not all team members will see or experience the complexity at the same time.

It may be necessary for the project team to work on multiple aspects of the project in parallel. However, this is a different concept to 'network crashing' a common project management technique where multiple independent tasks are worked on in parallel to increase speed of delivery, and different to 'fast-tracking' where a task is initiated before the one logically preceding it has been officially completed.

In this case, the parallelism is not to increase speed, but to increase opportunity. With multiple aspects of the project being concurrently developed, contextual change affecting one area might not stall the project as a whole, and work may be able to be continued in other areas. The balance between the use of problem-structuring and problem-solving methodologies would then adapt accordingly.

Furthermore, parallelism provides multiple delivery opportunities. Unlike many other kinds of project, in temporally complex projects timing of delivery is more important than speed. A colleague of the authors' refers to this as 'waiting for the planets to align'. It may only be by having multiple parallel options that the project team can be in a position to deliver when the opportunity presents itself.

Step by step

1. Train the project team to use selected problem-structuring and action-learning approaches. Seek advice from experienced facilitators in the field.
2. When aspects of the project stabilise, use problem-solving methodologies to progress aspects of the project towards delivery.
3. When part of the project becomes stalled as a result of contextual change, apply a problem-structuring methodology to clarify or develop understanding.
4. Repeat 2 and 3, progressing multiple aspects of the project towards possible solutions.
5. When the situation sufficiently stabilises, be in a position to deliver an adequate solution quickly.

Caution

Phase changes are often used as gateways or review points in projects, when go/no-go decisions are made. However, this model of the project life cycle does not include specific phases. An alternative way of checking the ongoing viability of the project, something which is a serious concern for a temporally complex project, is to ensure considerable stakeholder involvement.

Your stakeholders, if practically and regularly involved in the project, will be in a position to evaluate project viability. After all, your major stakeholders may be contributing to some of the factors which create the temporal complexity, or be more informed about the nature of the complexity than you are. Keep your stakeholders close!

Be clear and explicit about which methodology you are using at which time. These different kinds of methodologies are based on different philosophical positions, and entail very different emphases. Being explicit about the perspective you are working from will help others interpret your actions and to work with you.

Watch your own actions and those of the project team for indicators of which perspectives have predominantly been informing action. For many people, especially those who are action-oriented, problem-solving methodologies are more comfortable. It is the experience of the authors that there may also be reluctance to engage in problem-structuring activities towards the perceived end of the project. This can be related to a desire to just get the job done and avoid learning anything that might suggest that rework is required and the end is not as close as anticipated.

Examples in practice

One example of the use of this tool involved the combination of project management techniques and SSM in an information systems strategy development project in a public sector health agency in New South Wales, Australia. The project was set within the context of ongoing uncertainty regarding legislative change, potential relocation of the agency, and uncertainty regarding obligations to align with a variety of Government development initiatives (Pollack, 2005).

The project team regularly swapped between methodologies, progressing different aspects of the project when it was possible to do so. Although multiple different options were progressed at different times, and rework was required at some stages throughout the project, the final products delivered were appropriate to the agency's needs. The project has been shown to have provided considerable benefit to the organisation, in terms of effective strategic direction.

Another interesting example involved the UK taxation office (Brown et. al., 2006). In this case the project team regularly alternated between problem-structuring and problem-solving methodologies, as a way of successively exploring the context of the situation, then focusing on specific issues. This approach was used to provide recommendations for development to the taxation office.

References and further reading

Ackerman, F. and Eden, C. (2001), 'SODA – Journey Making and Mapping in Practice', in Rosenhead, J. and Mingers, J. (eds) *Rational Analysis for a Problematic World Revisited.* (Chichester, UK: John Wiley & Sons), 43–60.
Brown, J., Cooper, C. and Pidd, M. (2006), 'A Taxing Problem: The Complementary Use of Hard and Soft OR in the Public Sector', *European Journal of Operational Research* 172:2, 666–79.
Checkland, P. (1999), 'Soft Systems Methodology: A 30-year Retrospective', in Checkland, P. and Scholes, J. (eds) *Soft Systems Methodology in Action.* (Chichester, UK: John Wiley & Sons), A1–A65.
Eden, C. and Ackerman, F. (2001), 'SODA – The Principles', in Rosenhead, J. and Mingers, J. (eds) *Rational Analysis for a Problematic World Revisited: Problem Structuring Methods for Complexity, Uncertainty and Conflict.* (Chichester: John Wiley & Sons).
Jackson, M. (2000), *Systems Approaches to Management.* (NY: Plenum Publishers).

Midgley, G. (2000), *Systemic Intervention: Philosophy, Methodology, and Practice.* (NY: Plenum Publishers).

Miles, R. (1988), 'Combining "Soft" and "Hard" Systems Practice: Grafting or Embedding?' *Journal of Applied Systems Analysis* 15, 55-60.

Pidd, M. (2004), 'Bringing it all Together', in Pidd, M. (ed.) *Systems Modelling: Theory and Practice*, (Chichester, UK: John Wiley & Sons), 197-207.

Pollack, J. B. F. (2005), *Project pluralism: Combining the Hard and Soft Paradigms in IS/IT Strategy Development in the NSW Public Sector*, PhD Thesis. (Sydney, Australia: University of Technology Sydney).

16 *Virtual Gates*

Time to use:	At least once per project phase.
Level of difficulty:	
Group:	Involves the executive management group
Types of complexity suited for:	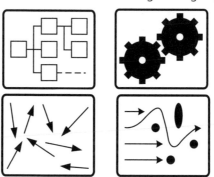

Problem

In large projects, risks can be triggered in such a way that positive reinforcement causes emergent properties of the system to have an avalanche effect on the project, reaching a point of no return when the only option is to close down the project.

Purpose

This tool was designed to help overcome these barriers by communicating a different ethos for these kinds of complex projects, which promotes and supports vigilant analysis and monitoring of emergent characteristics caused by the triggering of non-linear events.

Types of complexity

It is appropriate for any type of project complexity where the size and duration of the project are great enough to exhibit structural complexity.

Structural complexity, which can be found in any system that has many activities and many interdependencies, is particularly difficult to manage. Once a number of non-linear series of events have been triggered, the emergent properties, if unchecked at the right time, can cause what amounts to a phase change. This usually results in the project being altered significantly and sometimes being terminated. Added to these escalating problems may be reluctance on the part of promoters, owners and project personnel to acknowledge that they are approaching a point of no return.

Theoretical background

Risk analysis is the basis for risk management. Risk management devises strategies for reducing risks and treating risk events if they are triggered. Complex projects need very large contingencies in order to provide for cost overruns which are extremely likely to occur unless conditions can be guaranteed to be held stable and in many cases this is an impossible ask. Conditions which are very likely to change during a protracted project life cycle are political and regulatory environments, capital-market pressures, political and sector-policy conditions. Recently the World Bank commissioned a study of 92 projects. The study found that very few projects in the study demonstrated 'good practice' risk analysis (World Bank ECON Report, 29-30). Normally contingency for projects range in the order from ±10 per cent to ±20 per cent. Many scholars are now recommending much higher contingency sums. The Apollo aerospace programme is considered to be an exemplary case of megaproject planning and implementation. The cost overrun on the budgeted cost of US$21 billion was only 5 per cent. As Morris and Hough (1987) have pointed out, the contingency was US$8 billion. However, there is a widely held belief that setting high contingencies can invoke an atmosphere of complacency which might result in inefficiencies and a relaxation of rigour in project performance.

In best-practice risk assessment, the risk situations that might cause the project to change from being viable to being non-viable are identified and evaluated. The World Bank refers to these as 'switching values', which should be calculated for key variables. The 'switching value' is the level of the variable at which the project switches from being viable to being non-viable (World Bank, ECON Report, 22). However we would argue that it is not just the switching values that are important but the causal loops which can emerge in complex projects and which can push a number of the variables to a point of no return, causing a cascading effect as one risk reaching its switching value triggers another. Therefore we recommend that scenarios which illustrate the worst possible cases be investigated using both multi-variate analysis and causal mapping of the variables. The results might lead to the setting of more realistic contingencies for these high-risk projects.

Discussion

Currently it is common practice to define the project life cycle in terms of phases. At the end of each phase is a 'gate' with the function of promoting a formal appraisal of the project and a decision to continue as planned, re-plan, re-define or terminate the project is based on the appraisal of the project status to date. Planning projects to have multiple project phases and associated gates is widely recognised to be a useful mechanism for project control.

The project phases and associated gates are usually pre-determined based on logical handovers or funding cycles but less frequently on analysis of cost implications of emergent risk patterns which have been triggered by non-linear event scenarios. Instead we propose the pre-determination of potential or 'virtual gates' in the project that can be closed in response to the kind of analysis that might predict at which levels the project needs to be re-evaluated and possibly even re-defined. Thus the virtual gate is triggered in response to indicators, such as rapidly escalating costs, that have been predicted as levels beyond which the costs would be likely to increase exponentially if the project is not stopped and re-appraised.

We argue that in addition to increasing the planned number of phases and their associated gates in a complex project, the propensity for virtual gates, which are triggered by certain combinations of conditions, be planned into the project and communicated so that the process of monitoring these emergent conditions and then triggering the virtual gates becomes part of the project ethos.

NASA's flight systems and ground support projects are often the most visible and complex of NASA's product lines. Because of this, these projects must emphasise safety and mission success as primary drivers in order to justify the substantial time and resources they require. These projects typically have formulation periods of one to three years because of the need to conduct system analyses, select the best mission concept and retire technological risks to the point where implementation can begin. They typically have even longer implementation periods for design, development, testing and operations. Due to this, NASA has found it useful to decompose the project life cycle for flight systems and ground support projects into more incremental pieces that allow managers to assess management and engineering progress. Consequently, the document referenced (Flight Systems and Ground Support Projects) re-institutes the NASA project life cycle consisting of Phases A through F.

We recognise that there are significant disincentives to this approach. One is the difficulty in stopping project activities once contracts have been let and work has commenced. Contracts for work associated with the project should be written with this in mind. Contracts are often written with a 'termination for convenience' clause which gives the principal the right to terminate the contract if emergent conditions make the continuation of the contract untenable. Once the contract is discharged costs are normally calculated to the nearest milestone with compensation paid to enable the contractor to close and be paid for work done to date. This would be prescribed in the tender documents, and contractors would be advised to pass this risk on to sub-contractors. A slightly different approach might involve the contract being drafted in such a way that a confluence of certain events might be identified as part of the risk-allocation process and the effect on the contract identified in advance.

It goes without saying that during project implementation vigilant monitoring of risks is essential. However, standard risk registers are essentially lists, which are linear-thinking tools. It is extremely difficult to effectively monitor all risks in a proactive and integrated way from standard risk registers which may cite hundreds or even thousands of risks. If monitoring of the risks is difficult then understanding the causal links and possibilities for escalation due to potential positive feedback loops is impossible. It is essential that tools be adopted that promote connected thinking patterns, such as causal mapping and analysis. Software is now available to assist mapping of complex projects. For smaller projects mapping can be done by the relevant groups of stakeholders with sticky notes and felt pens and then translated to a simple software programme for preservation and monitoring.

Causal mapping has been suggested by scholars as one possibly useful procedure for analysis (Williams et al., 2003). We suggest the use of causal mapping with the addition of virtual gates which can be accommodated in contracts and identified when a confluence of risks is triggered. If people know that in addition to the defined project phases which should have control gates, there are other potential gates – virtual gates which can be closed when a confluence of risks is triggered – this might have the effect of increasing the vigilance of the monitoring process.

As with most aspects of project complexity the causes of cost overruns are many (see Flyvbjerg et al., 2003). Many of these cost overruns have been shown to have been influenced by perceptions or by key decision makers and promoters failing to believe the worst. Therefore it is vital that a new ethos be communicated for these kinds of complex projects, which not only promotes and supports vigilant analysis and monitoring of emergent and non-linear events, but also communicates that at some point the project might have to be terminated or radically re-defined if switching values are reached. The project life-cycle model for the project must support management of the emergent risks associated with such projects. This can be assisted through periodic revisiting of the life-cycle model, and breaking the life cycle down further, as emergent patterns of risks become apparent.

There are both time and cost implications associated with this model. Increased project duration overall and project cost reductions from letting huge contracts for the entire project may be offset by the ability to achieve tighter control and a higher level of confidence such that a healthy return of investment will be assured. Especially in the public sector there has been a tendency for the client project manager to take a hands-off approach by letting huge contracts which have long time frames. This would not work for this model. Using this model requires project directors/managers to commit to close and frequent monitoring of the project, and the project governance structure to support rapid escalation of issues and decision making.

The tool

The tool is actually a model which combines a number of existing, well-established tools:

- causal mapping to identify and assess emergent risk patterns;
- cost modelling using standard financial-modelling techniques to determine switching values;
- project organisation structure – involving decomposition techniques – utilizing the concept of virtual gates;
- procurement strategies to facilitate termination if risks accumulate;
- communication of the model – the key.

A form of causal mapping, known as Cognitive Mapping has been developed to a high level of sophistication for analysis of projects by Ackerman et al. (1997). The illustration in the example at the end of this chapter is a very simple example of causal mapping using sticky notes. Large projects might benefit substantially from the use of software (see Ackerman and Eden, 2001).

Standard financial-modelling techniques (which are not included here but are fully covered in a range of other texts) are then applied to the emergent patterns of risks identified in the causal map to establish the potential cost overruns in relation to return on investment. Switching values are determined. These indicate the cost overrun levels which, if exceeded, make the project no longer viable in its current form.

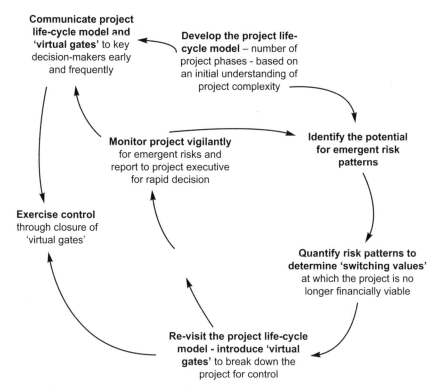

Figure 16.1 Virtual Gate process model

A project phase model is used initially and then revised to identify the structure of the project life cycle and the number of phases or control gates for the project at which decisions for procurement management are made. The model can be based on the type of complexity and anticipated risk patterns for the next phase. It may be agreed that the project would be better managed as a number of smaller projects in sequence, as a linear programme. In that way it might be easier to conceptualise the differences with different management strategies determined for each project. The project structure is very important in that it sets expectations. If the project is able to be broken down into a series of small projects, this significantly reduces the level of complexity – it is much easier to achieve the promised goals for each project. It is also easier to terminate the big project at the conclusion of one of the smaller ones, with some tangible deliverables, less loss of face and reduced potential financial impact.

If, however, the project cannot be broken down into separate smaller sequential projects then the phase breakdown and use of a programme structure can assist in determining different procurement strategies for each phase or project within the programme. Procurement strategies should reflect the type of complexity and include clauses allowing termination for convenience if switching values are reached. This is a less attractive option as any termination clause applied mid-way will involve the awarding of costs to the service provider or contractor for work partly committed plus loss of potential profit.

Virtual gates are potential gates that can be introduced in the project life-cycle model as the project progresses. Effectively they break up the project into smaller and smaller units for management and control. The virtual gate approach involves frequent and vigilant monitoring of risks, using a technique like causal mapping which can track patterns of risk, coupled with excellent communication. A termination for convenience clause in a contract should be exercised as a last resort.

Communication is the key to the success of this method. First is the idea that the project must have a structure which is geared to managing emergent patterns; risks need to be firmly and persistently communicated to the key stakeholders to prevent them from sliding into a false sense of security. This condition – now known as 'groupthink' following the analysis of the Challenger disaster, in which key personnel were unable to make others listen to vital messages about potential project failure – is very common on projects where a number of groups have high stakes in the project delivery. Second, issues and the likely emergent patterns of risk resulting must be communicated quickly to decision makers who must be prepared for rapid decision making. The pace of communication is vital as positive feedback loops can escalate rapidly.

Step by step

1. Determine the number of phases for the project.
2. Identify risks and potential positive loops using a causal-mapping technique, such as cognitive mapping.
3. Repeat this for each project phase.
4. Calculate the switching values beyond which the project is no longer viable.
5. Select an appropriate procurement method for each phase or each sub-project. Include termination clauses in all tender documents and contracts for supply of goods or services.
6. As the project progresses re-visit the phase model, breaking it down further as required using virtual gates.
7. Communicate the concept of switching values that can trigger virtual gates to the key stakeholders, including suppliers and sub-contractors.
8. Repeat the mapping process frequently throughout the project to assess emergent situations.
9. Communicate issues which might result in positive feedback loops and consequent emergent risks for immediate decision-making.

Caution

It will be difficult to predict when the switching values might be reached which would trigger the contract provisions; therefore it is essential that emergent risk patterns be vigilantly monitored.

Groupthink is a real phenomenon in practice and in the belief that things will right themselves, project teams and key decision makers succumb to denial. If the situation is allowed to progress beyond a certain point the project is unlikely to be able to be resurrected. Therefore communication of the concept is key to its success.

Reiterating earlier concerns, there are time and cost implications for this model. Increased project duration overall and project cost reductions from letting huge contracts for the entire project may be offset by the ability to achieve tighter control and a higher level of confidence that a healthy return of investment will be assured.

A hands-off approach by letting huge contracts which have long time frames would not work for this model. Using this model requires project directors/managers to commit to close and frequent monitoring of the project, and the project governance structure to support rapid escalation of issues and decision making.

Examples in practice

In a construction project, such a confluence of events causing non-linear escalation of the risks might have included: unforeseen adverse site conditions requiring the footings to be much deeper than anticipated, closely followed by unexpected wet weather causing flooding of the site, preventing piling from continuing as scheduled. Unforeseen site conditions would be expected to result in cost increases and delays. However when the weather suddenly changed during a particular project and there were unseasonable rainstorms, this resulted in further delays and costs associated with loss of time and repairing or replacing work already completed. Both of these events contributed substantially to increases in costs and delay construction. Due to a sudden drop in interest rates and the deployment of labour to other sites as a result of a temporary building boom, these two risks were closely followed by temporary but significant labour shortages. Labour costs therefore escalated and the project manager sought labour elsewhere. However, political pressures unexpectedly forced the government to temporarily withdraw access to short-entry visas for guest workers. On top of this an accident on site had been caused by the wet weather.

One or two of these events might have been able to be managed within the project contingency; however, if all were triggered, the combined effect switched the project from being viable to being non-viable. The confluence of these five variables was such that the project reached a tipping point at which it should have stopped and re-evaluated.

The causal map shown in Figure 16.2 is a simple way of understanding the possible effects that these events may have had. Each point of confluence on the map where a number of arrows descend on an item can be evaluated in terms of time delays and cost implications. Time delays can be converted to cost variances using tools like Earned Value Analysis. Using standard financial-modelling techniques the cumulative range of cost effects can then be estimated for worst-cost scenarios.

A causal map will help to uncover any positive feedback loops which will have the potential themselves to spiral out of control. In this simple example there is a positive feedback loop around the unexpected wet weather (shaded area on the right-hand side of the image) which caused damage to existing structures, which brought delays, which in turn made the project more vulnerable to damage from wet weather and so it continued around the loop. Each time there was a cost and time implication.

Another two positive feedback loops can be found in relation to the contractor's position (shaded area on the upper-left-hand side of the image). Here the mounting claims caused legal disputes which, together with other rising costs, drove the contractor into a cash-flow crisis, which in turn delayed the project, which was already delayed while the disputes were being settled. The longer the delays, the more likely it was that the contractor would go bankrupt and the project would be delayed for an even longer period. Each delay on a project will have implications for the project viability. For instance, the project might be a commercial venture whose profitability is based on being able to recover costs as soon as possible from sales or leasing of the facility. During this process the interactions between the people and within

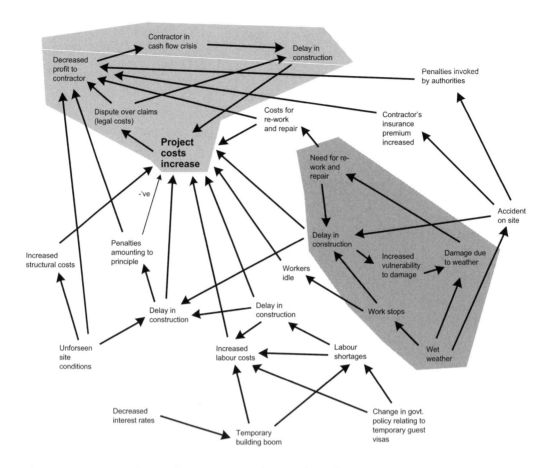

Figure 16.2 Causal map for a construction project that went wrong

individuals themselves also went through a phase change. Probably as a result of impending litigation, people started behaving differently to each other, which severely exacerbated already strained relations. The litigation cycle itself added significantly to the complexity. Eventually the contractor experienced a cash-flow crisis that further delayed construction and the further delays in construction caused an escalation of project costs which eventually forced the contractor into bankruptcy. The legal disputes are continuing and the project owner is now also facing bankruptcy.

Added to these escalating problems was reluctance on the part of promoters, owners and even some project personnel to acknowledge that they were approaching a point of no return.

In hindsight it would have been possible to break the project down into more phases for tighter control. However the developer was putting pressure on the project team to deliver in the earliest time. Standard risk-identification techniques were used but they failed to capture the emergent patterns of risk. These, and the potential for disastrous consequences, were not communicated to the developer as both the project team and the head contractor were keen to take the job. If the possible emergent patterns of risk had been identified and quantified they might have been mitigated slightly, but more importantly it would have been more likely that they would have been recognised. If the developer had been appraised of the results of positive feedback loops in the beginning, he might have been more responsive when alarm bells were finally rung. If the project had been procured as a series of smaller contracts and the contract contained appropriate termination clauses the project could have been suspended until conditions stabilised and it was possible to continue under a new contract.

References and further reading

Ackermann, F. and Eden, C. (2001), 'Using Causal Mapping with Computer Based Group Support System Technology for Eliciting an Understanding of Failure in Complex Projects: Some Implications for Organizational Research', *American Academy of Management Conference*, August, (Washington, AAM).

Ackerman, F., Eden, C. and Williams, T. (1997), 'Modelling for Litigation: Mixing Qualitative and Quantitative Approaches', *Interfaces* 2, 48-65.

AS/NZS4360: 1999, *Australian Standard for Risk Management.* (Australia: Standards Australia).

Eden, C. and Ackerman, F. (2004), 'Cognitive Mapping Expert Views for Policy Analysis in the Public Sector,' *European Journal of Operational Research* 152, 615-30.

Eden, C. (2004), 'Analyzing Cognitive Maps to Help Structure Issues or Problems', *European Journal of Operational Research.* 159, 673-86.

Eden, C. and Ackerman, F. (1998), *Making Strategy, The Journey of Strategic Management.* (London, UK: Sage).

Flyvbjerg, B., Bruzelius, N. and Rothengatter, W. (2003), *Megaprojects and Risk: An Anatomy of Ambition.* (Cambridge, UK: Cambridge University Press).

Morris, P and Hough, G. (1987), *The Anatomy of Major Projects: A Study of the Reality of Project Management.* (NY: John Wiley & Sons).

NASA (undated), 'Flight Systems and Ground Support Projects, 6.1.1', *Procedural Requirements* (accessed 20-12-06), http://nodis3.gsfc.nasa.gov/displayDir.cfm?Internal_ID=N_PR_7120_005C_&page_name=Chapter6.

World Bank (undated), 'Economic Analysis of Projects: Towards a Results-Oriented Approach to Evaluation', *ECON Report*, (Washington, DC: World Bank) 29-30.

Williams, T., Ackermann, F. and Eden, C. (2003), 'Structuring a Delay and Disruption Claim: An Application of Cause-mapping and System Dynamics', *European Journal of Operational Research.* 148:1, 192-204.

Williams, T. (2002), *Modelling Complex Projects.* (Chichester, UK: John Wiley & Sons).

17 *Risk Interdependencies*

Time to use:	20–60 minutes
Level of difficulty:	
Group:	Normally the project manager would engage a group of key stakeholders in this process
Types of complexity suited for:	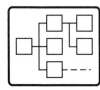 

Problem

For use in small- to medium-sized projects when it is necessary to monitor and track multiple risks that may be interdependent and have compound influences involving positive or negative feedback.

Purpose

This tool provides a simple way to facilitate the process of identifying and monitoring significant risks and the interdependencies between them. It aids in the process of identifying where multiple risks have the potential to compound upon each other, requiring special attention.

The intention is that this tool is a quick-to-use addition to standard risk-identification techniques that can be introduced at any meeting as part of the standard review of the risk/ issues log at the regular project status review meetings. It can also be used by the project team to identify any interdependencies which should be flagged in project status reports. In this respect it is a proactive tool, the aim being to identify potential risk hot-spots caused by the coming together of a number of risks before they arise so that preventative action may be taken to remove or mitigate the sources of risk or the interdependencies.

Types of complexity

Structural complexity: In structurally complex projects, complexity results from the number of interconnected factors. Although when taken in isolation, any of these factors may only be typified by simple relationships, when taken en masse the number of interconnections between factors give rise to complexity and emergent effects which are not apparent at a simple level. This tool helps in analysing interconnections between risks, so that areas where risks are likely to compound and create emergent risks can be identified.

Technical complexity: Technical complexity often involves significant risk associated with uncertainty concerning how particular design issues will be addressed, the time that it will take to develop adequate solutions and the costs that will be involved. Risks in one area can easily compound with others to create emergent risks, potentially affecting the viability of the project as a whole. The relationships between risks need to be managed, so that unforeseen factors do not either force design decisions away from ideal solutions or threaten the project as a whole.

Directional complexity: When different stakeholders perceive different risks, this can lead to them placing significantly different emphases on what they see as central to the project. This can in turn result in differing political agendas, creating directional complexity. This tool helps in creating a mutually developed understanding of risks within the project or programme, helping to resolve directional complexity.

Theoretical background

The main elements of the risk management process are as follows (see for example (AS/NZS4360: 1999):

- establish the context;
- identify the risks;
- analyse the risks;
- evaluate the risks;
- treat the risks.

This is an iterative process involving continuous communication and consultation and monitoring and review (see also Edwards and Bowen, 2005).

Risk identification is considered by many authors as the key to risk management. Risk identification methods can be broadly grouped as 'top-down' or 'bottom-up' approaches (Uher, 1993).

TOP-DOWN APPROACHES

- *Case-based approach* Uses experiences from similar projects, implemented under similar conditions as the starting point for identifying risk events.

- *Aggregate or bottom-line approach* Technique which simply adds on a certain percentage to the cost for contingency.

BOTTOM-UP APPROACHES

- *Prompt or check lists* Risks are identified from a list of categories previously defined based on past experience.
- *Brainstorming* Divergent-thinking technique, in which participants generate many issues without judgement. Classification takes place after the brainstorming sessions have generated the ideas.
- *Breakdown structure* The work, product or organisational breakdown structures are often used as the basis for identifying risks associated with the elements in the structure.
- *Flow chart* Graphic version of a process showing sequences of tasks and decision points is used as the basis for identifying where risk events may occur.
- *Delphi technique* Experts are identified and consulted individually in a systematic manner. Information is pooled. The technique's key characteristics include anonymity of response, use of experts and controlled feedback to respondents. The method can be used to structure group communication for the discussion of specific issues.
- *Scenario building* The formulation of risk management scenarios can be a complicated and iterative process. It consists of many different steps starting from the first conceptual idea to a final cost-efficient risk management scenario that is accepted by all stakeholders.
- *Causal mapping and cognitive mapping* A causal map can be used to capture the interrelationships between risk items, and helps towards a deeper understanding of the causality. Cognitive Mapping, primarily developed by Colin Eden and Fran Ackerman (for example 2004) is an operational research technique designed to help structure messy or complex data for problem solving. It is founded upon George Kelly's theory of personal constructs (1955), and inquires into the interrelationships between factors identified as significant to a situation. As with Systems Dynamics, Cognitive Mapping emphasises the significance of positive and negative feedback and causal loops. Ackerman, Eden and Williams (1997) and Williams (2002) have explored the use of cognitive mapping in conjunction with other software systems in reference to modelling very large complex projects.

Of the approaches to risk identification listed above, only scenario building and cognitive mapping offer effective ways of linking interdependent risks and exploring emergent patterns once risks are triggered.

Standard approaches to risk identification employ a series of linear-thinking approaches which usually culminate in a list of potential risks to the project. Sometimes these lists are enormous. Presented as they usually are as lists of risks, it becomes very difficult for those involved to picture interdependencies, potential positive feedback loops and other emergent characteristics before they occur.

For example, if you have identified 300 potential risks during a project risk-management session, from simply running down the list it is very difficult to detect that risk # 23 will have an impact on risk # 136 and risk # 264. Without a detailed causal analysis for each risk it is also very difficult to discover the contributing factors to each risk scenario. In a very large project there is only time to treat the risks with the highest impact and probability. They are usually carefully analysed and treated in some way. This involves mitigation of individual risks, replanning to avoid the cause of key risks with management plans in place to manage the risks if they are triggered.

Risk-management sessions usually involve a group of experts who are invited to participate because of their experience on previous projects. However, there is the issue that the thinking patterns of experts can actually be narrowed by their expertise. Although risks that have been encountered on previous projects may be identified, there is less likelihood that new or unusual risks or combinations of risks will be identified by groups of experts using standard risk-identification techniques.

This tool is influenced by work done in the systems field on ways of mapping interdependencies and interrelationships within a system by Forrester (1961), popularised by Peter Senge's (1990) *The Fifth Discipline*, together with later work with cognitive mapping by Ackerman, Eden and Williams (1997) and Williams (2002). However it simplifies some of those ideas into a very quick-to-use tool which is designed to encourage discussion about linkages and interdependencies.

Discussion

It is often considered to be a relatively simple task to identify isolated risks affecting a small- to medium-sized project. Panels of experts are often involved in the identification process. However, many of the more significant risks to affect a project or programme go undetected because they arise not from an unseen single cause, but from the interaction of multiple, more easily identifiable risks.

For instance, multiple small delays on semi-independent activities may not pose a risk as far as the evaluation of the success of those activities is concerned, and thus do not sound any warning bells. However, they may compound to quickly use up all the contingency originally written into the schedule. Compounded risks may contribute to a loss of face or trust if these results are seen as an indicator that you will not be able to deliver the project on time. This could be catastrophic if sponsor support is essential in the project.

At a programme level, it may be difficult to identify mounting risks when dealing with multiple project managers, working on multiple projects. People have different tendencies in reporting. Some only report exceptions. Some will give you more documentation than you could ever need. Some will do this with the intention of keeping you informed, while others may use reports with the intention of keeping the programme manager as far away from their project as possible. This can make the task of comparing, cross-tabulating and analysing multiple project managers' risk reports rather difficult. Using a consistent format to analyse risks in a group will aid the process of developing an across-programme understanding of how risks are developing.

As risks change during a project, it can be helpful to use this tool periodically. It has been specifically developed to be simple and fast, so that it takes a minimum of explanation and can be used as part of a meeting.

The tool

The Risk Interdependencies tool involves analysing the relationships between identified risks in a group setting. This tool is primarily for analysing the relationships between risks, not for identifying risks, although new risks may be identified through this process.

It is essential that appropriate stakeholders are included in this process. At a programme level, use of the tool should include not only the project managers, but the project director who has an overview, finance managers, legal personnel, environmental scientists and so on, in order to gain from cross-disciplinary input. If the group is large, it is possible to split the group, ask them to work on this separately, and later pool the results.

Some preparation is required. Users should start with a list of approximately 20 pre-prepared risks. These can either be risks which have separately been defined for the programme, or risks which the project managers have identified as particularly significant for their projects. If it is the latter, then a selection of risks from each project would be appropriate. Ideally have this list of 20 risks arranged before the meeting, for example:

1. withdrawal by major sponsor;
2. supply delay during manufacturing process;
3. action groups create negative press for the project;
4. breakdown of relationship with supplier.

The group will be divided into smaller sub-groups of twos or threes. For each of the groups it will be necessary to have a transparency slide prepared. These need to be pre-prepared, to ensure consistency when results are overlaid. Transparencies should resemble Figure 17.1, adjusted to suit the actual number of risks being examined.

In sub-groups, people will take the list of 20 risks and negotiate which seven risks they see as most significant. These should then be numbered in an eight-by-eight table, with the same risks listed along the column and row headers (Table 17.1). In fact the table can be any size depending on how many *significant* risks have been identified.

Participants then identify which risks can have an influence on another risk. Treat risks along the top as the influencing risks, while the risks along the side are the ones influenced. For instance, for the risks listed above, if it was seen that action groups creating negative press for the project could force our particularly media sensitive sponsor to withdraw from the project, then you would put a cross in the cell at the intersection of the action group's column (3) and the sponsor's row (1).

Do this for each link between the seven risks that the sub-group can see. If two risks affect each other, then put an entry in the column of each risk. This might be the case with risks 2 and 4 in our example.

Table 17.1 Interdependency matrix

RISKS	A	C	E	F	G	...	...
A	-	X					
C		-			X		
E			-	X			
F				-			
G	X				-		
...							
...							

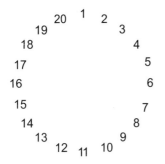

Figure 17.1   Circle of potential risks

Then take your transparency and circle the seven risks your sub-group identified as most significant. Now draw arrows representing these links on your transparency (Figure 17.2). So, if you have an entry in column 3, row 1, draw an arrow from risk 3 to risk 1. Draw double-ended arrows for risks which are mutually reinforcing.

When this has been completed by each sub-group, bring the transparencies together and align them on top of each other on an overhead projector so that all can see the results. Overlaying results will clearly demonstrate where different sub-groups see interconnections between risks. Results will be most clear if each sub-group has used a pen of a different colour. These interconnections can then be the focus of further discussion. Other aspects may become apparent when the group diagrams are overlaid.

Some risks may have many links attached which could mean that they are key risks that if triggered could have wide-ranging effects on the project. Or, alternatively, they could be triggered by many other risks and therefore the likelihood of being triggered can increase substantially.

If the process is repeated frequently, positive feedback loops may be revealed, such as the A-G-C loop indicated in Figure 17.2. This loop is a mutually reinforcing loop and consequences can escalate rapidly if one of the risks is triggered. If the loop is not broken in some way through intervention the compounded impact can be much greater than the impact of any of the risks taken singly, if they were not so connected.

Several variations of this tool are possible. For instance, if an overhead projector is not available, overlaying and photocopying the

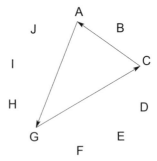

Figure 17.2   Risk interdependencies identified by one group

transparencies will produce a similar effect. If transparencies are not available, it would also be possible to produce a similar effect using a large piece of paper and a facilitator drawing the many risk relationships identified by participants. There is also the potential for computer support to this process.

The purpose of this exercise is to bring together a variety of views on where the most significant risks to the project or programme lie, and what the connections are between these risks. This allows you to monitor the relationship between risks, and if one risk becomes likely, or a reality, allows you to more easily compensate for consequences.

Step by step

1. You will need:

    (a) a list of approximately 20 risks which are significant to the project or programme;
    (b) identical transparencies pre-prepared with the risks in a circle, one for each sub-group;

(c) eight-by-eight matrices, one for each group;

(d) coloured pens.

2. Break the group into sub-groups of two or three.

3. Each sub-group identifies their top seven risks.

4. The relationships between these are identified on the table.

5. The top seven risks are circled on the transparency.

6. The relationships between them are drawn on the circle.

7. Transparencies are brought back to the group and overlaid so that the links drawn by different sub-groups can be compared.

8. Differences of opinion in significance of risks are debated, and the relationships between risks are monitored.

9. The process should be repeated regularly during the project planning and implementation phases.

Caution

This is a tool for small- to medium-sized projects only. This is not a suitable technique for medium to large projects which usually involve so many risks and potential linkages that appropriate causal mapping software and risk software programs are essential management tools.

On larger projects, this tool should not be used as a substitute for detailed approaches such as cognitive mapping, which map the causes, relationships and interdependencies over the whole project, or scenario analysis, which looks at 'what if' scenarios and can be used in conjunction with a technique like cognitive mapping.

It is important to repeat the use of the tool periodically. As the project or programme progresses, the relationships between significant risks may vary.

Be careful about how the top 20 risks which you start with are selected. It will facilitate use of this tool if the risks are predefined, but selecting the risks to focus on should still be a participative process. If it is not, then use of this tool may be subject to political steering.

References and further reading

Ackerman, F., Eden, C. and Williams, T. (1997), 'Modelling for Litigation: Mixing Qualitative and Quantitative Approaches', *Interfaces* 2, 48-65.

AS/NZS4360:1999, *Australian Standard for Risk Management*. (Sydney, Australia: Standards Australia).

Eden, C. and Ackerman, F. (2004), 'Cognitive Mapping expert views for policy analysis in the public sector,' *European Journal of Operational Research* 152, 615-30.

Edwards, P. J. and Bowen, P. (2005), *Risk management in project organisations*. (Sydney, Australia: UNSW Press).

Forrester, J. W. (1961), *Industrial Dynamics*. (Waltham, MA: Pegasus Communications).

Kelly, G. (1955), *The Psychology of Personal Constructs*, Vol. 1. (NY: Norton Press).

Lester, A. (2003), *Project Planning and Control*, 4th Edition. (Oxford, UK: Elsevier Butterworth-Heinemann).

Senge, P. (1990), *The Fifth Discipline*. (NY: Doubleday).

Turner, J. R. (1999), *The Handbook of Project-Based Management*. (Maidenhead, UK: McGraw-Hill).

Uher, T. E. (1993), 'Risk Management in the Building Industry', *Proceedings of the AIPM Conference*, Sydney, Australia, 278-83.

Williams, T. (2002), *Modelling Complex Projects*. (Chichester, UK: John Wiley & Sons).

18 *Temporal Cost/Time Comparison (TCTC)*

Time to use:	Depending upon the size of the project this could take from 3 hours to some days to use
Level of difficulty:	
	Use by an experienced manager who is able to plan projects using traditional scope, time and cost analysis and planning techniques
Group:	Single person or group. This can be performed by a single person. Project planning, especially in the initial phases, is more effective if the entire project team and other relevant stakeholders are involved in identifying items in scope and assigning durations in the schedule.
Types of complexity suited for:	

Problem

It is very difficult to predict a budget and schedule for a project which is experiencing either technical or temporal complexity particularly in the early phases of the project when senior executives, or the client, require a project budget figure for budget allocation.

Purpose

It will achieve a range of probable budgets and time frames based on anticipated likely options.

It will assist the executive board or client to plan if estimates are based on most likely scenarios rather than crude best/worst-case scenarios or averages.

Types of complexity

Projects are often found to be *technically complex* either because there is no obvious solution or because there are a number of possible solutions and no one is sure which one will be most appropriate or which one will satisfice. This tool is most appropriate for the latter because it entertains a range of options.

Projects facing *directional complexity* are also particularly difficult to plan because you don't have agreement on the objectives. Without agreement on the project objectives it is difficult to develop and assess options for delivering outcomes.

Temporally complex projects may also require you to keep a number of options waiting for a final decision to go ahead. However it may also be necessary to secure an approved realistic budget so that you can implement the project as soon as consent is obtained.

Theoretical background

This approach is similar to a feasibility study. It can be achieved quite quickly and using traditional project management tools for defining scope, schedule and project budget. Risks can be identified broadly but they are not explored in detail. The project management methods included in the tool may be found in any good standard project management textbook (such as Harrison and Lock, 2004; Turner, 1999; Cleland and Ireland, 2000; Kerzner, 2000). The traditional tools to be used are the Work Breakdown Structure for defining items in scope, a Precedence Network, to determine the critical path and assignment of resources, and estimates of resource time, supplies and sub-contracts to calculate a project budget. From experience, provided people with key expertise are present in the workshop, it is possible to construct a reasonably robust budget and schedule for a medium-sized project within a few hours using sticky notes, flip chart paper and markers.

The order of operations – scope, then schedule, then budget – is important because obtaining the budget depends upon information from both the scope definition and the schedule. Iteration will occur but the initial order of operations is important. It is important also to use a scheduling technique like a Precedence Network. It is a more effective planning tool which clearly shows dependencies. The tendency with simpler tools like Gantt Charts is to fit the project into the time available, without assessing the most likely durations and without considering interdependencies.

Discussion

To use traditional project management planning tools effectively the project objectives must be clearly defined and options agreed before detailed planning can take place. In some cases, particularly when technical and temporal complexity are present, the project manager must proceed with planning the project or at least provide some kind of plan to senior management before options have been fully explored and final outcomes agreed.

Even when outcomes are uncertain, managers may be expected to produce budgets for organisational purposes or so that clients or customers can plan their own expenditure portfolio. 'Just give us an idea of cost' is a common request of the project manager. As a project manager you know that the client will remember only the initial figure quoted and wisdom and orthodoxy would advise resisting any notion of a budget at this early stage, but expediency at the mercy of reality often places the manager in an impossible position. Therefore there is a tendency either to take a stab based on earlier projects, and triple it, or take the average of the least likely and most likely scenarios and add a contingency figure. Either method is riddled with problems, particularly if the project is unlike others you have managed or an average is not a truly representative estimate of the difference between the two extremes.

In a project with unclear objectives the aim is to increase the level of certainty so that budgets can be allocated. Project plans can be drawn up for the most likely scenarios. This provides the client with a realistic range of options so that a realistic range of budgets can be set. Rather than planning worst- and best-case scenarios, which tend to provide a very broad range of outcomes, it can be more effective to plan the most likely pathways. When presenting the options to senior management it is most important to state the assumptions made with each choice and the associated constraints.

The tool

This is essentially an extension of traditional project management tools which focus on decomposition or breaking-down of elements in order to increase the accuracy of each estimate. Experienced people are needed to help create a range of schedules and budgets based on the most likely options. In the report to the executive or the client the scenarios can be described in detail with associated risks and projected schedules and costs with appropriate contingencies. Knowledge at this level of detail also greatly helps decision makers to determine an option or preferred direction.

If you need to provide a project plan and budget for a project where there is a lack of agreement or approval on options for delivery or there are technical unknowns it is helpful to trace a path through a series of scenarios based on the most likely outcomes of each project phase. This might seem impossible in some instances of technical complexity but it is surprising how much useful information can be contributed by a team of experts in a short time. Remember the question to ask for each activity in the Precedence Network is not 'How do we do this?', but 'Based on past experience, approximately how long will it take to reach an acceptable solution?' Equally, unless the project requires the purchase of yet to be imagined technology, if the scope is broken down far enough it is often a matter of assigning time and the cost of resources to each activity, with appropriate assumptions and contingencies assigned to key activities or products in the network. Grey areas will remain but it is often possible to break those down to small unknowns to which a large contingency can be added.

PROCESS OVERVIEW

The first step is to get together as many subject experts as possible and brainstorm the possible number of options for delivery of the objectives, even if they are vague. This step is very important. Make sure that you establish the rules for brainstorming very clearly (no critical appraisal during idea generation, repeat the process as many times as necessary until enough people really do run out of ideas, and use a method that engages everyone, such as writing down ideas and pooling results each time to stimulate more ideas). Select the most likely options and create project plans for the most likely options. Try and keep your final selection to about five or six. This will provide a range of options from which to choose about three to plan.

For example, the project team might take an educated guess that a feasibility study might produce five possible options for delivery of the project objectives. B, D and E are likely, whereas A and C are possible but less likely. Rather than waste pre-planning time on the less likely options it is better to concentrate on those that are most likely.

It is apparently easier if you can reduce the most probable options to two. However it is more effective if you can select the three most likely options, especially if they are quite different as shown in the diagram. Three options are more likely to reveal the complexity of the situation. Also the outcome may be less likely to be simplified by decision makers, as differences will be more widely dispersed.

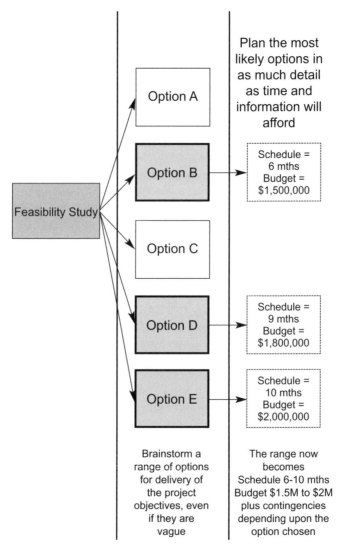

Figure 18.1   Temporal Cost/Time Comparison steps

If the group is large enough you can save time by dividing up the group during the planning phase, each sub-group planning one option. However it is important to bring the group back together to provide the maximum level of feedback to each plan. After critical appraisal by the group, each plan should be adjusted.

The report to the decision makers should briefly describe all options, which ones were selected for more detailed planning and why. Risk should be identified at a broad level for each option. Schedules and budgets should be adjusted for contingency and be presented for each option separately as in a feasibility study. Finally it should be emphasised in the report that the schedules and budget provided therein may be taken as a range with caution, bearing in mind that detailed planning is not possible at this stage.

The process can be repeated as more information becomes available and options are discarded or new options emerge.

Step by step

1. Gather a group of people with expertise about the project.
2. Brainstorm possible options for delivery.
3. Repeat process until people run out of ideas.
4. Try and come up with about five options.
5. Select the most likely. Three is a good number to work with.
6. Divide up the group if it is large enough and, using sticky notes and traditional project management tools, plan each option in as much detail as time permits. Use the following sequence:

    (a) plan the scope first (using a Work Breakdown Structure);
    (b) plan the schedule (using a Precedence Network);
    (c) find the Critical Path (the longest pathway through the network and the shortest time to completion);
    (d) plan the budget (add resources and costs to the network) and roll up.

7. Ask others in the group to critically appraise the plans that they were not involved with. Make adjustments based on the critical review.
8. Report, describing the scenarios explored, the broad risks associated and the range of schedules and times associated with each schedule, plus appropriate cautionary notes emphasizing the level of planning possible at this stage of the process.
9. Repeat the process if necessary as more information becomes apparent.

Caution

Decision makers are likely to simplify results for convenience. For that reason it is preferable to present the full range of scenarios planned.

As people generally simplify detail for memory purposes, each planned option should be given equal attention in the presentation or report.

Also as there is often a tendency to average numbers presented, avoid coming up with a single, often inappropriate estimate which tends to remain in people's minds.

Limitations of this method will result from the following:

- the number and expertise of the people gathering to do the planning – ideally someone with expertise in each particular discipline associated with or affected by the project should be present, including those representing functional areas of the organisation;
- experience and standing of the facilitator;
- relevant historical information to hand at the time of planning, such as costs of components in similar projects and availability of key personnel;
- amount of time available to spend on the planning process – but there is a limit to how much time should be spent when there are very many unknowns;
- the report must emphasise the limitations of the procedure and any assumptions made.

References and further reading

Cleland, D. I. and Ireland, L. R. (2000), *Project Manager's Portable Handbook*. (NY: McGraw Hill).

Harrison, F. and Lock, D. (2004), *Advanced Project Management. A Structured Approach*, 4th Edition. (Aldershot, UK: Gower Publishing).

Healy, P. L. (1997), *Project Management: Getting the Job Done on Time and in Budget*. (Port Melbourne, Australia: Butterworth-Heinemann).

Kerzner, H. (2000), *Applied Project Management: Best Practices On Implementation*. (NY: John Wiley & Sons).

Pinto, J. K. and Trailer, J. W. (eds) (1999), *Essentials of Project Control*. (Newton Square, PA: Project Management Institute).

Turner, J. R. (1999), *A Handbook of Project-Based Management. Improving the Processes for Achieving Strategic Objectives*, 2nd Edition. (London, UK: McGraw-Hill).

Turner, J. R and Simister, S. J. (eds) (2000), *Gower Book of Project Management*, 3rd Edition. (Aldershot, UK: Gower Publishing).

19 *Kokotovich Triad*

Time to use:	The length of time to use depends upon the complexity of the project and the number of stakeholders involved. As it comprises three main elements these can be used separately or iteratively as required. At least a day should be allocated to start such an activity. A number of shorter sessions over a longer period of time may be preferable to attempting to achieve an agreed solution in one session.
Level of difficulty:	
	The tool is of moderate difficulty. It must be explained to participants by the facilitator, however it is regularly taught to university students.
Group:	Group with facilitator
Types of complexity suited for:	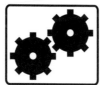 

Problem

Many complex projects require creative approaches to problem solving. Clients or customers may come with pre-conceived solutions which may not be sufficiently thought through to effectively deliver their needs. On the other hand, the solution offered might be valid but the technical design challenges may be daunting. Alternatively the goal of the project may be understood at a high level, or by a few, but key stakeholders remain with different and conflicting notions of the goal state. Any of these situations requires not only the ability to think creatively but a method to assist the players to arrive at an agreed solution. Without an agreed solution, nothing can be implemented and no useful outcomes can be achieved.

The approach described in this tool will be used most frequently at the front end of the project, during initiation or definition and planning. However, all, or elements, of it could be used at any phase in the project when the manager needs to stimulate divergent thinking and problem solving.

Purpose

Vasilije Kokotovich developed this approach as part of his ongoing research into design education. His aim in developing the method was to assist student industrial designers to enhance their ability to resolve complex design problems.

As some design problems exhibit similar characteristics to complex projects, the tool can be used to help project teams and stakeholder groups to explore options, develop solutions which satisfice and validate those solutions against agreed criteria. The approach achieves this by structuring the design process so that the kind of thinking that takes place is appropriate to the stage of the problem-solving process.

Types of complexity

The method is particularly appropriate for projects which exhibit characteristics of *technical* or *directional complexity*. Although all complex projects require creative thinking skills, projects which are technically or directionally complex are characterised by a period of extreme ambiguity. This can be particularly evident at the beginning of the project when managers and project teams are faced with problems which must be resolved in order to progress the project.

Theoretical background

In the pressure to deliver the project the period allocated for definition of the problem is often inadequate. Projects characterised by technical and/or directional complexity require sufficient time to negotiate the problem definition and solution space before planning can get underway.

Research into problem-solving behaviour in design, which has been described as a complex problem-solving activity (Lawson, 2000; Dorst, 2001) may give us insights into how complex projects can more effectively be defined. Comparing the behaviour exhibited by novice designers with that of expert designers has been particularly helpful. Mathias (1993) found that novice designers tended to rush towards a solution and then they tended to spend time justifying their design solutions. In so doing the novice designers were limiting their creative search space. Therefore there is an argument for using tools that delay solution finding as long as practically possible.

Christiaans (1992) reported from his study that the more time a subject spent in the process of defining and understanding the problem the more likely it was that a creative result was achieved. He found that time spent defining and framing the problem in terms of the problem solver's own frames of reference was a key aspect of creativity.

Matthias (1993) found that expert designers utilised an enriched problem-solving process/framework compared with novice designers. In particular the elements missing in the behaviour of the novice designers were in the areas of analysis of the problem statement, convergence and what he calls the 'solution concept'. Design-protocol studies (Ho, 2001) also suggest that expert designers tend to establish problem structure at the beginning of the design process and then they step back from the problem in order to contextualise the problem.

Kokotovich (2002) found that when problem solvers separated ideas from the embodiments of ideas in the early stages of the design process, the level of creative output substantially increased for both designers and non-designers. A greater number of creative responses were achieved when the problem solvers were forced to develop ideas mentally and forestall resolution of the problem.

Dorst (2001) argues, like Maher et al. (1996), that creative design seems to involve a co-evolution of the problem space with the solution space, developing and refining together, involving both the formulation of a problem and ideas for a solution. There was a constant iteration of analysis, synthesis and evaluation processes between the two notional spaces – problem space and solution space. Studies of expert designers (Cross and Cross, 1998) suggest that what Schön (1983) refers to as 'problem framing' ability is crucial to high-level performance in creative design.

Discussion

Projects which are characterised by either technical or directional complexity can benefit enormously from allowing extended time during project definition to allow for problem definition. However, in order to justify the extended time needed in creating the mental representations it is useful to structure the time as a series of tasks.

During early periods of problem definition, tools and approaches which encourage mental conceptualising and reasoning should take precedence over tools and approaches which might force premature containment of the problem space. Sketches and notes applied in rapid and unformed ways seem to be useful, predominantly as an aid to long-term memory. Tools that encourage freer problem exploration are important so that ideas can be generated for later evaluation.

Highly structured approaches, such as checklists which force analytical thinking, should be avoided in the early stages of problem structuring. However, as problem definition proceeds and solutions are proposed more structured analytical tools are useful. It is important at this time to prevent stakeholders from hanging on to solutions which need to be radically revised or discarded. When solutions are proposed they are validated using tools that encourage convergent and analytical thinking. This is where matrices and checklists are appropriate to make sure that all dependencies and interrelationships are addressed by the solutions proposed.

It is important to select the right problem-structuring tools at the right time. Kokotovich (2002; 2004) stresses that the process is iterative. It starts with exploration, which is a divergent-thinking activity, followed by validation, which is a convergent-thinking activity, and then as solutions are proposed and validated, the cycle begins again until a satisficing solution is achieved which addresses an agreed set of criteria.

Kokotovich (2004) has been exploring strategies and tools which might enable student designers to forestall development of the solution and focus early on the complex issues surrounding a given problem in order to develop more considered responses to a given design problem. He has structured the process to add a number of steps which encourage the problem solver to spend more time exploring the problem statement.

The tool

Kokotovich (2002; 2004) emphasises that most important is the purpose behind the selection of tools that make up this method. Other tools could be substituted as long as they achieve the same purpose.

1. EXPLORATION USING NON-HIERARCHICAL MIND MAPPING

Mind mapping was promoted by Tony Buzan in the mid 1970s and more recently (Buzan, 1995) as a tool for researching/analysing a problem. It involves placing ideas in a hierarchical structure which can be conveniently transformed into reports and so on. Kokotovich (2004) argues that this form of mind mapping may be suitable for highly structured problems but may not be so useful for problems that are ill-structured and ill-defined. Instead he suggests using a non-hierarchical form of mind map. Within ill-structured problems many different types of associations exist between the issues.

Kokotovich (2004) suggests four basic types of association:

- *Unidirectional* – like a straightforward causal relationship where A affects B.
- *Bidirectional* – where A and B affect each other.
- *Unidirectional intermittent* – where A might or might not affect B.
- *Bidirectional intermittent* – where A and B might or might not affect each other.

The mind map is built by the group of stakeholders either physically with sticky-notes or using non-hierarchical mind-mapping software. The elements can be colour-coded or grouped into topics, themes and sub-themes to further explore the problem. Text explanations can be added along the arrows, line weights can be changed and so on. An example developed for the community centre is shown in Figure 19.1:

There is no *right* way to do this. Stakeholders involved should be encouraged to freely explore connections and interrelationships. Once developed it can be progressively added to. As time is an important element it is helpful if the mind map can be left in a safe location so that participants can add to it over time, as ideas and connections become apparent to them.

Elements in the mind map can be grouped, coloured or given emphasis. For instance it is sometimes useful to colour or highlight nodes, elements which have multiple connections or elements in similar categories, such as 'user groups' or simply rearrange the map to reveal connections as shown in Figure 19.2.

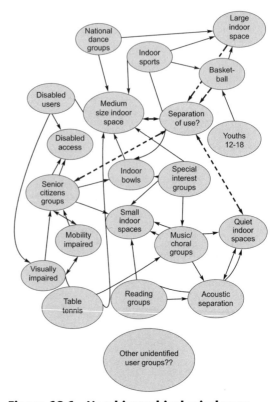

Figure 19.1 Non-hierarchical mind map

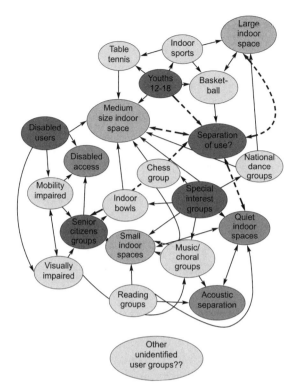

Figure 19.2 Non-hierarchical mind map showing grouping and highlighting

2. EXPLORATION AND SOLUTION FINDING THROUGH INTUITIVE LEAPFROGGING

The purpose of this stage is to encourage generation of unexpected ideas and combinations, offering creative insights but also revealing contradictions. It also delays solution finding and may assist in dislodging or at least unsettling or challenging some preconceived solutions. It is very probable that stakeholders will come to the project with preconceived solutions. Some of these are driven by vested interests. These may be particularly difficult to dislodge and must be revealed if the project is to proceed. Other stakeholders come with solutions which are based on their limited understanding of the possibilities. In both cases the search and construction space needs to be expanded so that all potential possibilities can be explored.

In the case of those who have vested interests or hidden agendas, experience suggests that the more time taken to explore the problem the more likely that hidden agendas will be revealed to other stakeholders. Therefore in order to delay premature signing off on deliverables until a satisficing solution involving all key stakeholders has been obtained, it is very useful to structure a number of problem-exploration activities during the early phases of the project. Whilst these kinds of activities may be frustrating and appear futile to those who have already made up their minds, they can be very useful ways of revealing the complexity of the project and dealing with power-based struggles.

Headings are chosen by the group. For example if the project is a new community-centre development, headings might be 'user demographics', 'environmental concerns', 'potential sponsors', 'stakeholders positive and negative', 'potential applications' and so on. The

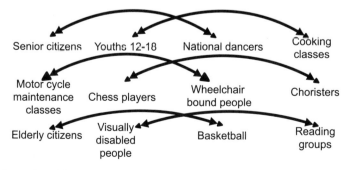

Figure 19.3 Sample of intuitive leapfrogging

participants are asked to list as many categories under each heading as possible. Categories are written on separate cards and then randomised and combined. Each person is then asked to describe using words or images, or both, what comes to mind when thinking about a centre to cater for the particular combination of categories. For instance a combination of categories could be 'elderly person from Latvia', a category under the heading of 'user demographics' and 'indoor basketball', a category under the heading of 'potential applications'. As play and creativity seem to be linked it can be more productive to ask participants to find something funny about the linkage as well as something serious.

Intuitive leapfrogging uses the notion of play as an extension to brainstorming in which participants are each asked what immediately comes to mind. It could be nothing to do with the project. For instance, one person might be thinking of a motorbike, another cooking the dinner and so on. These are listed and randomised, and participants, individually or in groups, are asked to conceptualise what might come out of these combinations; for instance 'cooking the dinner while riding a motorbike'.

Employing tools which structure exploration and encourage participants to play with ideas and seemingly absurd combinations allows participants the time to explore the problem mentally which will make solution finding easier and more effective.

3.   CONVERGENCE AND SOLUTION CONCEPT – MATRIX ANALYSIS

Often problem-solvers seem to be so happy at having arrived at a solution that seems to work that they become reluctant to test the veracity of the solution. Moreover resolution of the problem may be insufficient to guarantee a solution. Therefore, once the main objectives of the project are agreed and stated in functional terms, any potential solutions should be subjected to a 'dialectical' process which involves looking for contradictions (Dörner, 1999). For instance, in the case of a new community centre, the elderly Latvian residents want to use the centre for meetings and cultural activities; local teenage youths want to use the centre for indoor basketball matches. There is a contradiction in usage which, if not resolved in terms of elaboration and refinement of the solution space, will contribute to project failure, at least from the perception of one or more important stakeholder groups.

A tool, such as a link matrix, can be used to critically review the solution options. According to Kokotovich (2004) the use of a tool such as the Linkograph matrix greatly assists in moving the problem solvers towards convergence and validation of their ideas.

The link matrix provides a map of the important concepts and connections which can be used to test the solutions developed by the project team. Links can be weighted and notes can be attached to the links on the map are used to remind participants of the logic behind the decisions. The matrix can then be used a checklist to verify that interrelationships and connections have been addressed in a particular solution and to explore and validate decisions made earlier in the problem-solving process.

As options are evaluated, links can also be highlighted with different colours and given hierarchy by making the links larger or smaller as discussion and validation of options proceeds.

4.   AND BEYOND – ITERATION

Design, like complex problem solving, is an iterative process. It should be expected when scheduling this kind of activity that it will take some time and several iterations to arrive at a satisficing solution. The evidence is increasing (Christiaans, 1992; Mathias, 1993; Kokotovich,

2004) that allowing sufficient time for mental exploration of a problem, without forcing solution finding, will enhance the level of creativity. Therefore it might be helpful to allow for several sessions within several days in between to optimise the value obtained from mental exploration.

Step by step

1. *Exploration* Participants should be encouraged to explore the problem through issues that come to mind and link those issues as they see fit using a non-hierarchical mind map. A non-hierarchical mind map comprises issues, represented by bubbles with labels, and links, represented by one-way or two-way arrows. Agreement does not need to be reached. This stage is purely exploratory and should reveal dissonances.
2. *Exploration and solution finding* Intuitive leapfrogging is a process that randomises idea associations. It can be used to explore linkages and it can assist with idea generation. In both cases it involves making lists of related or unrelated categories and randomly combining them. Participants then explore the combinations in order to open up new possibilities and connections. An element of fun encourages playful thinking which is known to be linked with creativity.
3. *Convergence and solution concept* When solutions are proposed they must be validated, which requires convergent thinking and analysis. A matrix, such as a link matrix is constructed which forms a checklist against which solutions may be validated. Adding notes to the link matrix also records the rationale for decisions at various stages of problem solving.
4. *And beyond – iteration* The process is iterative, as are all design processes.

Caution

Although the process has been presented sequentially a design process is *not* linear. Participants need to be taught the process and recognise the triggers which tell them when they should be moving to the next iteration. Triggers include the following:

- The mind map contains very rich information and no new information is emerging. It might be useful at this stage to move to a tool like intuitive leapfrogging, which introduces an element of play, returning to the mind map from time to time to add any additional thoughts and connections.
- People offer predetermined solutions or solutions derived independently early in the process. The aim is to delay solution finding as long as possible to enable the largest number of connections and possibilities to be explored by the group. Therefore it is helpful to acknowledge and note the ideas but put them aside until all possibilities are explored.
- No really creative ideas have emerged from the process and no new ideas are emerging – this could mean that the ideas are exhausted or that people are hanging on to earlier thinking. It is useful at this stage to introduce any other tool which encourages explorative thinking.

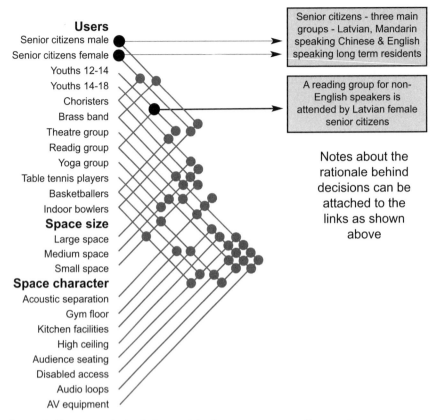

A partially complete link matrix for a community centre

Figure 19.4   Example of a link matrix

- People are justifying their solutions early in the process – this could mean that people have moved into analytical modes of thinking too early in the process. It is important to move them back to explorative thinking using any tool which encourages expansive thinking.
- Many ideas have been developed and the process is starting to slow down – this is the time to move to analysis using a tool such as the link matrix.

Both the pressure of time and the kind of analytical-thinking training that most of us receive at university may discourage people from taking enough time to explore the dimensions of the problem. If participants are tending towards premature solution finding and validation it is important to structure more activities which promote exploration until there is a measurable increase in the number of ideas being generated.

Evidence suggests that people are inclined to hang on to solutions once they have arrived at them. When people start to justify their solutions it is time to subject them to rigorous analysis using convergent tools and checklists, such as a matrix followed by a return to idea-generation activities.

Examples in practice

This approach has been used extensively in teaching design students, and observations suggest that it is very helpful in enhancing the level of creativity in problem solving. At the time of writing Kokotovich and his research team are conducting controlled trials with industrial design students at the University of Technology Sydney. The research results that have been analysed to date appear to strongly support the use of the approach in enhancing the overall quality of the design solutions, as judged by experts in the field.

References and further reading

Buzan, T. (1995), *The Mind Map Book*. (London, UK: BBC Books).

Christiaans, H. (1992), *Creativity in Design*, PhD Thesis. (Delft, The Netherlands: Delft University of Technology).

Cross, N. and Cross, A. C. (1998), 'Expert Designers', in Frankenburger, E., Badke-Schaub, P. and Birkhofer, H. (eds), *Designers – The Key to Successful Product Development*. (London, UK: Springer Verlag).

Dörner, D. (1999), 'Approaching Design Thinking Research', *Design Studies* 20, 407-15.

Dorst, K. (2001), 'Creativity in the Design Process: Co-Evolution of Problem-Solution', *Design Studies* 22, 425-37.

Ho, C. (2001), 'Some Phenomena of Problem Decomposition in Strategy for Design Thinking', *Design Studies* 22, 27-45.

Kokotovich, V. and Purcell, T. (2000), 'Ideas, the Embodiment of Ideas, and Drawing: An Experimental Investigation of Inventing', in Gero, J. S., Tversky, B. and Purcell, T. (Eds) *Visual and Spatial Reasoning in Design II*. (Sydney, Australia: Key Centre of Design Computing and Cognition, University of Sydney) 283-98.

Kokotovich, V. (2002), 'Mental Synthesis and Creativity in Design: An Experimental Examination', *Design Studies* 21:5, 437-49.

Kokotovich, V. (2004), 'Non-Hierarchical Mind-Mapping, Intuitive Leap-frogging, and the Matrix: Tools for a Three Phase Process of Problem Solving in Industrial Design', *Proceedings of the International Design Education Conference*, Sept. Delft, The Netherlands, 213-21.

Lawson, B. (1997), *Design in Mind*. (Oxford, UK: Architectural Press).

Lawson, B. (2000), *How Designers Think*. (Oxford, UK: The Architectural Press).

Maher, M. J., Poon, J. and Boulanger, S. (1996), 'Formalising Design Exploration As Co-Evolution: A Combined Gene Approach', in Gero, J. S. and Sudweeks, F. (Eds) *Advances in Formal Design Methods for CAD*. (London, UK: Chapman and Hall).

Mathias, J. R. (1993), *A Study of the Problem Solving Strategies Used by Expert and Novice Designers*, PhD Thesis. (Birmingham, UK: University of Aston).

Schön. D. A. (1983), *The Reflective Practitioner: How Professionals Think in Action*. (NY: Basic Books).

Schön, D. A. and Wiggins, G. (1992) , 'Kinds of Seeing and Their Function in Designing', *Design Studies* 13, 135-56.

20 *Stanislavski's Method*

Time to use:	Ongoing work over many days
Level of difficulty:	
Group:	Single person (this is a tool for personal development which will influence how you approach new situations).
Types of complexity suited for:	 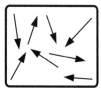

Problem

From time to time it becomes clear that new ways of looking at a situation are required in order to understand different perspectives.

Purpose

This tool will help you look at the working context and any problematic situations within it in new ways. It can be applied to any sufficiently complex perspective or set of concepts and helps to make these concepts or perspectives part of your lived experience. It involves a level of fun, which always helps.

Types of complexity

Technical complexity: Technically complex projects often require that managers demonstrate the ability to provide innovative solutions to problems. However, we are limited as much as we are empowered by our expertise. This is because the training we receive in education and in the workplace tends to encourage a deep but tight focus. This tool helps to broaden the range of ways in which we can look at the world, allowing us to see aspects of the world that were always there, but which were not previously apparent.

Directional complexity: Significant directional complexity arises in projects due to stakeholders' different perspectives on the world, an implicit assumption that theirs is the *right* way to view the world, and an inability to understand alternative perspectives. This tool helps people to manage directional complexity by broadening their capability of personally appreciating different perspectives.

Theoretical background

Konstantin Stanislavski was co-founder of the Moscow Art Theatre in 1897 where he started to develop what became known as his 'system' of acting. His approach to acting was based on the naturalist school of thought. His system was a significant challenge to the stylised characterisation popular with actors at the time, where characters were caricatures rather than representations of real people, with real emotions. 'Method acting' is a direct derivative of his work and Stanislavski is seen as one of the pioneering figures in modern theatre; his influence is still strong in drama circles. Hollywood actors who were most influenced include James Dean and Marlon Brando.

The 'Stanislavski Method' was a process of character development in which actors were required to develop a deep understanding of the characters they were to portray. 'An actor who is also a creative artist experiences everything that is felt by the character of his part' (Stanislavksi, cited in Margarshack, 1967: 121). Stanislavski declared for the true actor: 'The part and "I" no longer exist, but what exists is "I-the part", since his own individual "I" has disappeared' (Stanislavski, cited by Margarshack in Stanislavski, 1967: 174). Actors were first asked to understand changes in their character's objectives and emotions for each scene in a play. Understanding of the character was also often extended past the bounds of the script, to examine how the character would behave in a broader context.

Actors were required to find examples of the character's emotional state from their own personal history and use this as the basis for what they were to portray on stage. This was often achieved by actors in rehearsal constantly asking questions of their characters and themselves, examining how they would have reacted if in the same position as their character.

Bakalis (2001) identified elements of Stanislavski's acting system that can be incorporated in adult learning contexts which also require dramatic transformation of perspectives and personal views. Mezirow's (1991) concept of perspective transformation also reflects in Stanislaviski's characterisation and transformation. Within Mezirow's approach, transforming perspectives involves reorganising the individually constructed structures that create a person's model of the world (Conner (2003). Transforming perspectives involves using a prior interpretation to construct a new or a revised interpretation of the meaning of your experience in order to guide future action. It involves transforming your established frame of reference to allow a perspective that is more inclusive, differentiating, critically reflective, open to other points of view, and more integrative of experience. Some, like Kegan (1994) would even describe perspective transformation as movement toward a higher level of consciousness.

This tool involves perspective transformation and the resultant learning through method acting. The aim is to reduce the void between theory and practice or between work and outside life by significantly changing personal perspectives. However, changing personal perspectives is a difficult task. It requires reassessment of your understanding of self. Cognitive patterns, once established, do not change quickly. If you want a real shift, then you must work at the new perspective over time. If a new perspective is to really allow you to see a situation in a new way, then it requires significant effort.

Discussion

The purpose of this tool is to extend the range of ways in which a manager can view the world. This tool can be applied to any sufficiently complex perspective, and can lead to a deep and thorough understanding of the perspective, but it takes time to develop.

This tool can be applied to almost any kind of perspective that it might be useful to adopt. A perspective, in this sense, refers to an ability to see the world in a particular way. For instance, this tool could be used to develop the capability to see the world with a perspective that focuses on one of the four kinds of complexity examined in this book.

If you tend to think of the world in terms of structure you might look at the project in terms of organisational structure. If your project were running late, you might think of ways of altering the project structure to increase efficiency. If you were engaged in an organisational change programme you might think of possibilities for change in terms of how the structure of the organisation could be altered. This might be a useful approach, but it is only one of many possible ways of addressing the situation. On realising this, you might use the tool to develop a perspective which focuses on social networks, which would provide a different kind of insight into the situation.

Very simply, the more ways in which you are able to look at a situation, the more likely you are to be able to find a solution to your problem which appreciates the wider problem. It is not that one perspective is better than another, or even that a perspective is more appropriate to a situation than any other. It is simply about increasing perspective views.

Examples of possible perspectives that could be developed using this tool include:

- complexity: such as the four kinds of complexity described throughout this book;
- economic focus: seeing the world in terms of transactions;
- information systems: looking for flows of data and information, and how this is transformed;
- structuralist: understanding the formal structure of how society and organisations operate;
- functionalist: looking at the world in terms of the function that systems perform;
- mechanistic: viewing your environment as a machine to be engineered;
- organic: understanding the world as an interconnected organism;
- interpretive: looking for the influence of interpretation in how reality is understood.

There is a wide variety of possible perspectives to which this tool can be applied. Each of those listed above is associated with a wide literature. More suggestions for possible perspectives can be found in Gareth Morgan's book *Images of Organization* (1997), which looks at different ways in which organisations can be perceived. The concept is also used by Bolman and Deal (2003) in their reframing model.

The tool

The intention of this tool is to develop a deep understanding of a topic. It is intended to provoke a more comprehensive range of ways in which the world can be understood.

Before a perspective can be applied to a working situation successfully, it needs to be experienced. It is not enough to simply read about an idea or a potentially useful perspective, and to assume that when the call comes, it will be ready at hand. Instead, it is necessary to slowly build up an understanding of the idea in different contexts, if it is to truly be useful in a work setting. You need to incorporate the perspective into your daily life, regularly and in a variety of situations, before it can be applied to a work context.

This is necessary for two reasons. Firstly, technically or directionally complex project work typically involves uncertainty. It is impossible to determine what will emerge out of the fitness landscape, and how we will be required to respond. Because of this, it is necessary to understand a new perspective from many different angles if it is to be useful in the face of uncertainty.

Secondly, powerful perspectives and ideas are never simple. They may be sold as simple, or may look simple when we look back on them, but incorporating and coming to understand a perspective which is significantly different to our current one is always a complex and difficult task.

The first step is to choose the particular perspective to be developed and learn as much as possible about it. Read about it and discuss it with others. However, to make this perspective relevant to your life you will need to actively look at the world through it. Learning to do this is a slow process, which requires repetition.

At regular intervals, stop and look around you. Take a minute to bring the perspective to mind, then ask yourself questions:

* What evidence of the phenomena described by the perspective can you see around you?
* What going on around you can be described using the perspective? How would you see the world from this perspective?

It is important to flesh out the perspective as thoroughly and in as many different ways as possible. You may like to keep a diary, describing the events of the day from the chosen perspective. You may like to paint or draw a picture of a situation from the perspective. Or stand on a street corner for a minute, watching the scene around you and listing what stands out to you when you look at the world through the chosen perspective.

Repeat this over many days. Each day stop a few times, for a few minutes each time. Before long you will have developed a thorough understanding of the concepts involved, one which is significantly deeper and more flexible than could be achieved by reading about it alone.

Step by step

1. Choose a perspective to develop.
2. Become familiar with the theory behind the perspective.
3. Observe the world from within the perspective regularly, outside the project environment.
4. Repeat Step 3 until you are comfortable with the perspective in many different environments.
5. Take the perspective back to the project environment.

Caution

Benefits from this tool will not be immediately apparent, and it is not something which can be rushed. It is important to spend time to develop the perspective fully, before its validity is questioned.

It is more effective to spend five minutes every day examining the perspective, than one hour each week. This will embed the perspective much more thoroughly as the natural way that you perceive the world.

Developing one different perspective is the start. In order to be able to 'reframe' as a matter of course it is necessary to develop a number of working perspectives.

Examples in practice

Murray was from a finance background. Everything was about the dollars and cents. He had recently been seconded to an internal development project, and although the project had started well, it had quickly slowed to a crawl as disagreements about the goals of the project surfaced, and an inability to find solutions to the few problems people actually agreed upon threatened to prevent any further headway.

Murray was sick of hearing the same arguments play themselves out. In a moment of self-reflection he noticed that he was as much to blame as anyone else. Just like everyone else, he was always pushing the same line, and it wasn't getting them anywhere.

He decided he needed to change his perspective. He'd come across references to 'structuralism' a couple of times, and always thought it sounded interesting, but hadn't looked into it in any depth. He decided it was time for a change.

Murray spent a few late nights reading about structuralism. He told himself that he was going to start looking at the world from a structuralist perspective, but he was always busy and before long he was back to his old working pattern, with barely a difference. He'd received little benefit from the reading alone.

He decided to set a daily reminder on his mobile phone. When it rang he would stop whatever he was doing and try to see the world form a structuralist perspective. While sitting at dinner with his family, he would think about the implicit power structure around the dinner table. When the alarm went off while in his car waiting at the traffic lights, he would think about the formal way the lights imposed structure on the right of passage.

Before long Murray was seeing 'structure' all around him, wherever he went and whatever he did. After this it wasn't any effort to apply the perspective to work. It had become a natural way for him to perceive the world. His next challenge was to take up another perspective frame, such as power relations, and add that to his repertoire.

References and further reading

Bakalis, M. B. (2001), The *Stanislavski System of Acting: An Adult Education Learning Methodology*. Ed.D. (Illinois, USA: Northern Illinois University).

Bolman, L. G. and Deal, T. E. (2003), *Reframing Organizations: Artistry, Choice, and Leadership*. (San Francisco, CA: Jossey-Bass).

Carnicke, S. M. (1998), *Stanislavski in Focus*. (Amsterdam, The Netherlands: Harwood Academic Publishers), 235.

Conner, F. L. (2003), *Transformation as a Sociocultural Phenomenon: A Study of Adult Learning in Leadership Development*, Ph.D. Thesis. (Michigan, USA: Michigan State University).

Hughes, R. I. G. (1993), 'Tolstoy, Stanislavski, and the Art of Acting', *The Journal of Aesthetics and Art Criticism* 51:1, 39-48.

Kegan, R. (1994), *In Over Our Heads*. (Cambridge, MA: Harvard University Press).

Mezirow, J. (1991), *Transformative Dimensions of Adult Learning*. (San Francisco, CA: Jossey-Bass).

Morgan, G. (1997), *Images of Organization*. (Thousand Oaks, CA: Sage Publications).

Stanislavksi, K. (1967), 'The System and Methods of Creative Art', in Margarshack, D. (trans. and ed.) *Stanislavski and the Art of the Stage* 2nd Edition. (London, UK: Faber and Faber).

Stanislavksi, K. (1980), *An Actor Prepares,* 2nd Edition (Hapgood, E. R. trans. and ed.). (London, UK: Methuen).

21 *Discursive Universe*

Time to use:	It will take the length of the conversation
Level of difficulty:	
	It takes a bit of practice to use
Group:	Group
Types of complexity suited for:	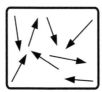

Problem

In complex projects we often need to communicate complex and difficult ideas to others. This could occur in any phase of a project life cycle but is more likely to be prevalent at the beginning of a project.

Purpose

The tool will help us frame communication appropriately so that it makes more sense from the other person's point of view.

Types of complexity

This tool is applicable to any situation that requires you to reach a shared agreement on a way forward. Therefore it is particularly relevant to directional complexity.

Directional complexity: Directionally complex projects are characterised by ambiguity, unshared goals and goal paths, and hidden agendas. Associated management challenges tend to be related to sharing of meanings in order to reach agreement. Part of the difficulty in sharing meanings is in the communication process itself, especially when the ideas themselves might be complex and foreign to the parties with whom you are trying to communicate.

Theoretical background

The tool combines two frameworks. We originally developed this tool, with much help from our colleague, Katherin Coster, to use with Project Management Masters students, to help them develop skills in managing communications in complex situations, particularly where there is lack of agreement on which way to proceed. The first framework examines context and focus in relation to you and others and the boundaries created by those positions. The second framework experientially places you in the others' position.

Research from fields such as marketing suggests that building relationships through communication, rather than persuasion, is most effective (Duncan and Moriaty, 1998). Communication involves the intention to influence, at some level, even when the intention is simply to make sure that information is transferred and shared by the parties involved. When managing a complex project, particularly one characterised by directional complexity, the project manager needs help to build trust amongst the participants in order to maximise the potential for information sharing.

Dialogue has been used extensively in organisations to help people to explore positions. Hazen (1993) argues that dialogue is essential for effective organisational change. She describes an organisation as comprising many dialogues occurring simultaneously and sequentially, all participants viewing themselves as central to the action; that is, they all exist within their own particular bubbles determined by their history, experience, their position and influence in the organisation and their own value and beliefs system. There is also considerable evidence that people interpret information in ways which seem to conform to their pre-existing beliefs, attitudes and concerns (Chapman and Chapman, 1967; Lord et al., 1979).

Levine (1994) distinguishes discussion from dialogue. Most of what occurs in meetings in organisations is discussion. It is focused on outcomes. Dialogue, on the other hand, is exploratory, probing and open-ended. Kotter and Cohen (2002) describe dialogue as the key to building trust among members of a group.

Cooperrider and Srivastra (1987) coined the term 'Appreciative Inquiry'. It draws upon and extends dialogue and involves three steps. It aims to discover the best practices in the organisation, understand what factors contribute to best practice, reinforce and amplify the factors, and encourage the people who can best support and promote best practice. Appreciative Inquiry places great importance on the words used in the dialogue; in particular words that are shared by individuals that show respect, value and recognition for the contribution they make to all members of the discussion. The intention is to build a constructive bridge between and among members of the stakeholder group, with emphasis on the achievements, potentials, innovations, strengths, and visions of valued and possible futures (Cooperrider and Whitney, 2001).

Discussion

There is now clear evidence that relationship building through trust enhances the level of disclosure. However, dialogue and more structured approaches, such as Appreciative Inquiry, may not always be helpful when some parties, for one reason or another, choose not to participate fully, holding back information that might benefit the project to support their own political agendas. The battles that ensue as a direct result of non-disclosure of issues are very common in directionally complex projects. Gergen (1999) and other protagonists of dialogical approaches also acknowledge the difficulties resulting from the social reality that not all stakeholders are willing participants in the dialogue. In these circumstances the project manager must focus on building strong personal relationships with key stakeholders.

For practical reasons we looked for other tools, in addition to dialogical tools, to find ways of assisting project managers. One avenue we investigated was Neuro Linguistic Programming (NLP). First developed by Bandler and Grinder in the 1970s (Bandler and Grinder, 1975; 1979), NLP has been through many iterations since that time and received some bad press when the techniques were appropriated by some for purposes of manipulation.

However NLP provides a very useful range of tools and techniques which are central to influencing. At this point it needs to be emphasised that in a directionally complex project influencing is not about getting people to do things that they don't want to do, and it has nothing to do with manipulation. That would be counter-productive and unsustainable in the long term. Rather it is about pacing and leading people so that you come to an appropriate position together. In this respect NLP theory recognises that the outcome you want will only be achieved by being in a powerful relationship with the other stakeholders. With this as a context, the tool draws upon two NLP techniques, the Perceptual Position model and Pacing and Leading (Grinder and Delozier ,1987).

In order to communicate effectively with others in your universe it is important first to understand your own position in the scheme of things. This means being very clear about your areas of concern. Second you should be clear about the position in the universe of the other person or group with whom you wish to communicate, including their concerns and the organisational context from which you all need to view the issues. Context and concerns may vary considerably from person to person within an organisation.

For instance, finance managers might be concerned with finance generally but sitting in the strategic management level of the organisation they will have to report to the CEO, board and possibly even government. Their focus will therefore be on strategic rather than operational issues, in which case they may be less focused on cost issues from an operational perspective. This does not mean that they are not interested in operational issues but your dialogue with such people will be more effective if it has a strategic focus.

In addition, people in different roles in the organisation use different language and approach problems from different levels of abstraction. You are more likely to be listened to if you talk in a way which is aligned with their own areas of concern – in this case this means their roles in the organisation, their levels of abstraction and their positions within or outside the organisation.

The tool

The Perceptual Position model is also known as '1st person, 2nd person, 3rd person shifts' in the NLP literature. In 1st position you are concerned with 'I', in 2nd position you are concerned with 'the other' and in 3rd position you are concerned with the whole system.

1st person is your own Perceptual Position as you, yourself, experience it. It is often called a fully associated position. That is, you are fully in your own experience, living it as if it is happening right now – which it is. If you communicate from your own perspective you will be less likely to *coincide* with the concerns of the other person or group and they will be less likely to *hear* you.

2nd person is the Perceptual Position of an 'other'. It's the walking, seeing, hearing, feeling, thinking and believing in another person's shoes. Second position can be that of an object or even a theoretical position, mathematical principle or an idea, so long as it is represented as *other* than the *you* in first position. If you communicate from their perspective you will be more likely to *coincide* with the concerns of the other person or group and they will be more likely to *hear* you.

3rd position is the position of the 'neutral observer'. It is outside the first two positions. Beliefs or assumptions about both first and second positions are suspended. In this position it is possible to see the whole system, such as the project, the programme, organisation or the broader context. The 3rd position is detached; it is the helicopter view. If you communicate from 3rd position you will be in holistic problem-solving mode, more interested in the patterns of communication that develop than the content of individual utterances.

Pacing and Leading is a technique used in psychotherapy in which the therapist empathically communicates with the patient using the same tone, speed, language and content until the patient is ready to *move* to a new understanding of the problem. At that time the therapist will test the waters by leading the patient to a new perspective view of the problem using appropriate questions, body language and so on.

This tool applies both concepts, the Perceptual Position model and Pacing and Leading.

STEP 1: KNOW YOUR OWN UNIVERSE

Ask yourself:

- Where am I?
- What is my area of concern?
- What am I talking about?
- What do I think about this?
- What do I feel about this?
- What would I like to do about this?
- What structures do I use to defend my position?
- What personal barriers do I have to the communication?
- What options do I have?
- What would I accept? What is my fall-back position?
- How big is my circle of focus?
- Do I talk about it in 1st, 2nd or 3rd position?

STEP 2: TRY AND APPRECIATE THE OTHER PERSON'S UNIVERSE

Ask yourself before the communication event:

- Who am I talking to?
- Where are they?
- What is their area of concern? What do they focus on?
- How big is their circle of focus?
- What do they want?
- What would they settle for?

- During the communication:
  - Are they talking/writing about it in 1st, 2nd or 3rd position?
  - What kind of language are they using?
  - What is their language telling me about what is going on for them?

STEP 3: ASCERTAIN THE STATE OF THE WIDER UNIVERSE

Ask yourself:

- What are the big issues?
- How does this affect everyone?
- What would benefit everyone?
- How does it affect the whole system?
- What are the environmental constraints that might affect this issue?
- What is the most equitable/fair/neutral position with respect to this issue?
- What is the most sustainable solution to this?

STEP 4: MONITOR THE DIALOGUE

Listen carefully to the person with whom you are communicating. If you are communicating by email look carefully at what is written. Pay close attention to the words used. Is the other person using 1st person, 2nd person or 3rd person or a combination? Has the dialogue moved or changed in focus?

STEP 5: MATCH THEIR DIALOGUE

Reframe what you want to communicate to be conscious of harmonizing with what the other person is paying attention to. Be very careful to use words and concepts that they will be familiar with. The aim is to get across what you want to say by saying it in a way the other person will want to hear and respond to. If you have a concern at your level, and your level is different to the level which concerns the other person questions that might be helpful are:

- What are the consequences for your level/area?
- Who do you see this affecting?

STEP 6: REPOSITION THE DIALOGUE

However, it is counter-productive to continue a dialogue if the participants are in different perceptual positions. The second concept, Pacing and Leading, acknowledges and respects the other person's position and only moves to a new position when the other person is ready.

Try to move the dialogue to a wider problem-exploration or problem-solving frame when you sense the other person is ready. You might ask:

- What options do you think can be explored?
- What are the consequences for the project/organisation?
- How do you think we might progress this for the benefit of the project?

If the other person responds to this question you may continue in a problem-solving mode. On the other hand if the person is still voicing concerns about local (individual 1st person) concerns you should return to matching position and building the relationship until you are both ready to see the situation from a new position.

Step by step

1. *Know your own universe* – your own concerns, requirements, feelings, belief system, values and so on.
2. *Try and appreciate the other person's universe* – 'walk in their shoes' and think about their concerns, requirements and so on.
3. *Ascertain the state of the wider universe* – take the helicopter view and look at the problem from a whole-of-systems viewpoint.
4. *Monitor the dialogue* – listen carefully to what the other person is saying, the language being used, the subject matter and so on.
5. *Match their dialogue* – reframe what you want to say in terms of their concerns, using their language, models and so on.
6. *Reposition the dialogue* – after pacing the other person for an appropriate length of time, move the dialogue to a wider problem-focused mode when you sense the other person is ready.

Caution

It is really important to note carefully what positions both you and the other person are in at the moment. Words like 'I' and 'me' are give-away indicators that the persons with whom you are communicating are in their own 1st position and you can respond accordingly by matching their language and framing your issue around their concerns. However, communication is usually much more subtle and you will have to listen very carefully for the content of what is being said, which may not be obvious. For instance, communication may be couched in the guise of 3rd person, but really address the needs of the 1st person. This approach is sometimes used when issues are too personal or confronting for the talker to identify with them directly. It is also used by people wishing to give their opinion the appearance of objective fact. Be aware that you may need to address this from a 2nd person position, satisfying the 1st person needs of the other party, while using language from a 3rd person perspective.

For example, a stakeholder who wants personal recognition or self-gratification from the project can be difficult to deal with. Often, if the stakeholder is powerful, the needs of the stakeholder must be addressed in some way. Reframing the real need for personal kudos into a project success factor such as 'a high level of positive media for the project' addresses the 1st person need of the stakeholder but it is couched in acceptable 3rd person, project-focused language for the 'greater good'.

If you are really interested in honing these skills, this is a very brief introduction. There are many specialist courses in NLP which go into the practice of influencing in much greater depth.

Example in practice

The situation involves a conversation between a project manager and the finance manager. From the perspective of a project manager working on a long project who tends to focus on the project and consequences (1st position), your statement might be expressed as:

> *'We are behind schedule and we need a $40 000 increase in budget to obtain more resources in order to bring the project back on track.'*

Being concerned about the team, the project manager (in 2nd position on behalf of the project team) might say:

'My concern is the well-being of the project team because I know that my team members are stressed and some are developing health issues.'

However, neither your own 1st nor 2nd position might be relevant for the finance manager, whose main concern is financial implications for the organisation as a whole. Therefore a broader organisation perspective and consequences from their perspective (1st position) might be more effective. Long-term cost impact to the whole organisation and how it will reflect upon them when reported to the managing director is likely to be a major focus of concern. The issue might restated as:

'It is important that you are aware that current resourcing levels for this project are creating high levels of stress amongst team members. This is already starting to manifest as health issues that have the propensity for long-term losses to the organisation in term of staff retention, sick leave, injuries and low productivity. How does the organisation wish to deal with the issue now to prevent long-term consequences?'

This statement now combines 2nd position (the finance manager's own 1st position) and 3rd position (the organisational perspective).

References and further reading

Bouwen, R. and Steyaert, C. (1990), 'Constructing Organizational Texture in Young Entrepreneurial Firms', *Journal of Management Studies* 26.

Bandler, R., Grinder, J. and Satir, V. (1976), *Changing with Families*. (Palo Alto, CA: Science & Behavior Books).

Bandler, R. and Grinder, J. (1975), *The Structure of Magic I: A Book About Language and Therapy*. (Palo Alto, CA: Science & Behavior Books).

Bandler, R. and Grinder, J. (1979), *Frogs into Princes: Neuro Linguistic Programming*. (Moab, UT: Real People Press), 15, 24, 30, 45, 52.

Chapman, L. and Chapman, J. (1967), 'The Genesis of Popular but Erroneous Psychodiagnostic Observations', *Journal of Abnormal Psychology* 72, 193-204.

Cooperrider, D. and Srivastra, S. (1987), 'Appreciative Inquiry in Organizational life', in Passmore, W. and Wodman, R. (eds), *Research in Organization Change and Development* Vol. 1. (Greenwich, CT: JAI Press).

Cooperrider, D and Whitney, D. (2001), *Appreciative Inquiry. An Emerging Direction for Organizational Development*. (Champaign, Il: Stipes Publishing).

Duncan, T. and Moriaty, S.E. (1998), 'A Communication-Based Marketing Model for Managing Relationships', *Journal of Marketing* 62:2, 1-13.

Gergen, K. (1999), *An Invitation to Social Construction*. (Thousand Oaks, CA.: Sage Publications) 154.

Grinder, J. and Delozier, J. (1987), *Turtles All the Way Down, Pre-requisites to personal genius*. (Scots Valley, CA: Grinder & Associates).

Hazen, M. A. (1993), 'Towards Polyphonic Organization', *Journal of Organizational Change Management*, 6:5, 15-6.

Isaacs, William N. (1993), 'Taking Flight: Dialogue, Collective Thinking, and Organizational Learning', *Organizational Dynamics* 22:2.

Kotter, J. and Cohen, D. S. (2002), *The Heart of Change. Real Life Stories of How People Change Their Organizations*. (LLC, USA: John Kotter and Deloitte Consulting).

Levine, L. (1994), 'Listening with Spirit and the Art of Team Dialogue', *Journal of Organizational Change Management* 7:1, 61-73.

Lord, C. G., Ross, L. and Leer, M. (1979), 'Biased Assimilation and Attitude Polarization', *Journal of Personality and Social Psychology* 37, 2098-262.

Maccoby, M. (1996), *Interactive Dialogue as a Tool for Change*. Research Technology Management, v. 39, Sept/Oct 1996, 57–9.

Schein, E. H. (1993), 'On Dialogue, Culture, and Organizational Learning', *Organizational Dynamics*, Autumn Vol. 22, Issue 2.

22 *Conclusion*

Many theorists and practitioners now agree that complex projects exist in a different universe from that on which much project management theory has been based. This is not to say that existing project methodologies should be discarded. Rather it points to the fact that project managers must manage from a pluralistic perspective, drawing upon a much wider range of models to help them cope with the various sources of complexity. In this book we have attempted to apply ideas from Complexity Theory to project management with the aim of throwing some light on why complex projects are so difficult to manage. We have done so by suggesting that the source of complexity might be a useful way of thinking about the complex issues to be managed in many projects. To this end we have defined four types of project complexity, building upon the work of many others. However, we recognise that any process of categorisation is fraught with problems through omissions in the process of classification or because many projects will fall between the categories or, more likely, exhibit any number of combinations of the categories we have defined. Nevertheless categories are useful to help us think about the different management challenges that might be associated with each source of complexity.

The examples of tools have come from practitioners and academics kind enough to share their knowledge and experience, and from our own experience in practice, consulting and teaching Masters of Project Management students, many of whom come to the university with many years of practical experience. The tools section contains just a small selection of the many methods and approaches that might be used to help manage different aspects of project complexity. We hope you will find some of the ideas contained in them useful or at least interesting.

Index

Figures are indicated by bold page numbers, tables by italic.

A
Ackerman, F. 158, 167
acting system 190
action research 20
Adam, Douglas 4
adaptiveness
    in complex adaptive systems 6
    and structural complexity 30–1
Alderman, N. 65, 70
Allen, T.J. 42
ambiguity 20–2, **21, 22,** 23
    directional complexity **52,** 52–3
    structural complexity **28,** 28–9
    technical complexity 40, **40**
    temporal complexity 62–4, **63**
anatomy-based engineering process (ABEP)
    95–102, **97, 98, 99**
Appreciative Inquiry 55, 196–7
Arrow, H. 68

B
Bagnall, J. 55
Bakalis, M.B. 190
Bandler, R. 197
Baskerville, R. 20
Bastien, D.T. 134
Beatles, The 5–6
Benner, M.J. 42
Bolman, L.G. 191
Bowker, S.L. 18
brains and neurons 21
Brocklesby, J. 77
Brown, S.L. 69, 134, 139
Büchel, B. 45
budgeting 173–8, **176**
Build Operate Transfer (BOT) contracts 70
butterfly effect 6

C
categorisation of projects 17–18

causal mapping 157–8, 161, **162,** 167
challenges for project management
    directional complexity 55–8
    structural complexity 32–6
    technical complexity 42–7
    temporal complexity 65–70
Champion, D. 20
chaos to order continuum 9–10
    directional complexity 53–4
    structural complexity 31–2
    technical complexity 42
    temporal complexity 64
    time-linked semi-structures 134–9
Checkland, Peter 1, 20, 77
Christiaans, H. 180
city planning, Europe 16-17th century 10
Cochrane, R.A. 86
Cognitive Mapping 149, 158, 167
Cohen, D.S. 196
Collaborative Working Arrangements (CWAs)
    103, 104, 105–12, **107, 109**
communication
    building relationships through 196–7
    in complex adaptive systems 4
    Neuro Linguistic Programming (NLP) 197
    rule-bound 29
    structural complexity 29–30
    structured in directional complexity 54–5
    technical complexity 41–2, 44–5
    temporal complexity 64, 67, 135–6
    virtual gates tool 160
complex adaptive systems, characteristics of
    4–6
complexity
    combination of types in projects 8–9
    different perspectives 18–19, **19**
    identifying sources of 87
    mapping 85–92, **86–7, 89–92**
    navigation via markers 18
    and perception 17
    reflection on 20
    types of 5–8
    see also directional complexity; structural
        complexity; technical complexity;

temporal complexity
Complexity Theory 2, 3
  edge of chaos 11
  fitness landscapes 10–11
  order to chaos continuum 9–10
construction projects 103–4, 161–3, **162**
contingencies 156
contracts
  Build Operate Transfer (BOT) 70
  Collaborative Working Arrangements
    (CWAs) 105–6
  delaying of 70
  in fast-track projects 47
  non-traditional forms 47, 53, 58
  Refurbish Operate Transfer (ROT) 70
  and termination of projects 36, 157
control
  in complex adaptive systems 5
  directional complexity 54–5, 57
  financial 34, 45, 57
  structural complexity 30–1
  technical complexity 41–2
control-based approaches 1
Cooperrider, D. 196
cost estimation 32, 33, 34, 69
Coster, Katherin 196
creative thinking 179
critical phase transitions
  temporal complexity 64, 65
  tools to use per phase 155–63
critical project phases 32–3
  directional complexity 56
  technical complexity 43
  temporal complexity 66
critical systems heuristics 55
Critical Systems Thinking (CST) 1–2, 142

D
Davis, C. 45
Deal, T.E. 191
decision-making 33
decision tree analysis 45
Delphi technique 167
dependencies, functional 96
Descartes 5
design, problem-solving in 180–1
dialogue 196
difficulty, level of 79
directional complexity 7–8
  control in 54–5
  discursive universe 195–6
  edge of chaos 53–4
  executive support 56

financial issues 57
hospital services project 91–2
Kokotovich Triad 180
mapping the complexity 88
multimethodology in series 141–2, 143
order to chaos continuum 53–4
procurement issues 58
programme tool 114, 118
project management challenges 55–8
project manager capabilities 56–7
risk interdependencies 166
risk management 58
role definition 124
scheduling issues 58
and sensitivity to initial conditions 54
solution/problem spaces 52
Stanislavski's method 189–90
structured communication in 54–5
team support 57
temporal cost/time comparison (TCTC)
  174
traps and consequences 58–9
and uncertainty **52,** 52–3, 53
unclear aims and objectives 51–2
virtual gates 155
discursive universe 195–202
Distributed Software Development (DSD) 95
domain construction process (DCP) 95–6,
  99–100
Dorst, K. 181
Dua, Raf 106, 112
Dvir, D. 56, 57

E
Earned Value Management (EVM) 34
Earned Value Performance Measurement 106
Eden, Colin 167
edge of chaos 11
  directional complexity 53–4
  and organisational structure 135
  structural complexity 31–2
  technical complexity 42
Eisenhardt, K.M. 69, 134, 139
emergence 29
  in complex adaptive systems 5
  and risk 35–6
entrainment 69
executive sponsor role 126, *127–8*
executive support 33
  directional complexity 56
  structural complexity 33
  technical complexity 44
  temporal complexity 66–7

F

Faems, D. 47
fast-tracked projects 35
Fifth Discipline, The (Senge) 168
Filareti, Antonio 10
financial control
    directional complexity 57
    structural complexity 34
    technical complexity 45
    temporal complexity 68–9
fitness landscapes 10–11
    and temporal complexity 63–4
Flood, R. 2, 142
Flyvbjerg, B. 32
Forrester, J.W. 168
Foucault, M. 18
Francis, D. 107
Frost, P.J. 134
functional dependencies 96

G

Gently, Dirk 4
Gergen, K. 197
Global Software Development (GSD) 95
Goals and Methods matrix 86, **86**
Griffin, D. 2
Grinder, J. 197
group norms in complex adaptive systems 5
Gunz, H. 17

H

Hagemeijer, R.E. 69
hard systems thinking 1
Hatch, J. 134
Hazen, M.A. 196
hierarchies 29
    in complex adaptive systems 4
    flat in technical complexity 40
    of theory, methodology and tools 75–6,
    76
Hobbs, B. 69
Holwell, S. 20
hospital services project 90–2, **90–2**
Hostager, T.J. 134
Huygens, Christian 69

I

Images of Organisation (Morgan) 191
improvisation 134
influencing 197
information transfer. *see* communication
Integration Centric Development (ICD) 95–6

interconnectedness 20–2, **21, 22,** 29
intuitive leapfrogging **183,** 183–4
iteration 184–5
Ivory, C. 65, 70

J

Jackson, M. 2, 142
Jarvis, P. 20
jazz (time linked semi-structures) 133–40,
    137
Jokinen, T. 68

K

Katz, R. 42
Kegan, R. 190
Kelly, George 167
Keys, P. 142
Khurana, A. 46
Kiesler, S. 42
knowledge, project 66
Koberg, D. 55
Kokotovich Triad 179–87, **182, 183, 186**
Kotter, J. 196
Kuhn, T. 76

L

Lai, L. 145
Latham Report 105
leapfrogging, intuitive **183,** 183–4
Lechler, T. 56, 57
Letiche, H. 69
level of difficulty 79
Levine, L. 196
Lewin, R. 2
Lilliesköld, J. 95, 96
link matrix 184, **186**
Lissack, M. 2, 17

M

mapping complexity 85–92, **86–7, 89–92**
markers, navigation via 18
Mathias, J.R. 180
matrix analysis 184
McGrath, J.E. 68
Meditations (Descartes) 5
meetings as form of control 136–7
method acting 190
methodology
    defined 77
    and theory and tools 75–6, **76,** 77–8
methods 77–8, **78**
Meyer, A. 134

Mezirow, J. 190
Middleton, E. 22
Midgley, G. 2, 55, 77
Miles, R. 143
milestone dates 136–8
Miller, R. 69
mind mapping 182, **182, 183**
Mingers, J. 2, 77, 143
Minor, A.S. 135
Moorman, C. 135
Morgan, Gareth 191
multimethodology
 in parallel 147–53, **150**
 in series 141–6, **144**

N
NASA flight systems and ground support
 projects 157
navigation via markers 18
Neal, R.A. 145
net present value (NPV) 45
net present value risk-adjusted (NPVR) 45
Neuro Linguistic Programming (NLP) 197
neurons in brains 21
non-hierarchical mind mapping 182
non-linearity in complex adaptive systems
 5–6

O
Offshore Development 95
options analysis 32, 33, 70
options planning 65
order to chaos continuum 9–10
 directional complexity 53–4
 structural complexity 31–2
 technical complexity 42
 temporal complexity 64
 time-linked semi-structures 134–9
Organisation Science 134
organisational structure 134–5

P
Pacing and Leading 198–201
paradigm, defined 76
partnering. *see* Collaborative Working
 Arrangements (CWAs)
Paton, G. 77–8
Payne, J.H. 115
perception and complexity 17
Perceptual Position model 197–201
perspectives, changing 18–19, **19**, 33, 190–4
 and team-working 34

phase transitions in complex adaptive
 systems 5
philosophy
 defined 76
 realist/positivist 142–3
pluralistic approach 2, 78–9
precedence networks 174
problem solving/structuring methods 142–3,
 143–5, 148, 149–52, **150**, 181
problem spaces 23, **23**, 29
 directional complexity 52
 structural complexity 29
 technical complexity 40
 temporal complexity 62–3, **63**
procurement issues
 directional complexity 58
 structural complexity 36
 target outturn costs tool 104, 105–12,
  107, 109
 technical complexity 47
 temporal complexity 70
programme director 132
programme tool 113–21, **116, 118**
project management challenges
 directional complexity 55–8
 structural complexity 32–6
 technical complexity 42–7
 temporal complexity 65–70
project manager capabilities 33–4
 directional complexity 56–7
 structural complexity 33–4
 technical complexity 44
 temporal complexity 67–8
project manager role 124–5, 128, *129–31*
projects
 attributes of 3
 categorisation of 17–18
 critical project phases 32–3
 fast-tracked 35
 large 113–21
 reflection on 20
 structural complexity 32–3
 as systems 2
 types of complexity of 6–8

Q
quantity of uncertainty 20–2, **21, 22**

R
real options 45
redundancy in temporal complexity 67
reflective practice 20
Refurbish Operate Transfer (ROT) contracts 70

relationships, building through
      communication 196–7
risk analysis 32, 33
risk identification 166–8
risk interdependencies 165–71, **169, 170**
risk management
      contingencies 156
      directional complexity 58
      monitoring of risks 157–8
      process 166
      technical complexity 46–7
      temporal complexity 69–70
Rix, S. 105
role definition 123–32, *127–31*
Roos, J. 2
Rosenthal, S.R. 46
rule-bound communication 29

S
satisficing zones 22–3
scenario building 167
scheduling
      directional complexity 58
      structural complexity 35
      technical complexity 45–6
      temporal complexity 69
      temporal cost/time comparison 173–8,
      176
Schön, D.A. 181
semi-structure 136, **137**
Senge, Peter 168
sensitivity to initial conditions
      in complex adaptive systems 6
      directional complexity 54
      structural complexity 30–1
ship-building 31
Simon, Herbert 22
Söderlund, J. 66
Soft Systems Methodology (SSM) 143–4, 145,
      149
solution spaces 23, **23,** 29
      directional complexity 52
      structural complexity 29
      technical complexity 40
      temporal complexity 62–3, **63**
Sproull, L. 42
Srivastra, S. 196
Stacey, Ralph 2
Stanislavski's method 189–94
Star, S.L. 18
Stowell, F. 20
Strategic Options Development and Analysis
      (SODA) 143–4, 149

Stringer, E.T. 20
structural complexity 7
      and adaptiveness 30–1
      and ambiguity 28, **28**
      characteristics of projects 28–9
      communication in 29–30
      and control 30–1
      critical project phases 32–3
      executive support 33
      finance control 34
      hospital services project 91–2
      mapping the complexity 88
      number of elements in project 27–8
      and order/chaos continuum 31–2
      problem/solution spaces 29
      and procurement issues 36
      programme tool 114, 117
      project management challenges 32–6
      project manager capabilities 33–4
      risk interdependencies 166
      and risk management 35–6
      scheduling in 35
      and sensitivity to initial conditions 30–1
      system anatomy 94
      target outturn costs tool 104
      team support 34
      traps and consequences 36–7
      virtual gates 155–6
structure
      organisational 134–5
      in temporal complexity 65
Swepson, P. 20
switching values 156
System Anatomy 93–102, **97–100**
System of Systems Methodologies 142
systemic pluralism 1–2, 78–9
systems thinking 3–4

T
target outturn cost 103–12, **107, 109**
Taxén, L. 95–6
team support
      directional complexity 57
      and structural complexity 34
      technical complexity 40–1, 44–5
      temporal complexity 68
technical complexity 7
      and communication 41–2, 44–5
      control in 41–2
      critical project phases in 43
      edge of chaos 42
      and executive support 44
      financial issues 45

hospital services project 91–2
jazz (time linked semi-structures) 133–4
Kokotovich Triad 180
mapping the complexity 88
problems with 39
procurement issues 47
programme tool 114, 117–8
project management challenges 42–7
project manager capabilities 44
risk interdependencies 166
risk management 46–7
role definition 124
scheduling issues 45–6
and solution/problem spaces 40
Stanislavski's method 189–90
structure and control in 42–3
system anatomy 94
target outturn costs tool 104–5
team structure and characteristics 40–1
team support in 44–5
temporal cost/time comparison (TCTC) 174
traps and consequences 47–8
uncertainty in 40, **40**
virtual gates 155
telecommunications network 95, 101–2
temporal complexity 8
  and communication 64, 67, 135–6
  critical project phases 64, 65, 66
  entrainment 69
  executive support 66–7
  financial control 68–9
  fitness landscapes and time 63–4
  hospital services project 91–2
  impact of changes 67
  jazz (time linked semi-structures) 133–4
  managing project knowledge 66
  mapping as interconnected nodes 65, 70
  mapping the complexity 88
  multimethodology in parallel 147–8, 149, 150
  order to chaos continuum 64
  planning by options 65, 70
  problem/solution spaces in 62–3, **63**
  procurement issues 70
  programme tool 114
  project management challenges 65–70
  project manager capabilities 67–8
  risk management 69–70
  role definition 124
  scheduling issues 69
  sources of complexity 61–2
  structure 65

system anatomy 94
target outturn costs tool 104
team support 68
temporal cost/time comparison (TCTC) 174
traps and consequences 70–1
uncertainty in **63**
virtual gates 155
temporal cost/time comparison (TCTC) 173–8, **176**
theory
  mapping complexity 86, **86**
  and methodology and tools 75–6, **76**, 77–8
  system anatomy 95
time linked semi-structures (jazz) 133–40, **137**
tools
  changing personal perspectives 189–94
  defined 77
  Goals and Methods matrix 86, **86**
  jazz (time linked semi-structures) 133–40
  Kokotovich Triad 179–87, **182, 183, 186**
  multimethodology in parallel 147–53, **150**
  multimethodology in series 141–6, **144**
  programme tool **116, 118**
  risk interdependencies 165–71, **169, 170**
  role definition 123–32, *127–31*
  Stanislavski's Method 189–94
  summary of *80–1*
  System Anatomy 93–102, **97–100**
  target outturn cost 103–12, **107, 109**
  temporal cost/time comparison (TCTC) 173–8, **176**
  and theory and methodology 75–6, **76**, 77–8
  type of complexity 82
  use of 79
  virtual gates 155–63, **159, 162**
Total Systems Intervention 142
traps and consequences
  directional complexity 58–9
  structural complexity 36–7
  technical complexity 47–8
  temporal complexity 70–1
Trattato di architettura (Filareti) 10
Turner, J.R. 86, 115, 143
Turner, Rodney 58
Tushman, M.L. 42

U
uncertainty 20–2, **21, 22**, 23
  directional complexity **52**, 52–3, 53

structural complexity 28–9
technical complexity 40, **40**
temporal complexity 62–4, **63**

V
Value Management 55
Van Oorschot, K.E. 46
variance control 34
    switching values 156
Verner, J.M. 33
virtual gates 155–63, **159, 162**

W
Weick, K.E. 134

whole of project approaches
    jazz (time linked semi-structures) 79,
        133–40
    mapping the complexity 85–92, **86–7,
        89–92**
    programme tool 113–21, **116, 118**
    role definition 123–32, *127–31*
    System Anatomy 94–102, **97–100**
    target outturn cost 103–12, **107, 109**
Whybrew, K. 44
Williams, T. 32, 167
Wood-Harper, A.T. 20
workpractices 95
World Bank 156

About the Authors

Dr Kaye Remington is as much a practitioner as an academic with a career involving 25 years in project and senior management, then becoming Director of Post-graduate Project Management at the University of Technology Sydney. Firmly believing that theory and practice are inseparable she now writes, consults and lectures internationally.

Dr Julien Pollack integrates practice with theory through action research, post-graduate teaching and consulting. Focussing on complexity and systems thinking he is the author of many papers and articles. He has won national and international awards for his work linking project management, systems thinking and multi-methodology in practice.